"Scott Klusendorf takes the insights and methods for defending the right to life he so effectively communicates in his teaching presentations into a book that provides a clear and cogent biblical rationale for the sanctity and dignity of life, born or unborn. This is a great tool for the layman who knows he or she is pro-life, but doesn't understand the presuppositions on which his or her beliefs are based or who doesn't feel equipped to defend or discuss the issue with others."

    —CHUCK COLSON, Founder, Prison Fellowship

"*The Case for Life* is *prophetic* and *practical*. It is *prophetic* in the sense that it makes a clear and undeniable argument based on truth about human value. It gives a biblically informed pro-life view. It is *practical* because it provides pro-life advocates a toolbox for offering understandable defenses for the unborn. It shows how to logically answer objections and move a debate to a dialogue. As a pastor, I was challenged, informed, and inspired to confidently and graciously make a difference in my generation for the cause of life."

    —JIMMY DALE PATTERSON, Senior Pastor, First Baptist Church, Newman, Georgia

"Scott Klusendorf has produced a marvelous resource that will equip pro-lifers to communicate more creatively and effectively as they engage our culture. *The Case for Life* is well-researched, well-written, logical, and clear, containing many pithy and memorable statements. Those already pro-life will be equipped; those on the fence will likely be persuaded. Readers looking to speak up for those who cannot speak for themselves will find much here to say. I highly recommend this book."

    —RANDY ALCORN, best-selling author

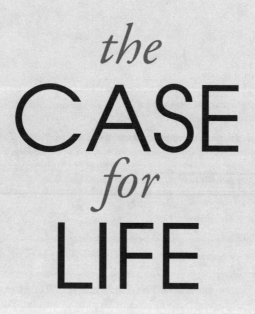

the
CASE
for
LIFE

Equipping Christians to Engage the Culture

SCOTT KLUSENDORF

CROSSWAY BOOKS
WHEATON, ILLINOIS

Library of Congress Cataloging-in-Publication Data
Klusendorf, Scott, 1960–
   The case for life : equipping Christians to engage the culture / Scott Klusendorf.
      p. cm.
   Includes bibliographical references and index.
   ISBN 978-1-4335-0320-7 (tpb)
   1. Abortion—Religious aspects—Christianity. 2. Pro-life movement—United States. II. Title
HQ767.25.K58   2009
261.8'36—dc22   2008041696

VP		18	17	16	15	14	13	12	11	10	09
14	13	12	11	10	9	8	7	6	5	4	3	2	1

To Stephanie,
my beloved wife,
*who has never wavered in her support for my pro-life work
and whose love gives me courage to confront ideas
that diminish us all*

CONTENTS

PREFACE

THIS BOOK BEARS THE MARKS of two men who mentored my early development as a pro-life apologist.

Gregg Cunningham, executive director of the Center for Bio-Ethical Reform, made the first investment, though I doubt he knew it the first time we met.

The setting was a Saturday breakfast for pastors in November 1990. At the time I was an associate pastor in Southern California, and organizers from the local crisis pregnancy center and right-to-life affiliate invited me and a hundred others to hear a pro-life message aimed at equipping church leaders to think strategically about abortion.

Four of us showed up.

Undeterred by the dismal attendance, Gregg, with his background in law and politics (he served two terms in the Pennsylvania House of Representatives where he wrote the bill ending tax-financed abortions in that state), launched into the most articulate case for the lives of the unborn I'd ever heard. That was impressive enough.

But then he showed the pictures. Horrible pictures that made you cry.

In the course of one seven-minute video depicting abortion, my career aspirations were forever altered, though it took me a few months to realize it. Gregg asked us to think of the two religious leaders in the Parable of the Good Samaritan who, although they most likely *felt* pity for the beating victim, did not *act* like they felt pity. Only the Good Samaritan took pity, thus proving he truly did love his neighbor.

For the next several months, I followed Gregg to many of his Southern California speaking events. I memorized huge portions of his talks and devoured his writings. Six months later I left my job as an associate pastor (with the blessing of the church) and hounded Gregg even more until he put me on staff as his understudy, a position I was privileged to hold for six years. Watching him dismantle abortion-choice arguments in front of hostile audiences, I lost my fear of opposition. Watching him sacrifice the comforts of this life so he could save unborn humans, I lost my desire for an easy job. Both losses have served me well.

Gregg's signature quote haunts me to this day: "*Most people who say they oppose abortion do just enough to salve the conscience but not enough to stop the killing.*" That's a staggering truth. Every time I am tempted to quit, I remember it.

While Gregg Cunningham taught me courage, Greg Koukl taught me to be a gracious ambassador for the Christian worldview. Koukl is not only a top-notch apologist, he's also one of the most winsome guys you'll ever meet. His mission is to equip Christians to graciously and incisively defend truth. That's refreshing, as too many Christians lack the diplomatic skills needed to effectively engage listeners.

I first heard Greg on the radio back in 1989. I thought, *Wow, this guy is really smart!* By 1993 his Sunday afternoon show was my personal clinic in clear thinking. In 1996 we met for the first time at a pro-life conference in Pasadena, where we were both presenters. In 1997 we met again, this time for lunch. Later that same year I joined his staff at Stand to Reason.

Shortly thereafter, Greg taught me a valuable lesson that continues to pay off each time I write or speak. The setting was the University of Illinois (Champaign), where I was scheduled to debate author and political science professor Eileen McDonagh. (I discuss McDonagh's views in Chapter 15.) Campus abortion-choice advocates did not want the debate to transpire and tried numerous ploys to stop it. First, they claimed that debates only serve to legitimize the "anti-choice" position. If you won't debate slavery advocates, why on earth debate pro-lifers? When that didn't fly, they went after me personally with a series of editorials in the school newspaper. Every one of those stories falsely claimed I was associated with groups advocating violence against abortion doctors, while some even claimed that I hated gays.

In response, I typed out a heated reply that shot down each of those lies and sent it off to Greg for a quick review before faxing it to the school paper.

That was a smart move. Greg graciously suggested that I tone things down a bit, or a lot. Instead of anger, I should communicate sadness that a fine university committed to the free exchange of ideas would even think of censoring a debate over a legitimate public policy question. His advice saved the day. I revised the letter, and instead of looking like angry victims, the pro-lifers on campus now appeared reasonable and willing to debate while the abortion-choicers looked like cowards out to suppress academic freedom. The school paper even hinted as much in a subsequent write-up after the debate was canceled. (I showed up anyway and after making a defense for the pro-life view took questions from critics, which made abortion-choicers look even more unreasonable.) The comic drawing alongside the story suggested that those censoring the event were "pansies."

From that day forward I had a Koukl filter. Even if I'm hundreds of miles away, I hear Greg asking if the piece I've just written or the talk I've just given communicates in a winsome and attractive manner. When the answer is no, guess where I go?

Back to his radio show. Back to the CDs. Back to the commentaries on the Stand to Reason website. It's there I recover my ambassador skills.

I thank God for both of these men. They are responsible for saving countless lives and equipping many others for effective Christian service. I am but one they've impacted for eternity.

I am also indebted to others who played a direct role in this book. Steve Weimar, my associate and friend at Life Training Institute, not only works tirelessly organizing (and promoting) my speaking events, he's also my number one sounding board. Many pages in this book were strengthened with his critical eye.

Throughout the writing process, Jay Watts, Stephanie Gray, Steve Wagner, and Rich Poupard made valuable contributions, refining the contents of the original manuscript. Patrick Lee at the Franciscan University of Steubenville also made helpful suggestions.

These are challenging days for pro-life advocates. The executive and legislative branches of the federal government are now firmly in the hands of those deeply committed to the proposition that an entire class of human beings can be killed simply because they are in the way of something we want. Even as I write, liberal lawmakers are crafting legislation designed to sweep away every limitation on abortion and destructive embryo research. If that weren't bad enough, a small but vocal group of "pro-life" leaders now says we might as well give up the fight to legally protect unborn humans.

Yes, they are right about one thing. Things are bad.

But surrender is not an option. We must equip ourselves to engage.

My prayer is that the words found in this book will give you courage to do just that.

INTRODUCTION

RIGHT NOW AS YOU ARE reading this sentence, the United States (and to some degree, Great Britain and Canada) is having a huge argument over two key questions that will impact you, your children, and even your grandchildren for decades to come. How we answer these questions will do nothing less than determine the future of human beings.

First, we're arguing about truth. Is moral truth real and knowable, or is it just a preference like choosing chocolate ice cream over vanilla? Second, we're arguing over human value. Are you and I valuable for what we *are* intrinsically or only valuable for what we can *do* functionally?

The question of truth and the question of human value are driving our national debates on abortion, cloning, and embryonic stem cell research (ESCR). The debates are contentious because they involve deep worldview commitments that get to the heart of who and what we are as people. But the debate itself is not complex. Either you believe that each and every human being has an equal right to life or you don't.

Pro-life Christians provide one answer. Although humans differ in their respective degrees of development, they are nonetheless equal because they share a common human nature that bears the image of their Creator. Humans have value simply because they are human.

Secular critics like David Boonin provide a radically different perspective: Although you are identical to the embryo you once were—meaning you are the same being now as you were then—it does not follow that you had the same right to life then as you do now. Being human is nothing special, meaning your right to life is strictly accidental. You have it because of some acquired characteristic you have that embryos do not. To make sure we get the point, Boonin includes this chilling passage:

> On my desk in my office where most of this book [*A Defense of Abortion*]
> was written and revised, there are several pictures of my son, Eli. In one, he
> is gleefully dancing on the sand along the Gulf of Mexico, the cool ocean

breeze wreaking havoc with his wispy hair. In a second, he is tentatively seated in the grass in his grandparents' backyard, still working to master the feat of sitting up on his own. In a third, he is only a few weeks old, clinging firmly to the arms that are holding him and still wearing the tiny hat for preserving body heat that he wore home from the hospital. Through all of the remarkable changes that these pictures preserve, he remains unmistakably the same little boy. In the top drawer of my desk, I keep another picture of Eli. This picture was taken . . . 24 weeks before he was born. The sonogram image is murky, but it reveals clearly enough a small head tilted back slightly, and an arm raised up and bent, with the hand pointing back toward the face and the thumb extended out toward the mouth. There is no doubt in my mind that this picture, too, shows the same little boy at a very early stage in his physical development. And there is no question that the position I defend in this book entails that it would have been morally permissible to end his life at this point.[1]

So what makes us equal? Here's Boonin's problem: If humans only have fundamental value because of some characteristic they possess in varying degrees, those with more of it have greater value than those with less.

My own thesis is that a biblically informed pro-life view explains human equality, human rights, and moral obligations better than its secular rivals and that rank-and-file pro-life Christians can make an immediate impact provided they're equipped to engage the culture with a robust but graciously communicated case for life.

Making that case is what this book is about.

Part 1 helps pro-life Christians simplify debates over abortion and embryonic stem cell research. These issues are not morally complex, though they are often presented that way. Can we kill the unborn? Yes, I think we can, *if.* If what? If the unborn are not human beings.

Part 2 explains why moral neutrality is impossible. In a typical abortion debate, the pro-life advocate will be grilled incessantly on every one of his starting points. His critics will demand to know how a right to life can stand apart from fundamental religious underpinnings, why those underpinnings should be allowed to inform public policy, and why anyone should suppose that just because I exist as a human, I have a right to life that others are obliged to respect. The truth is, both sides bring prior metaphysical commitments to the debate and are asking the same exact question: What makes humans valuable in the first place?

---

[1]David Boonin, *A Defense of Abortion* (Cambridge: Cambridge University Press, 2003), xiii–xiv.

For Christians fearful they'll get caught with nothing to say on abortion, Part 3 provides answers to the most common objections including appeals to the hard cases, assertions of bodily autonomy, and personal attacks that ignore the real issue. Pro-lifers who stay focused on the one question that truly matters, the status of the unborn, won't be sidetracked.

Part 4 addresses questions related to the pastoral side of pro-life advocacy. First, what is the role of the pro-life pastor? To make an impact on culture, pro-life pastors must not only understand the times but pursue four vital tasks that I outline in some detail. Second, are evangelicals who work with Catholics, Jews, and others to reform culture compromising the gospel? Some evangelicals say yes. I say no, provided we draw careful lines between co-belligerence and co-confession. Third, how can post-abortion women and men find hope? Many precious pro-life advocates I meet are trying to atone for past abortions with tireless activity. There's a better way. It's called grace. Finally, I conclude with three goals designed to lay a foundation for victory.

I do not pretend to have written an exhaustive defense of the pro-life view. That's been done already by selected authors I cite throughout the text. My purpose is different. This book will take those sophisticated pro-life defenses and put them in a form that hopefully equips and inspires lay Christians (with or without academic sophistication) to engage the debate with friends, coworkers, and fellow believers.

Admittedly, a book about pro-life apologetics may not appeal to some lay Christians. It seems many believers would rather focus on end times rather than these times. That's a mistake. Humans who ignore questions about truth and human value may soon learn what it really means to be left behind.

PART ONE

Pro-Life
Christians Clarify
the Debate

1

WHAT'S THE ISSUE?

The abortion controversy is not a debate between those who are pro-choice and those who are anti-choice. It's not about privacy. It's not about trusting women to decide. It's not about forcing one's morality. It's about one question that trumps all others.

EMILY NEVER SAW IT COMING. A fifteen-year friendship was on the brink of disaster over one word. *Abortion.*

She met Pam at a Christian college, and the relationship paid off immediately. Emily excelled at language and history, while Pam was a math and science whiz. Together they could tackle any required course, and they did. Both graduated with honors a semester ahead of their classmates. Within a year they both married their college sweethearts. Later, when kids came along and budgets got tight, they swapped baby clothes and enjoyed occasional sack lunches together. Even when a job change forced Pam to move fifty miles away, they still managed to meet for coffee at least once a month. Emily looked forward to her times with Pam. She needed escape from the kids, not to mention the endless grind of household chores. Pam was easy to talk to, optimistic, and always lifted Emily's spirits. Sometimes they shared prayer requests.

Now Emily wondered if they would ever feel connected again. For the hundredth time that night, she replayed the conversation that started it all.

Pam: Emily, did I tell you that my niece, Sarah, is pregnant?
Emily: What? You mean the one in California? We've never met, but you talk about her a lot.
Pam: Yes, that's the one. You'd love her. She's nineteen and a freshman at college. Sweet, sweet girl. Smart as a whip and drop-dead gorgeous. I would have never thought . . .

Emily: Did her parents have any clue she was in trouble?

Pam: None. Sarah attends church religiously and never had a serious boyfriend before Jack. They met over the summer and attend the same university. He swept her right off her feet.

Emily: What about his parents?

Pam: Seldom home and very liberal. Sarah told Jack she wanted to wait, but with no adults around, well, you can guess the rest.

Emily: I don't have to. Have they talked to their pastor?

Pam: Well, Sarah has one, but Jack's not the churchgoing type. He's very liberal, like his parents. Says Christianity is a bunch of fairy tales, a crutch for the weak.

Emily: You mean she's romantically involved with a non-Christian?

Pam: Yep. I tried to warn her, but she insisted she could change him. Even now, she thinks he'll change if given enough time.

Emily: Oh dear. Since when has that ever worked? We used to call that missionary dating.

Pam: Yeah, only in this case, the "missionary" is pregnant. And her mission "project" wants out. He'll pay for the abortion, but that's it.

Emily: But what if she doesn't want one? What if she keeps the child?

Pam: I guess he won't stick around to find out.

Emily: What a loser! He's going to bolt no matter what she does. What's she thinking?

Pam: Right now, only about keeping him, whatever it takes.

Emily: How about her parents?

Pam: Funny you ask. They're supportive but think Jack has a point.

Emily: What? You mean they think abortion might be an option?

Pam: Jack told Sarah that if she has this baby, she'll never finish college and won't make enough money to support herself. She'll also forfeit a promising modeling career and cause her parents untold embarrassment in the community. Her dad's a deacon, you know. Maybe Jack's on to something.

Emily: What did you say?

Pam: Only that Sarah stands to lose a lot and needs to think about what Jack said.

Emily: What do you mean by that? You aren't saying you buy what Jack's telling her, are you?

Pam: Personally, no. I oppose abortion and would never have one. But if Sarah thinks it's the right decision for her at this time, it's not my place to judge. I've never walked in her shoes.

Emily: Pam, I'm shocked. How could killing an innocent human being ever be the right call?

Pam: I personally don't think it is. Like I said, I don't like abortion one bit. I hope she keeps the baby. But it's not my decision. If you and I don't like abortion, we shouldn't have one. But Sarah may feel differently, and we shouldn't force our views on her.

Emily: I still don't understand. How can a Christian ever say abortion is okay just because it would solve a difficult life problem?

Pam: No, no, you've got me all wrong. I hate abortion. Like I said, I personally think she should keep the baby. That's what my preference would be. But she has to decide for herself what's best in this situation. It's not my place to say what's right or wrong. None of us are in a position to judge. And you certainly don't want the government getting involved in her personal life, do you?

Emily: Pam, it's not about that.

Pam: Consider the consequences, Emily. If abortion is made illegal, Sarah and girls like her will be forced to get dangerous illegal abortions. They'll get thrown in jail if caught. I can't even imagine that. And if they're raped, they'll be forced to give birth to a child that will forever remind them of that terrible event.

Emily: I still don't understand. How does any of that make abortion right?

Pam: Think about it, Emily. If your daughter gets in a tough spot, do you want her going to some guy with a rusty coat hanger in a back alley? You never know—she could get pregnant, like Sarah.

Emily: Let's hope not, but even if she does, right and wrong don't change just because we dislike the consequences of our choices. God might have something to say about this, you know.

Pam: Emily, don't think it can't happen to your kids or mine. I seem to remember both of us getting into some tough spots in college.

Emily: Yes, but . . .

Pam: So why should it be any different with our daughters? Besides, the Bible never says abortion is wrong. It doesn't even mention the word. I'm sure that's why my pastor never talks about it.

Emily: Wait . . . Are you saying the Bible is okay with abortion?

Pam: Again, I just don't think we should force our morals on others, and you aren't going to change my mind about that. Sarah has a right to make her own private decisions. Besides, how's she going to care for this baby anyway? There are so many abused and abandoned kids out there. Who's going to pay for them all? Besides, Sarah could become dirt-poor trying to raise this kid on her own. She needs to think about all this. It's not our place to judge her.

Emily: Pam, let's talk about this later. Nothing I say right now will convince you.

Although the above conversation is contrived, the content of the exchange is very real. When it comes to abortion, many pro-life Christians don't know what to say. They're caught completely off-guard just like Emily was. Sure, they have pro-life convictions, but defending those convictions with friends and co-workers is another matter altogether. Better to stay silent and avoid embarrassment. Who wants to stir up a hornet's nest the way Emily did?

The good news is, you don't have to surrender in silence. There's a better way. Simplify the debate by focusing on the one question that truly matters: *What is the unborn?*

HIDDEN ASSUMPTIONS

Emily didn't realize it, but Pam was cheating. Not that Pam meant to—she was just repeating what she'd heard abortion-choice advocates say in the popular media. Nevertheless, she was cheating by assuming the very thing she was trying to prove.

Put simply, each of her objections *assumed* that the unborn are not human beings. However, instead of proving that conclusion with facts and arguments, she merely assumed it within the course of her rhetoric. We call this begging the question, and as Francis J. Beckwith points out, it's a logical fallacy that lurks behind many arguments for abortion.[2] For example, consider Pam's claim that we shouldn't force our views on others. Do you think she would say such a thing if someone wanted the right to choose to kill toddlers? There's no way. Only by assuming the unborn aren't human can she make such a claim. Or take her objection that government shouldn't get involved in our personal decisions. Can you imagine, even for a moment, Pam arguing this way if the topic were child abuse? Again her objection only flies if she assumes the unborn isn't already a child. If he is one, abortion is the worst kind of child abuse imaginable. Pam also asserts that if we restrict abortion, women will be forced to get dangerous back-alley abortions. We'll take up that specific objection in a later chapter, but notice that it, too, assumes that the unborn are not human. Otherwise she is claiming that

---

[2]Francis J. Beckwith, *Politically Correct Death: Answering Arguments for Abortion Rights* (Grand Rapids, MI: Baker Books, 1993), 59.

because some people will die attempting to kill others, the state should make it safe and legal for them to do so.

I AGREE, IF . . .

Nadine Strossen is the former president of the ACLU, and I consider her a friend. She is pleasant, and I enjoy her company each time we debate. I wish more of my opponents were like her.

During a January 2008 Worldview Forum at Malone College (in Canton, Ohio), Nadine and I debated abortion in front of a full house of a thousand students, faculty, and others. The ACLU of Ohio even reserved one hundred seats in advance. This was our second debate in the course of a year. The theme of our exchange was "Abortion: Legal Right or Moral Wrong?"

The coin toss went to Nadine, which meant she got to speak first. She tried to frame the debate with an appeal to reproductive freedom. To paraphrase her case, reproductive freedom means the ability to choose whether or not to have children according to one's own personal religious beliefs. That freedom is necessary if all persons are to lead lives of self-determination, opportunity, and human dignity. She repeatedly stressed our need to work together to reduce the high number of abortions, by which she meant pro-lifers should support tax-funded birth control programs.

Notice the question-begging nature of her claim. She simply assumed that the unborn are not human beings. Would she make this same claim for human freedom and self-determination if the debate were about killing toddlers instead of fetuses?

To help the audience see the problem, I began my own opening speech by saying the following (paraphrased for brevity):

> Men and women, I agree completely with everything Nadine just said. She's right that abortion is a personal, private matter that should not be restricted in any way. She's right that we shouldn't interfere with personal choices. She's right that pro-lifers should stay out of this decision. Yes, I agree completely *if*. *If* what? If the unborn are not human beings. And if Nadine can demonstrate that the unborn are not members of the human family, I will concede this exchange, and so should everyone else who is pro-life.

Contrary to what some may think, the issue that divides Nadine and me is not that she is pro-choice and I am anti-choice. Truth is, I am vigorously "pro-choice" when it comes to women choosing a number of moral goods. I support a woman's right to choose her own health care provider, to choose her own school, to choose her own husband, to choose her own job, to choose her own religion, and to choose her own career, to name a few. These are among the many choices that I fully support for the women of our country. But some choices are wrong, like killing innocent human beings simply because they are in the way and cannot defend themselves. No, we shouldn't be allowed to choose that. So, again, the issue that separates Nadine and me is not that she is pro-choice and I am anti-choice. The issue that divides us is just one question: What is the unborn? Let me be clear: If the unborn is a human being, killing him or her to benefit others is a serious moral wrong. It treats the distinct human being, with his or her own inherent moral worth, as nothing more than a disposable instrument. Conversely, if the unborn are not human, killing them through elective abortion requires no more justification than having your tooth pulled.

In short, I was willing to buy her argument for freedom and self-determination, but only if she could demonstrate that the unborn are not human beings. I then argued scientifically that the unborn are distinct, living, and whole human beings, a case we'll take up in the next chapter.

Framing the exchange around the status of the unborn set the tone for the entire evening and allowed me to ask good questions later in the debate. For example, during cross-examination I asked Nadine why the high number of abortions troubled her. After all, if abortion does not take the life of a defenseless human being, why worry about reducing it?

Notice that I made my case in two steps. First, I simplified the debate by focusing public attention on just one question: What is the unborn? Second, I argued for my pro-life view.

This two-part strategy is the same whether your audience has one person or a thousand. Consider Pam's objection to Emily's pro-life stance: "You certainly don't want the government getting involved in Sarah's personal life, do you?" Suppose Emily replied as follows: "Pam, if Sarah were talking about killing her toddler to solve a difficult life problem, would you object to the government telling her she can't do that?" There's no way Pam's going to say yes. Instead, she'll likely say, "Well, that's different—it's not the same thing."

Oh, really? Not the same? How so? As you can see, Pam is assuming that the unborn are not human. Emily's question exposed that assumption and refocused the discussion on the status of the unborn. The strategy is clear: first simplify, then argue. Let's examine those two steps in more detail.

STEP #1: SIMPLIFY THE ISSUE

If you think a particular argument for elective abortion begs the question regarding the status of the unborn, here's how to clarify things: *Ask if this particular justification for abortion also works as a justification for killing toddlers.* If not, the argument assumes that the unborn are not fully human. I call this tactic "Trot out the Toddler," and it's illustrated in the dialogue below. The purpose is not to argue for the humanity of the unborn (you'll do that later) but to frame the debate around one question: What is the unborn?

Let's revisit the exchange between Pam and Emily. Pam justified abortion with an appeal to privacy. She also said that poor women can't afford any additional children. Again, only by assuming that the unborn are not human do these appeals have any force whatsoever. Here's how Emily might have clarified the issue and exposed Pam's hidden assumptions about the unborn:[3]

Emily: Pam, you say that privacy is the issue. Pretend that I have a two-year-old in front of me. (She holds out her hand at waist level to illustrate this.) May I kill him as long as I do it in the privacy of the bedroom?

Pam: That's silly—of course not!

Emily: Why not?

Pam: Because he's a human being.

Emily: Ah. If the unborn are human, like the toddler, we shouldn't kill the unborn in the name of privacy any more than we'd kill a toddler for that reason.

Pam: You're comparing apples with oranges, two things that are completely unrelated. Look, killing toddlers is one thing. Killing a fetus that is not a human being is quite another.

Emily: Ah. That's the issue, isn't it? Are the unborn human beings, like toddlers? That is the one issue that matters.

Pam: But many poor women cannot afford to raise another child.

Emily: When human beings get expensive, may we kill them? Getting back to my toddler example, suppose a large family collectively decides to

---

[3]Portions of this dialogue, with some modification, first appeared in Gregory Koukl and Scott Klusendorf, "The Vanishing Pro-Life Apologist," *Clear Thinking*, Spring 1999.

quietly dispose of its three youngest children to help ease the family budget. Would this be okay?

Pam: Well, no, but aborting a fetus is not the same as killing children.

Emily: So once again the issue is, what is the unborn? Is the fetus the same as a human being? We can't escape that question, can we?

Again, notice that Emily has not yet argued for the humanity of the unborn or made any case for the pro-life view whatsoever. She'll do that later. For now all she's doing is framing the issue around one question: What is the unborn? That is the crux of the debate, and it clarifies many of the toughest questions, including the rape objection.

Pam: But what about a woman who's been raped? Every time she looks at that kid she's going to remember what happened to her. If that's not hardship, what is?

Emily: I agree that we should provide compassionate care for the victim, and it should be the best care possible. That's not at issue here. It's your proposed solution I'm struggling to understand. Tell me, how should a civil society treat innocent human beings who remind us of a painful event? (She pauses and lets the question sink in.) Is it okay to kill them so we can feel better? Can we, for example, kill a toddler who reminds her mother of a rape?

Pam: No, I wouldn't do that.

Emily: I wouldn't either. But again, isn't that because you and I both agree that it's wrong to kill innocent human beings, even if they do remind us of a painful event?

Pam: But you don't understand how much this woman has suffered. Put yourself in her shoes. How would you feel?

Emily: You're right. I don't understand her feelings. How could I? How could anyone? I'm just asking if hardship justifies homicide. Can we, for instance, kill toddlers who remind us of painful events? Again my claim here is really quite modest. If the unborn are members of the human family, like toddlers, we should not kill them to make someone else feel better. It's better to suffer evil rather than to inflict it.[4] Personally, I wish I could give a different answer, but I can't without trashing the principle that my right to life shouldn't depend on how others feel about me. In the end, sometimes the right thing to do is not the easy thing to do. And what's right depends on the question, what is the unborn? We can't get around it.

---

[4]See Peter Kreeft, *The Unaborted Socrates* (Downers Grove, IL: InterVarsity Press, 1983).

In this revised dialogue, Emily stays focused like a laser beam on the status of the unborn. She graciously yet incisively exposes the hidden assumptions in Pam's rhetoric, forcing each objection back to the question, what is the unborn? She doesn't let Pam distract her with appeals to privacy, economic hardship, or rape, all of which assume that the unborn are not human beings. She sticks to just one issue.

Until you clarify what's really at stake—namely, that we can't answer the question, can we kill the unborn? until we answer the question, what is the unborn?—there's no point advancing your case. Gregg Cunningham is correct. For too long the pro-life movement has been shouting conclusions rather than establishing facts.[5] Staying focused on the status of the unborn brings moral clarity to the abortion debate. It allows you to engage friends and critics in conversation so that you do not talk past each other.

Admittedly, trotting out a toddler won't persuade everyone there's only one issue to resolve. Some abortion-choice advocates bite the bullet and concede the humanity of the unborn but justify elective abortion with an appeal to bodily autonomy. Judith Jarvis Thomson's famous violinist argument is a prime example of those who argue this way. I'll take up that particular objection later in chapter 15, but you won't hear it often outside academic circles. Most people on the street simply assume that the unborn are not human beings.

STEP #2: MAKE A CASE FOR LIFE

Once you've framed the discussion around the status of the unborn, you can present a basic case for the pro-life position. We'll explore that case in more detail in the next two chapters, but for now here's a summary of what that case looks like.

Pro-life advocates contend that elective abortion unjustly takes the life of a defenseless human being. This simplifies the abortion controversy by focusing public attention on just one question: Is the unborn a member of the human family? If so, killing him or her to benefit others is a serious moral wrong. It treats the distinct human being, with his or her own inherent moral worth, as nothing more than a disposable instrument. Conversely, if the unborn are not human, elective abortion requires no more justification than having a tooth pulled.

---

[5]Gregg Cunningham, the executive director of The Center for Bio-Ethical Reform, has said this in various public presentations; www.abortionno.org.

Pro-life advocates defend their case using science and philosophy. Scientifically, they argue that from the earliest stages of development, the unborn are distinct, living, and whole human beings. True, they have yet to grow and mature, but they are whole human beings nonetheless. Leading embryology textbooks affirm this.[6] For example, Keith L. Moore and T. V. N. Persaud write, "A zygote is the beginning of a new human being."[7]

Philosophically, there is no morally significant difference between the embryo you once were and the adult you are today. As Stephen Schwarz points out using the acronym SLED, differences of size, level of development, environment, and degree of dependency are not relevant in the way that abortion advocates need them to be:[8]

Size: Yes, embryos are smaller than newborns and adults, but why is that relevant? Do we really want to say that large people are more human than small ones? Men are generally larger than women, but that doesn't mean they deserve more rights. Size doesn't equal value.

Level of development: True, embryos and fetuses are less developed than you and I. But again, why is this relevant? Four-year-old girls are less developed than fourteen-year-old ones. Should older children have more rights than their younger siblings? Some people say that self-awareness makes one human. But if that is true, newborns do not qualify as valuable human beings. Remember, six-week-old infants lack the immediate capacity for performing human mental functions, as do the reversibly comatose, the sleeping, and those with Alzheimer's disease.

Environment: Where you are has no bearing on who you are. Does your value change when you cross the street or roll over in bed? If not, how can a journey of eight inches down the birth canal suddenly change the essential nature of the unborn from non-human to human? If the unborn are not already human, merely changing their location can't make them valuable.

Degree of dependency: If viability makes us valuable human beings, then all those who depend on insulin or kidney medication are not valuable, and we may kill them. Conjoined twins who share blood type and bodily systems also have no right to life.

---

[6]See T. W. Sadler, *Langman's Embryology*, 5th ed. (Philadelphia: W. B. Saunders, 1993), 3; Keith L. Moore and T. V. N. Persaud, *The Developing Human: Clinically Oriented Embryology* (Philadelphia: W. B. Saunders Company, 1998), 2–18; Ronan O'Rahilly and Fabiola Müller, *Human Embryology and Teratology*, 2nd ed. (New York: Wiley-Liss, 1996), 8, 29.
[7]Moore and Persaud, *The Developing Human*, 2.
[8]Stephen Schwarz, *The Moral Question of Abortion* (Chicago: Loyola University Press, 1990), 18. The SLED test was initially suggested by Schwarz but is modified and explained here by me.

In short, pro-life advocates contend that although humans differ immensely with respect to talents, accomplishments, and degrees of development, they are nonetheless equal because they share a common human nature.

IS KILLING ALWAYS WRONG?

Let me clarify two points. First, the pro-life view is not that it's always wrong to take human life, a position only a strict pacifist would hold. Our view is that it's always wrong to take human life without proper justification, and we believe (for reasons we'll discuss in this book) that elective abortion does just that.

Francis J. Beckwith outlines a basic pro-life syllogism as follows:

1. The unborn entity, from the moment of conception, is a full-fledged member of the human community.
2. It is prima facie morally wrong to kill any member of that community.
3. Every successful abortion kills an unborn entity, a full-fledged member of the human community.
4. Therefore, every successful abortion is prima facie morally wrong.[9]

By "full-fledged member of the human community" (premise #1), Beckwith means that the unborn are the same kind of being as you and I and thus have the same basic rights we do. True, they differ from us in terms of size, level of development, environment, and degree of dependency, but these differences are not morally relevant to their status as human beings. Thus, depriving them of life requires the same strict justification needed for killing a ten-year-old or any other human being. Note again that he is not arguing we can never take human life, only that it's *prima facie* wrong to do so, meaning that under normal circumstances we are not justified in killing another human being. That last point is a key distinction, one often missed by some abortion-choice advocates who insist that pro-lifers are inconsistent for opposing elective abortion but not opposing the death penalty, the killing of animals, or war. In this case, the abortion-choice advocate is attacking a straw man. As stated above, most pro-lifers do not say it's always wrong to take life, but that it's always wrong to take human life *without* justification.

---

[9]Francis J. Beckwith, *Defending Life: A Moral and Legal Case Against Abortion Choice* (New York: Cambridge University Press, 2007), xii. In using the term "successful" abortion, Beckwith is not saying unsuccessful abortions are morally permissible.

We believe elective abortion takes human life without justification, and thus we oppose it.

Second, by elective abortion I mean those abortions *not* medically necessary to save the mother's physical life. As reported in the journal *International Family Planning Perspectives*, the vast majority of abortions worldwide are *not* done for medical necessity but to delay giving birth:

> [T]he most commonly reported reason women cite for having an abortion is to postpone or stop childbearing. The second most common reason—socioeconomic concerns—includes disruption of education or employment; lack of support from the father; desire to provide schooling for existing children; and poverty, unemployment or inability to afford additional children. In addition, relationship problems with a husband or partner and a woman's perception that she is too young constitute other important categories of reasons. Women's characteristics are associated with their reasons for having an abortion: With few exceptions, older women and married women are the most likely to identify limiting childbearing as their main reason for abortion.[10]

Abortion clinic workers have acknowledged the "elective" nature of their trade for years. Dr. Warren Hern, whose 1984 book *Abortion Practice* is the standard medical teaching text on late-term abortion procedures, writes:

> A study of motivations for abortion has found that the majority are sought for socioeconomic reasons. Women seeking abortions seldom give the real reason for doing so to investigators studying the issue. The impression from clinical practice is that all but a few women seek abortions for reasons that can broadly be defined as socioeconomic, and many cite strictly economic reasons. . . . As a rule, women do not make decisions about pregnancy prevention or treatment on the basis of statistical evaluations and medical advice but rather on the basis of personal attitudes and necessities. At times medical considerations enter into the picture, but decisions are usually made on the basis of such factors as desire or lack of desire for parenthood, stability of relationships, educational status, emotional status, or economic status, among others.[11]

---

[10]Akinrinola Bankole, Susheela Singh, and Taylor Haas, "Reasons Why Women Have Induced Abortions: Evidence from 27 Countries," *International Family Planning Perspectives*, Vol. 24, No. 3, September 1998.
[11]Warren Hern, *Abortion Practice* (Boulder, CO: Alpenglo Graphics, 1990), 10, 39. During the 1995 Congressional debate over partial-birth abortion (clinically termed "Intact D&X abortion"), opponents of a proposed ban on the procedure asserted it was rarely performed and was used only in extreme cases when a woman's life was at risk or the fetus suffered from severe anomalies. However, Ron Fitzsimmons, executive

Suppose, however, that the pregnancy does in fact pose a grave threat to the mother's life. What is the morally correct way to proceed?

Ectopic pregnancy (EP) is a clear case in point. With EP, the developing human embryo implants somewhere other than the uterus, usually on the inner wall of the fallopian tube. This is an extremely dangerous situation for the mother. When the EP outgrows the limits of the narrow fallopian tube enclosing it, the tube bursts, resulting in massive internal hemorrhaging. In fact, EP is the leading cause of pregnancy-related death during the first trimester.[12] The accepted medical protocols in this case are to end the pregnancy through chemical (Methotrexate) or surgical intervention.[13] There is no way the developing human can survive EP. If the mother dies from internal bleeding, the embryo dies also, given he's too young to survive on his own. At the same time, the limits of current medical technology do not allow transfer to a more suitable environment. Despite our best intentions, we simply can't save the child.

What is the greatest moral good we can achieve in this situation? Is it best to do nothing and let two humans (likely) die, or is it best to act in such a way that we save one life even though the unintended and unavoidable consequence of acting is the death of the human embryo?

Pro-life advocates almost universally agree we should do the latter. It is better to save one life than lose two. Notice, however, that the *intent* of the physician is not to directly kill the embryo but to save the mother's life. The unintended and unavoidable consequence of that lifesaving act is the death of the embryo. Perhaps in the future we can transplant the embryo to a more desirable location. If that day comes, we should do that. But for now, ending the pregnancy is our only course of action. If we do nothing, both mother and child die. It's best that one should live. But again, notice that the intent in ending the pregnancy is to save the mother, not directly and purposefully to kill the child.[14]

As for other alleged threats to the mother's life, few are truly life-

---

director of the National Coalition of Abortion Providers, later admitted that not only was the actual number of partial-birth procedures much higher than he originally stated but that his own contacts with many of the physicians performing these procedures indicated that the vast majority were done on healthy mothers carrying healthy fetuses. Diane Gianelli, "Abortion Rights Leader Urges End to 'Half Truths,'" *American Medical News*, March 3, 1997.

[12]T. E. Goldner, H. W. Lawson, Z. Xia, H. K. Atrash, "Surveillance for Ectopic Pregnancy—United States, 1970–1989," *MMWR CDC Surveillance Summaries* 42 (6) (December 1993): 73–85.

[13]Eric Daiter, MD, "Ectopic Pregnancy: Overview," Obgyn.net, http://www.obgyn.net/women/women. asp?page=/pb/cotm/9902/9902.

[14]As a result, some pro-life advocates think we should avoid the term *abortion* in this case because the intent is radically different from abortions performed for socioeconomic reasons.

threatening. Most can be managed with proper physician oversight. Dr. Thomas Murphy Goodwin oversees the largest high-risk pregnancy clinic in the United States, averaging between fifteen thousand to sixteen thousand births annually. Excluding cases diagnosed late in pregnancy, only one or two cases a year pose an immediate lethal threat to the mother's life. Goodwin writes that even women suffering from cancer can often be treated with chemotherapy, and the fetus tolerates the treatment.[15]

SUMMARY: STAY HITCHED TO YOUR TODDLER

Again, whenever you hear an argument for elective abortion, stop and ask this question: Would this justification for killing the unborn work for killing a toddler? If not, your critic is assuming that the unborn aren't human, a point for which he needs to argue. Trot out your toddler to expose the hidden (and perhaps unrecognized) assumptions in the argument.

You may need to do this more than once. Your critic may toss numerous objections your way, none of which address the status of the unborn. You'll hear about rape, severely disabled kids, economic hardship, foster care problems, child abuse, and every other hard-case scenario imaginable. Be gracious, but don't fall for it. Keep trotting out your toddler. Stay focused on the one question that really matters: What is the unborn? Until that question is answered, everything else is a distraction.

Finally, remember that arguments are seldom won on the spot. Even after you make a compelling case for the pro-life view, critics—even intelligent ones—may balk. That shouldn't surprise us. Let's be honest: How many of us upon hearing a powerful rejoinder to one of our most cherished beliefs immediately concedes the point? To the contrary, we typically fight on. Thus, if the argument is won, it's won later when your critic is alone with his thoughts and quietly abandons his former position.

Conservative columnist and expert debater William Rusher writes that a genuine change of mind on a subject important to us can be painful:

> Nobody, when confronted with a really devastating argument against something in which he has hitherto deeply believed, slaps himself on the thigh and shouts, "By gosh, I never thought of that!" On the contrary, the blow will be resented. Very often it will be sustained in obstinate silence. The ego needs time to marshal its defenses—either to try to restore the

---

[15] Thomas Murphy Goodwin, "Medicalizing Abortion Decisions," *First Things*, March 1996; http://www.firstthings.com/article.php3?id_article=3835.

toppled idol, or to come to terms with the toppling, or (at the very least) to regain its own shattered composure.

It is precisely then, however—in the silent weeks or months after the argument, when perhaps no one else is present and the defeated arguer confronts only himself in the recollection of his defeat—that the argument may truly be said to be "won." Because then, if ever, is when the loser of the argument will tacitly abandon his former position. He may never admit to having changed his mind at all; but at the very least he will have rearranged his mental furniture, to insure that he does not hereafter sit, so often or so heavily, on that all too demonstrably fragile chair.[16]

Don't worry that you can't change everyone's mind. Truth is, hard-core abortion-choicers are not your primary customers. You're after the 60 percent of Americans in the mushy middle who think of themselves as "pro-choice" because they've never thought seriously about the choice they're advocating. Your job is to bring clarification and get them thinking. Just keep trotting out your toddler.

REVIEW QUESTIONS

1. What do pro-lifers contend about abortion? How does this help simplify the debate?

2. Why is the pro-choice/anti-choice distinction misleading?

3. In what ways are pro-lifers pro-choice? When it comes to choosing abortion, what makes that choice right or wrong?

4. Why do appeals to privacy and choice miss the point in the abortion debate?

5. What does *begging the question* mean? Why is this a logical fallacy?

6. What assumption seems to lurk behind many of the typical defenses for abortion?

7. How does "trotting out the toddler" help simplify the debate? What is its primary purpose?

8. A friend says, "Poor women cannot afford another child and should therefore have a right to an abortion." What is she assuming about the unborn? Use a *trot out the toddler* example to show that the status of the unborn is the real issue in the debate, not the poverty of the mother.

9. When abortion advocates argue for abortion in cases of rape, what are they assuming about the unborn? What question can you ask to expose that assumption?

---

[16]William Rusher, *How to Win Arguments More Often than Not* (New York: Doubleday, 1981), 44–45.

10. When pro-life advocates say it's a *prima facie* wrong to take human life, what do they mean?

11. What does William Rusher say about winning arguments?

HELPFUL RESOURCES

Randy Alcorn. *Why Pro-Life?: Caring for the Unborn and Their Mothers*. Colorado Springs: Multnomah, 2004.

Scott Klusendorf. *Pro-Life 101: A Step by Step Guide to Making Your Case Persuasively*. Signal Hill, CA: Stand to Reason Press, 2002.

Gregory Koukl. *Precious Unborn Human Persons*. Signal Hill, CA: Stand to Reason Press, 1997. (Call 1-800-2-REASON to order, or visit www.str.org.)

Gregory Koukl and Scott Klusendorf. *Making Abortion Unthinkable: The Art of Pro-Life Persuasion*. Signal Hill, CA: Stand to Reason Press, 2001.

Peter Kreeft. *The Unaborted Socrates: A Dramatic Debate on the Issues Surrounding Abortion*. Downers Grove, IL: InterVarsity Press, 1983.

2

WHAT IS THE UNBORN?

The science of embryology is clear. From the earliest stages of development, the unborn are distinct, living, and whole human beings. Therefore, every "successful" abortion ends the life of a living human being.

AS MENTIONED IN CHAPTER 1, we can't answer the question, can we kill the unborn? until we answer a prior question, what is the unborn?

The question is not mysterious. The science of embryology establishes a set of facts about the developing human, and as Robert P. George points out, "these facts are stubborn; there is no running away from them."[1]

"Human embryos are not creatures different in kind from human beings (like rocks, or potatoes, or alligators)," George writes. "They are, rather, human beings—distinct living members of the species Homo sapiens—at the earliest stage of their natural development. They differ from human beings at later developmental stages not in virtue of the kind of entity they are, but rather by degree of development."[2]

Leading embryology textbooks affirm this. Keith Moore and T. V. N. Persaud, in *The Developing Human: Clinically Oriented Embryology*, a widely used embryology text, write that "human development begins at fertilization when a male gamete or sperm (spermatozoon) unites with a female gamete or oocyte (ovum) to form a single cell—a zygote. *This highly specialized, totipotent cell marked the beginning of each of us as a unique individual*."[3]

Another text, T. W. Sadler's *Langman's Embryology*, states, "The devel-

---

[1]Cited in Robert P. George's blog debate with John Hood in National Review Online's The Corner, August 9, 2005; http://corner.nationalreview.com/post/?q=M2Y1MzAxZTFhMjczNDhlOWU5Yzc4YjFkZjRmNGFkYWI=.
[2]Ibid.
[3]Keith Moore and T. V. N. Persaud, *The Developing Human: Clinically Oriented Embryology* (Philadelphia: Saunders/Elsevier, 2008), 15 (emphasis added).

opment of a human begins with fertilization, a process by which the spermatozoon from the male and the oocyte from the female unite to give rise
to a new organism, the zygote."[4]

We've known these basic scientific facts for years. Prior to advocating elective abortion, former Planned Parenthood president Dr. Alan
Guttmacher was perplexed that anyone, much less a medical doctor, would
question them. "This all seems so simple and evident that it is difficult to
picture a time when it wasn't part of the common knowledge," he wrote in
his 1933 book *Life in the Making*.[5]

As early as 1868, Dr. Horatio Storer, the head of the American Medical
Association's Committee on Criminal Abortion, along with coauthor
Franklin F. Heard, confidently stated, "Physicians have now arrived at the
unanimous opinion that the foetus in utero is alive from the very moment
of conception. . . . [T]he willful killing of a human being at any stage of its
existence is murder."[6]

In 1981, a U.S. Senate judiciary subcommittee heard expert testimony
on when human life begins. Professor Micheline Matthews-Roth of Harvard
University Medical School told the subcommittee, "It is incorrect to say that
biological data cannot be decisive. . . . It is scientifically correct to say that
an individual human life begins at conception." Dr. Watson A. Bowes of the
University of Colorado Medical School stated, "The beginning of a single
human life is from a biological point of view a simple and straightforward
matter—the beginning is conception." The subcommittee report concludes,
"Physicians, biologists, and other scientists agree that conception marks the
beginning of the life of a human being—a being that is alive and is a member
of the human species. There is overwhelming agreement on this point in
countless medical, biological, and scientific writings."[7]

In short, you didn't come from an embryo. You once were an embryo.
At no point in your prenatal development did you undergo a substantial
change or change of nature. You began as a human being and will remain
so until death. Sure, you lacked maturity at that early stage of your life (as
does an infant), but you were human nonetheless. "Living things do not

---

[4]T. W. Sadler, *Langman's Embryology*, 5th ed. (Philadelphia: W. B. Saunders, 1993).
[5]Alan Guttmacher, *Life in the Making: The Story of Human Procreation* (New York: Viking Press, 1933), 3.
[6]Horatio Storer and Franklin Heard, *Criminal Abortion: Its Nature, Its Evidence & Its Law* (out of print);
cited in Stephen Krason, *Abortion: Politics, Morality, and the Constitution* (Lanham, MD: University Press in
America, 1984), 171.
[7]Subcommittee on Separation of Powers to Senate Judiciary Committee S-158, Report, 97th Congress, 1st
Session, 1981.

become entirely different creatures in the process of changing their form," writes Gregory Koukl. "Rather, they develop according to a certain physical pattern precisely because of the kind of being they already are."[8]

DISTINCT, LIVING, AND WHOLE

Again, no one is claiming that embryos are *mature* human beings. Rather, my claim is that they are distinct, living, and whole members of the human species regardless of their size or location. As is true of infants, toddlers, and teenagers, embryos are human individuals at a particular stage of their development, and thus they do not differ in kind from the mature adults they will one day become.

Each of these points should be clarified. To say the embryo is *distinct* means it is different in kind from any cell of its parents. Sperm and egg, for example, cease to exist at fertilization, their role being restricted to surrendering their constituents into the makeup of a new entity, the embryo. From the start this new entity not only directs its own internal development, it has something completely different from both parents—its own unique chromosomal structure. Later it will bear other distinctions such as a different blood type and different internal organs.

That the embryo is *living* seems obvious on the face of it, as dead things don't grow. Scientists generally agree that anything that exhibits irritability (reaction to stimuli), metabolism (converting food to energy), and cellular reproduction (growth) is alive. Not only does the embryo exhibit all of these things, it develops itself in ways conducive to its own survival and maturation. True, there is some limited disagreement about how we should define "life," as some things have only some of the characteristics of living things (for example, viruses). However, just because we don't know if a *specific* thing is alive does not mean we can't know if *anything* is alive. And anything that exhibits the three qualities above is living.[9]

It's also clear that the embryo is *human* since it comes from human parents and has the genetic constitution characteristic of human beings. Put simply, human parents produce human offspring. To deny this, one must explain how two human parents can produce offspring that is not human but later becomes so. Most importantly, the embryo is a *complete* or *whole* human organism rather than part of another living entity. All of its cells

---

[8]Gregory Koukl, *Precious Unborn Human Persons* (Signal Hill, CA: Stand to Reason Press, 1997), 21.
[9]Steve Wagner and David Lee, *Abortion: From Debate to Dialogue* (Wichita: Justice for All, 2005), 16.

work together in tandem toward the growth of a single entity, the embryo. "From conception onward, the human embryo is fully programmed, and has the active disposition, to develop himself or herself to the next mature stage of a human being," write Robert George and Patrick Lee.[10]

ANY OL' CELL WILL DO?

Nonetheless, Ronald Bailey of *Reason* magazine insists that we gain no real knowledge from these basic scientific facts. Sure, human embryos carry the full genetic code, but so do ordinary somatic (body) cells. Using cloning technology, we can generate an entire human embryo from one of these cells, thus demonstrating that early embryos are no different in kind from any other bodily cell that's routinely discarded.[11]

This is bad biology. As Lee and George point out, Bailey is making the rather elementary mistake of confusing *parts* with *wholes*.[12] The difference in kind between each of our cells and a human embryo is clear: An individual cell's functions are subordinated to the survival of the larger organism of which it is merely a part. The human embryo, however, is already a whole human entity. True, it's an immature human, as is an infant, but it's a whole human organism nonetheless.

That is to say, although Bailey is right that a somatic cell contains a complete genetic code, left alone it will never develop itself to the mature stage of a human. If you plant it in a uterus or a test tube, it remains what it is—a bodily cell. Even in a cloning process, it must be acted upon externally so its constituents can be merged with an enucleated ovum, thus forming a new living organism. In that sense, each of our cells is analogous to sperm and egg, not to a whole human embryo. Just as sperm and egg contribute genetic material that becomes a human being, so adult cells, through cloning, can contribute material used to form a new human. An organism, on the other hand, only needs a proper environment and adequate nutrition and it will grow through its various stages.

It makes no sense to say that you were once a sperm or somatic cell. However, the facts of science make clear that you were once a human embryo. Lee and George say it well: "Somatic cells are not, and embryonic

---

[10]Robert P. George and Patrick Lee, "Acorns and Embryos," *The New Atlantis*, No. 7, Fall 2004/Winter 2005, 90-100; http://www.thenewatlantis.com/publications/acorns-and-embryos.

[11]Ronald Bailey, "Are Stem Cells Babies?" *Reason*, July 11, 2001.

[12]Robert George and Patrick Lee, "Reason, Science, and Stem Cells," *National Review Online*, July 20, 2001.

human beings are, distinct, self-integrating organisms capable of directing their own maturation as members of the human species."[13]

ARE HUMAN EMBRYOS MERE CLUMPS OF CELLS?

Imagine a Halloween visit to the local morgue—alone. Inside are dozens of bodies with living cells, but no one offers you candy (thankfully). Why do we call the occupants dead and you living?

Strictly speaking, the biological differences aren't that great between a person five minutes before death and five minutes after. Immediately after death, cells remain alive and, for a time, function normally. Yet something has clearly changed. What is it?

Dr. Maureen Condic, assistant professor of neurobiology and anatomy at the University of Utah, states that "death occurs when the body ceases to act in a coordinated manner to support the continued healthy function of all bodily organs. Cellular life may continue for some time following the loss of integrated bodily function, but once the ability to act in a coordinated manner has been lost, 'life' cannot be restored to a corpse—no matter how 'alive' the cells composing the body may yet be."[14]

Condic goes on to say that embryos are nothing like a corpse, which merely contains clumps of cells. Rather, they are living human beings because

> they possess the single defining feature of human life that is lost in the moment of death—the ability to function as a coordinated organism rather than merely as a group of living human cells. . . . It is precisely this ability that breaks down at the moment of death, however death might occur. Dead bodies may have plenty of live cells, but their cells no longer function together in a coordinated manner.[15]

In other words, Ronald Bailey is just plain wrong when he claims embryos are no different in kind from ordinary body cells. As Condic points out, from conception forward, human embryos clearly function as whole living organisms.[16] They are not mere collections of cells like those on a corpse but are "living creatures with all the properties that define any organism as distinct from a group of cells; embryos are capable of growing,

---

[13]Ibid.
[14]Maureen L. Condic, "Life: Defining the Beginning by the End," *First Things*, May 2003.
[15]Ibid.
[16]Frozen embryos, though not appearing to function as organisms, actually are.

maturing, maintaining a physiologic balance between various organ systems, adapting to changing circumstances, and repairing injury. Mere groups of human cells do nothing like this under any circumstances."[17]

BAD SCIENCE: SIX COMMON OBJECTIONS

1) Twinning. Cloning advocates sometimes claim that because an early embryo may split into twins (up until fourteen days after conception), there is no reason to suppose that it's an individual human being prior to that time. Hence, early embryo research prior to day 14 is morally permissible. The flaws in this argument are easy to spot.

First, how does it follow that because an entity may split (or even recombine) that it was not a whole living organism prior to the split? As Patrick Lee points out, if we cut a flatworm in half we get two flatworms.[18] Would advocates of destructive embryo research argue that prior to the split, there was no distinct flatworm? I agree that twinning is a mystery. We don't know if the original entity dies and gives rise to two new organisms or if the original survives and simply engages in some kind of asexual reproduction. Either way, this does nothing to call into question the existence of a distinct human organism prior to splitting.

Second, if the early embryo (prior to twinning) is merely a hunk of cells and not a unitary organism, why doesn't each individual cell develop individually? Robert George writes:

> The clearest evidence that the embryo in the first two weeks is not a mere mass of cells but is a unitary organism is this: if the individual cells within the embryo before twinning were each independent of the others, there would be no reason why each would not regularly develop on its own. Instead, these allegedly independent, non-communicating cells regularly function together to develop into a single, more mature member of the human species. This fact shows that interaction is taking place between the cells from the very beginning (even within the zona pellucida, before implantation), restraining them from individually developing as whole organisms and directing each of them to function as a relevant part of a single, whole organism continuous with the zygote. Thus, prior to an extrinsic division of the cells of the embryo, these cells together do constitute a single organism. So, the fact of twinning does not show that

---

[17]Condic, "Life: Defining the Beginning by the End."
[18]Patrick Lee, *Abortion and Unborn Human Life* (Washington, DC: Catholic University Press in America, 1996), 93.

the embryo is a mere incidental mass of cells. Rather the evidence clearly indicates that the human embryo, from the zygote stage forward, is a distinct, unitary human organism—a human being.[19]

The key point is that even though the cells in the early embryo are totipotent (that is, able to develop into any kind of bodily cell), they function in a coordinated manner as parts of a unified organism, the embryo.

Third, cloning technology renders the twinning objection absurd. Put simply, cloning is twinning. An ordinary skin cell taken from any one of us can be used to form an embryo with the donor's genetic code. "If an embryo has no right to life because a twin can be formed from it, and a twin can be formed from any of us, it follows that nobody has a right to life," writes Ramesh Ponnuru.[20]

Fourth, there's plausible scientific evidence that only a small percentage of embryos have the capacity to split. Thus, in the vast majority of cases, the twinning objection vanishes altogether.[21]

2) Miscarriage. Cloning advocates cite the high number of miscarriages as proof that a) embryos are not individual human organisms, and b) destructive research is morally permissible. Suppose miscarriages are common—how does this fact refute the claim that embryos are human beings? Many Third-World countries have high infant mortality rates. Are we to conclude that those infants who die early were never whole human beings? Moreover, how does it follow that because nature may *spontaneously* abort an embryo I may *deliberately* kill one? Admittedly, these miscarriages are tragic events. But as journalist Andrew Sullivan points out, just because earthquakes happen doesn't mean massacres are justified.[22]

3) The burning research lab. Advocates of embryonic stem cell research such as Ellen Goodman use this objection to justify destroying embryos for medical research. It goes like this: Suppose a research lab is on fire. Whom should you save—a vial full of frozen embryos or a two-year-old? Goodman is banking that our moral intuitions will drive us to choose the toddler, thus proving we don't really think the embryo is human after all.[23]

[19]George posted these comments at National Review's website The Corner on August 8, 2005, in his reply to John Hood.
[20]Ramesh Ponnuru, *Party of Death: The Democrats, the Media, the Courts, and the Disregard for Human Life* (Washington, DC: Regnery, 2006), 156.
[21]Edwin C. Hui, *At the Beginning of Life: Dilemmas in Theological Bioethics* (Downers Grove, IL: InterVarsity Press, 2002), 69–70.
[22]Andrew Sullivan, "Only Human," *The New Republic*, July 19, 2001.
[23]Ellen Goodman, "Weathering the Embryo Debate," *Boston Globe*, June 12, 2005.

The objection fails for three reasons. First, how does choosing to save one human being over another prove the one left behind is not human? Given a choice between saving my daughter and a building full of other people, I would save my own kid. Would that prove the others were not human beings?

Second, the debate over embryonic stem cell research is not about choosing whom we're going to *save*, as in the case of the burning lab. It's about whom we're going to deliberately *kill* to benefit us. Saving my own kid first is permissible. Shooting those left behind is not, even if it would increase my chances of escape.

Third, moral intuitions are important, but they are not infallible. We must examine them in light of reason. A little over a century ago, many whites thought it unthinkable that anyone would consider black slaves human beings.[24] Hadley Arkes recounts one such example from Chapter 32 of *The Adventures of Huckleberry Finn*, where Huck contrives a story to explain to Aunt Sally his late arrival by boat:

> "We blowed out a cylinder head."
> "Good gracious! Anybody hurt?"
> "No'm. Killed a nigger."
> "Well, it's lucky; because sometimes people do get hurt."[25]

Notice it's simply assumed that the black man is not one of us. Thus, it's no stretch to imagine a proponent of slavery putting the following challenge to a northern abolitionist: "Your barn is burning. You have a choice of saving a Negro slave or a white schoolboy. Which would you choose?" If a majority of abolitionists leave the black kid behind, does that change the kind of thing he is or, more to the point, justify our killing him to get the white kid out?

4) "The sperm and egg are alive." Like the "every cell is alive" objection above, this one fails to distinguish between parts and wholes. Unlike the embryo, which is already a whole human organism, sperm and egg are merely parts of larger human organisms. The capacity of each is restricted to fulfilling a given purpose within the larger context of a human body. For this reason they differ radically from the capacity of the human embryo.

---

[24]See, for example, the various essays published in Eric L. McKitrick, ed., *Slavery Defended: The View of the Old South* (Englewood Cliffs, NJ: Prentice-Hall, 1963).

[25]Mark Twain, *The Adventures of Huckleberry Finn* (New York: Harper-Collins, 1994), 258. Cited in Hadley Arkes, *Natural Rights and the Right to Choose* (New York: Cambridge University Press, 2002), 126–127.

Again, when we say the human embryo already is a whole human organism, we don't mean it's a mature human organism. But it's a human organism nonetheless with the inherent capacity to develop into a fetus, infant, toddler, teenager, and adult. This capacity to develop into all stages of human existence is not something external to the embryo but is inherent in its very nature.[26] In the case of sperm and egg, each dies in the act of contributing its parts to the makeup of a new, whole living organism—the embryo.[27]

5) Ignorance. Philosopher David Boonin discounts the pro-lifer's claim that the newly conceived zygote is a distinct, living, and whole human organism. How can this be, he argues, when we don't know the precise moment during the conception process at which the new zygotic human being comes into existence?[28] Here Boonin is both right and wrong. True, we don't know exactly when during the conception process the zygote comes to be. Some embryologists argue that it happens when the sperm penetrates the ovum, while others point to syngamy, when the maternal and parental chromosomes cross over and form a diploid set.

But as Francis J. Beckwith points out, although Boonin raises an important *epistemological* question (when do we know that sperm and egg cease to be and a new organism arises?), he's mistaken that his skepticism successfully undermines the pro-lifer's strongly supported *ontological* claim that the zygote is a distinct, living, and whole human being. "It may be that one cannot, with confidence, pick out the precise point at which a new being comes into existence between the time at which the sperm initially penetrates the ovum and a complete and living zygote is present. But how does it follow from this acknowledgment of agnosticism that one cannot say that zygote X is a human being?"[29]

Moreover, Boonin's skepticism cuts both ways and serves to undermine his own case. Abortion advocates typically claim that until a fetus has value-giving properties such as self-awareness, rationality, and sentience, it does not have a right to life. But since when can we know the precise moment

---

[26]Note, though, that the capacity to develop through these stages is not the thing that gives the embryo value. How it develops simply helps us see the kind of thing it is. The capacity to develop (as well as all other capacities) are markers for the kind of thing we are. And it's the kind of thing we are that makes us valuable. See Chapter 3.

[27]For more, see George and Lee, "Reason, Science, and Stem Cells." I owe my thoughts in this paragraph to their excellent analysis.

[28]David Boonin, *A Defense of Abortion* (Cambridge: Cambridge University Press, 2003), 37–40.

[29]Francis J. Beckwith, "Defending Abortion Philosophically: A Review of David Boonin's *A Defense of Abortion*," *Journal of Medicine & Philosophy* 31 (April 2006): 177–203.

that those properties come to be in the fetus? That is, at what *exact* point in the pregnancy does the unborn become rational enough to warrant a right to life? No one can say, though abortion advocates suggest that it's somewhere between twenty-four to thirty weeks. Despite their lack of certitude on these questions, few abortion advocates are willing to surrender their views. However, if the pro-life position is refuted by a lack of certitude, so is the abortion-choice one.[30]

6) *"The term 'human being' is hard to define precisely; it may not apply to embryos."* This is simply false. Peter Singer, who supports not only elective abortion but also the killing of some newborns, writes:

> It is possible to give 'human being' a precise meaning. We can use it as equivalent to 'member of the species *Homo Sapiens*.' Whether a being is a member of a given species is something that can be determined scientifically, by an examination of the nature of the chromosomes in the cells of living organisms. In this sense, there is no doubt that from the first moments of its existence an embryo conceived from human sperm and egg is a human being.[31]

Like Singer, philosopher Wayne Sumner does not contest the scientific evidence for the humanity of the unborn, though he defends elective abortion in other ways. "A human fetus is not a non-human animal; it is a stage of human being."[32]

A FINAL CONSIDERATION: CONSTRUCTION VERSUS DEVELOPMENT

Philosopher Richard Stith asks an important question: are human embryos and fetuses constructed or do they develop

Stith asks us to consider the example of a car. When does the car come to be? Some might say it's when the body is welded to the frame, giving the appearance of a vehicle. Others insist there can be no car until the engine and transmission are installed, thus enabling the car to move. Others point to the addition of wheels, without which a vehicle cannot make functional contact with the road.

But no one argues that the car is there from the very beginning, as, for example, when the first two metal plates are welded together. After all, those

---

[30]Ibid.

[31]Peter Singer, *Practical Ethics*, 2nd ed. (Cambridge: Cambridge University Press, 1993), 85–86.

[32]Wayne Sumner, *Abortion and Moral Theory* (Princeton, NJ: Princeton University Press, 1981), 10.

same metal plates can be used to construct some other object like a boat or a plane. Only gradually does the assemblage of random parts result in the construction of a car.

According to a 2005 *New York Times* op-ed piece cited by Stith, most Americans see the fetus exactly the same way—as something that's constructed part by part. It's precisely this understanding, he writes, that renders pro-life arguments absurd to so many people. As they see it, embryos are no more human beings in early stages of their construction than metal plates are cars in the early stages of theirs.[33]

Virginia Postrel, the former editor of *Reason* magazine, is a case in point. In a December 2001 *Wall Street Journal* op-ed piece defending destructive embryo research, she takes aim at pro-lifers who treat microscopic cells with no past or present consciousness, no organs or tissues, as people. A vocal minority of Americans, of course, do find compelling the argument that a fertilized egg is someone who deserves protection from harm. That view animates the anti-abortion movement and exercises considerable influence in Republican politics. But most Americans don't believe we should sacrifice the lives and well-being of actual people to save cells. Human identity must rest on something more compelling than the right string of proteins in a petri dish, detectable only with high-tech equipment. We will never get a moral consensus that a single cell, or a clump of 100 cells, is a human being. That definition defies moral sense, rational argument, and several major religious traditions.[34]

Besides Postrel's obvious category mistake (she answers a scientific question—"What kind of thing is the embryo?"—with appeals to non-scientific categories of morality, theology, and public opinion), the construction analogy she employs is deeply flawed. As Stith points out, embryos aren't constructed piece by piece from the outside; they develop themselves from within. That is to say, they do something no constructed thing could ever do: they direct their own internal growth and maturation, and this entails continuity of being. Unlike cars, developing embryos have no outside builder. They're all there just as soon as growth begins from within. In short, living organisms define and form themselves. An oak tree is the same entity that was once a shoot in the ground, years before it had branches and leaves.

---

[33]Richard Stith, "Does Making Babies Make Sense? Why so Many People Find it Difficult to See Humanity in a Developing Foetus," *Mercatornet,* September 2, 2008; http://www.mercatornet.com/articles/docs_making_babies_make_sense/.

[34]Virginia Postrel, "Yes, Don't Impede Medical Progress," *Wall Street Journal,* December 5, 2001; http://www.dynamist.com/articles-speeches/opeds/cloning.html.

Stith illustrates the difference between constructing and developing this way:

> Suppose that we are back in the pre-digital photo days and you have a Polaroid camera and you have taken a picture that you think is unique and valuable—let's say a picture of a jaguar darting out from a Mexican jungle. The jaguar has now disappeared, and so you are never going to get that picture again in your life, and you really care about it. (I am trying to make this example parallel to a human being, for we say that every human being is uniquely valuable.) You pull the tab out and as you are waiting for it to develop, I grab it away from you and rip it open, thus destroying it. When you get really angry at me, I just say blithely, "You're crazy. That was just a brown smudge. I cannot fathom why anyone would care about brown smudges." Wouldn't you think that I were the insane one? Your photo was already there. We just couldn't see it yet.[35]

Likewise, whenever critics of the pro-life view describe the embryo solely in terms of its appearance, they fall into a constructionism. It's an easy error to make. Our intuitions are not immediately impressed by the image of an eight-celled embryo with its dynamic self-directed development obscured.

However, our initial intuitions about the embryo can change dramatically upon reflection, as Stith explains:

> When we look backwards in time or otherwise have in mind a living entity's final concrete form, development becomes intuitively compelling. Knowing that the developing Polaroid picture would have been a jaguar helped us to see that calling it a "brown smudge" was inadequate. If we somehow had an old photo taken of our friend Jim just after he had been conceived, and was thus just a little ball, we'd have no trouble saying, "Look, Jim. That's you!" Thus the most arresting way to put the developmental case against embryo-destructive research would be something like this: "Each of your friends was once an embryo. Each embryo destroyed could one day have been your friend."[36]

To sum up, human beings develop. To say they are constructed is simply false. Nevertheless, the construction view remains intuitively plausible to large numbers of philosophers, whose views we turn to next.

---

[35]Stith, "Does Making Babies Make Sense?"
[36]Ibid.

The real fight is about the foundation for human value. Are you and I valuable for what we are or only valuable for what we can do? We'll take up that question in Chapter 3.

REVIEW QUESTIONS

1. Describe in a sentence what the science of embryology tells us about the unborn.

2. Ronald Bailey confuses parts with wholes. What do we mean by that?

3. Dr. Maureen Condic describes the critical difference between a mere group of cells and the embryonic human being. What is that difference?

4. What's wrong with the claim that sperm and egg are alive, like the embryo?

5. How does the definition of death help us clarify the status of the embryo?

6. Why are the objections based on twinning and miscarriage not persuasive?

7. Why does the burning research lab example fail to justify ESCR?

8. What does the *Huckleberry Finn* example teach us about moral intuitions?

9. How does Richard Stith's distinction between construction and development help clarify how we view embryos?

HELPFUL RESOURCES

Maureen L. Condic. "Life: Defining the Beginning by the End." *First Things* (May 2003); http://www.firstthings.com/ftissues/ft0305/articles/condic.html.

Robert George and Patrick Lee. "Reason, Science, and Stem Cells." *National Review Online*, July 20, 2001; http://www.nationalreview.com/comment/comment-george072001.shtml. (The article is part of a series of debates with Ronald Bailey.)

Robert P. George and Christopher Tollefsen. *Embryo: A Defense of Human Life.* New York: Doubleday, 2008.

3

WHAT MAKES HUMANS VALUABLE?

Humans have value simply because they are human, not because of some acquired property that they may gain or lose during their lifetime. If you deny this, it's difficult to account for fundamental human equality for anyone.

TO REVIEW, PRO-LIFE ADVOCATES contend that from the earliest stages of development, the unborn are distinct, living, and whole human organisms. They are not parts of larger human beings (like skin cells are) but are whole human entities capable of directing their own internal growth and development. Pro-lifers don't look to theology to tell them these things but to the science of embryology.

Admittedly, science cannot tell us how we should treat unborn humans. It can't tell us what's right and what's wrong. Is it wrong to torture toddlers for fun after beating your wife? Science can't help you with that question. Nor can it tell us why the unborn human (or for that matter, any human) has value and a right to life.

In short, science alone cannot justify the pro-life position, though it can give us the facts we need to draw moral conclusions on a host of controversial issues, including abortion, embryonic stem cell research, and cloning. Thus, the first step in resolving these issues is to state the proper scientific facts about the biological nature of the unborn entity. As we have seen, those facts are not in dispute. Embryology textbooks uniformly state that new human life comes into existence upon completion of fertilization (or after a successful cloning process).

That leaves us with an important philosophical question: Do all human beings regardless of size, level of development, environment, or degree of dependency have an equal right to life?

Pro-life Christians contend that human beings are valuable in virtue of the kind of thing they are, creatures endowed by their Creator with an unalienable right to life. That right to life comes to be when they come to be. The science of embryology establishes that we each come to be at conception or at the completion of a cloning process. From this it follows that we had the same basic right to life then as we do now. As we shall see in this chapter, secular critics deny this, insisting that mere membership in the human species is not enough to confirm a right to life. Rather, they say, humans come to be at one point but only become intrinsically valuable after they acquire some immediately exercisable capacity—usually self-awareness or sentience—that embryos and fetuses lack. Thus, embryos and fetuses do not have a right to life that we are obliged to respect.

SUBSTANCE THINGS VERSUS PROPERTY THINGS

The pro-life case for human equality is grounded in the substance view of human persons.[1] Substances are living organisms that maintain their identities through time, while property things, such as cars and machinery, do not. What moves a puppy to maturity or a fetus to an adult is not an external collection of parts but an internal, defining nature or essence. As a substance develops, it does not become more of its kind but matures *according to* its kind. It remains what it is from the moment it begins to exist. Consequently, a substance functions in light of what it is and maintains its identity even if its ultimate capacities are never realized due to disability or injury. A dog that never develops his capacity to bark is still a dog by nature.

In sharp contrast, a property thing, like my car, is nothing more than the sum total of its parts. Change the motor or replace a tire, and you technically have a different vehicle from the one that rolled off the assembly line. There is no internal nature (or essence) that orders its development and grounds its identity through change.

Applied to the pro-life case, the substance view tells us that you are identical to the embryo you once were. You were the same being then as you are now, though your functional abilities and physical characteristics have

---

[1]Contemporary proponents of this view include philosophers Robert P. George, J. P. Moreland, Patrick Lee, and Francis J. Beckwith, to name a few. I owe my own thoughts in this section primarily to Francis J. Beckwith's *Defending Life: A Moral and Legal Case Against Abortion Choice* (New York: Cambridge University Press, 2007), 49–50, 131–171 and Robert P. George, "Embryo Ethics," *Daedalus*, Winter 2008.

changed. From the moment you began to exist, there's been no substantial change in your essential nature. Moreover, you are intrinsically valuable in virtue of being you, not in virtue of some attribute you acquire at some point, such as nice looks, intelligence, etc. Thus, if you are intrinsically valuable now, you were intrinsically valuable at the embryonic stage as well.

True, a human embryo will develop accidental properties (such as self-awareness, sentience, and physical structure) as it matures, but these properties are nonessential and can be changed (or never fully expressed) without altering the nature of the thing itself. If you lose an arm or never learn to think abstractly, you remain yourself even though your ability to immediately exercise certain ultimate capacities is never fully realized.

Suppose you are in a terrible motorcycle accident that leaves you comatose for two years.[2] During that time, you lack the immediately exercisable capacity for self-awareness and have no sense of yourself existing over time. Are you the same person even though your functional abilities have changed? Imagine further that when the two years are up, you emerge from the coma with no memory of your past life. Your wife and kids are strangers. You touch the hot stove and get burned. You must relearn everything from speaking to eating to working with your hands. In many ways you are much like the standard fetus: You possess a basic capacity for self-awareness, rational thought, and language but lack the immediate capacity to exercise these things. Like the fetus, all of your life experience and memories will be new.

Through all of these changes, would you still be you? Could doctors have justifiably killed you during your extended sleep because you couldn't immediately exercise your capacity for self-awareness or sentience? If your right to life is based on your current functional abilities rather than on our common human nature, it's difficult to say why it would be wrong to kill you while you are comatose. Yet, clearly it would be morally wrong to kill you in that state, and the substance view can explain why: You never stopped being you through all of these changes because you have a human nature that grounds your identity through time and change.

In short, humans are equal by nature, not function.

HUMAN NON-PERSONS?

Most critics of the pro-life position reject the substance view of human persons outlined above. Instead, they ground human rights and human equal-

---

[2] I owe this example to Beckwith, *Defending Life*, 134–139.

ity in one's ability to immediately exercise certain capacities that embryos and fetuses, in virtue of their immature stage of development, cannot yet immediately exercise.

Abortion-choice advocate Mary Anne Warren says we should distinguish between human non-persons that we can destroy and human persons whom we can't. A person, she asserts, is a living entity with feelings, self-awareness, consciousness, and the ability to interact with his or her environment. Because a human fetus has none of these capabilities, it cannot be a person with rights.[3] Warren makes an assumption here that she does not defend. That is to say, even if she is correct about the distinction between a human being and a human person, she fails to tell us *why* a human being must possess self-awareness and consciousness in order to qualify as a person. In other words, she merely *asserts* that these traits are necessary for personhood but never says why these alleged value-giving properties are value-giving in the first place.[4]

Like Warren, Paul D. Simmons concedes that zygotes (early embryos) are biologically human but denies they are "complex" or "developed enough" to qualify as "persons" in a biblical or philosophical sense. "No one can deny the continuum from fertilization to maturity and adulthood," writes Simmons. "That does not mean, however, that every step on the continuum has the same value or constitutes the same entity."[5]

Simmons's larger purpose is to defend abortion rights by telling us who does and does not bear God's image. He argues that humans bear that image (and hence have value as "persons") not in virtue of the kind of thing they are (members of a natural kind or species) but only because of an acquired property, in this case the immediate capacity for self-awareness. A "person," he contends, "has capacities of reflective choice, relational responses, social experience, moral perception, and self-awareness." Human embryos, as mere clusters of human cells, do not have this capacity and therefore do not bear God's image.

Right away there are counter-examples that underscore the arbitrary nature of Simmons's claim.

First, newborns cannot make conscious, reflective choices until several

[3]Mary Anne Warren, "On the Moral and Legal Status of Abortion," in *The Problem of Abortion*, ed. Joel Feinberg (Belmont, CA: Wadsworth, 1984).
[4]See Patrick Lee, *Abortion and Unborn Human Life* (Washington, DC: Catholic University Press in America, 1996) for more on Warren's failure to argue for her view.
[5]Paul D. Simmons, "Personhood, the Bible, and the Abortion Debate," published by the Religious Coalition for Reproductive Choice; http://www.rcrc.org/pdf/RCRC_EdSeries_Personhood.pdf.

months after birth, so what's wrong with infanticide?[6] What principled reason can he give for saying, "No, you can't do that"? As Peter Singer points out in *Practical Ethics,* if self-awareness makes one valuable as a person, and newborns, like fetuses, lack that property, it follows that the fetus and newborn are both disqualified. You can't draw an arbitrary line at birth and spare the newborn.[7]

Abraham Lincoln raised a similar point with slavery, noting that any argument used to disqualify blacks as valuable human beings works equally well to disqualify whites.

> You say "A" is white and "B" is black. It is color, then: the lighter having the right to enslave the darker? Take care. By this rule, you are a slave to the first man you meet with a fairer skin than your own.
>
> You do not mean color exactly—You mean the whites are intellectually the superiors of the blacks, and therefore have the right to enslave them? Take care again: By this rule you are to be a slave to the first man you meet with an intellect superior to your own.
>
> But you say it is a question of interest, and, if you can make it your interest, you have the right to enslave another. Very well. And if he can make it his interest, he has the right to enslave you.[8]

Second, Simmons cannot account for basic human equality. As Patrick Lee and Robert George point out, if humans have value only because of some acquired property like skin color or consciousness and not in virtue of the kind of thing they are, then it follows that since these acquired properties come in varying degrees, basic human rights come in varying degrees. Do we really want to say that those with more self-consciousness are more human (and more valuable) than those with less? This relegates the proposition that all men are created equal to the ash heap of history.[9] Theologically and philosophically, it's far more reasonable to argue that although humans differ immensely with respect to talents, accomplishments, and degrees of development, they are nonetheless equal in fundamental dignity because they share a common human nature. In short, humans have value simply because they are human, not because of some acquired property they may

---

[6]Conor Liston and Jerome Kagan, "Brain Development: Memory Enhancement in Early Childhood," *Nature* 419, 896 (October 31, 2002). See also Ronan O'Rahilly and Fabiola Müller, *Human Embryology and Teratology,* 2nd ed. (New York: Wiley-Liss, 1996), 8.

[7]Peter Singer, *Practical Ethics* (Cambridge: Cambridge University Press, 1997), 169–171.

[8]*The Collected Works of Abraham Lincoln,* Vol. 2 (Piscataway, NJ: Rutgers University Press, 1953), 222.

[9]Robert P. George, "Cloning Addendum," *National Review Online,* July 15, 2002; Patrick Lee, "The Pro-Life Argument from Substantial Identity," Tollefsen Lecture, St. Anselm's College, November 14, 2002.

gain or lose during their lifetime. If you deny this, it's difficult to say why objective human rights apply to anyone.

Third, if the immediate capacity for consciousness makes one valuable, many non-human animals qualify as persons. Consequently, dogs, cats, and pigs are valuable persons, while fetuses, newborns, and victims of Alzheimer's disease are not. It's hard to see how Simmons can escape this conclusion given his belief that God's image in man is grounded in self-awareness and the capacity for reflective choice, not in human nature.

Fourth, human embryos have a basic (root) capacity for self-consciousness, lacking only the immediate capacity to exercise it. As George points out, human embryos possess this basic capacity in virtue of the kind of thing they are—members of a natural kind, a biological species whose members (if not prevented by some extrinsic cause) in due course develop the immediate capacity for such mental acts.[10] We can therefore distinguish two types of capacities for mental functions: 1) immediate and 2) basic or natural. On what basis can Simmons require for the recognition of full moral respect the first sort of capacity, which is an accidental attribute, and not the second, which is grounded in the kind of thing one already is?[11] I cannot think of any non-arbitrary justification.

Moreover, the difference between the two types of capacities is merely a difference of *degree*, not a difference of *kind*. The immediate capacity for mental functions is only the development of an underlying capacity that was there all along in virtue of the kind of entity the unborn already is.

In the end, Simmons's case for human value (as well as Warren's) is ad hoc and arbitrary. Why is some development needed? And why is this particular degree of development, self-awareness, the morally relevant factor rather than another? These questions are left unanswered.

"NO MORE" VERSUS "NOT YET"

John Hood asks, "If we can agree that brain death is the end of a person, then can we not agree that brain function is the beginning of a person?"[12] I'm often asked a variation of that same question: If the embryo (who doesn't even have a brain yet) is so valuable it cannot be killed by abortion, how do you justify pulling the plug on brain-dead individuals? Neither one has a functioning brain.

---

[10]George, "Cloning Addendum."
[11]Patrick Lee asks this question (though not addressing Simmons) in "The Pro-Life Argument from Substantial Identity."
[12]Posted on National Review's website The Corner, August 7, 2005.

I dealt with so-called personhood arguments above (the main problem being they are arbitrary and prove too much), but for starters, "pulling the plug" can mean a couple of different things, one moral, one immoral. First, it can mean disconnecting life support from a brain-dead individual. To be clear, a brain-dead person is in fact dead, meaning he's suffered (and this is key) an *irreversible* loss of all coordinated bodily function, including brain function.[13] His bodily systems no longer work together in an integrated manner the way they do in living organisms. In this case, all so-called life-support is doing is preventing the body from decomposing. There may, in fact, be good reasons for doing this—as, for example, when organs can be recovered for transplantation (with, of course, the patient's prior consent) or when a pregnant woman has an otherwise survivable fetus who will die if she is "unplugged." However, barring those types of cases, I see no moral requirement for using life-support to delay the decomposing process. After all, the person is already dead. Second, "pulling the plug" can mean (erroneously) active euthanasia on a person who is not brain-dead but merely brain-damaged, such as a mentally disabled person or perhaps someone in a persistent vegetative state. While both these states are lamentable, we are not dealing here with a corpse but a damaged human being. And we should not kill humans for their injuries.

Here's the key point: The embryo is nothing like the brain-dead person because the embryo, unlike you and I, does not need a brain to live. For the embryo, something else coordinates the bodily systems so that it functions as a coordinated whole. In short, embryos function as living organisms; brain-dead people do not. Hence, there is no parallel between the brain-dead person and the embryonic human beings you and I once were. As Stephen Schwarz points out, the embryo's brain is in the category of "not yet," while the brain-dead person's brain is in the category of "no more."[14] The latter has an irreversible loss of brain function resulting in death; the former does not yet need a brain to live.

If we thought the brain-dead person would (or even might) awaken several months later, we couldn't justify taking his organs. And that is exactly the condition of the embryo: it's a living organism, developing, fully human, though not yet fully mature. "We don't treat brain-dead people as dead because they are living human organisms who happen no longer to

---

[13]Maureen Condic, "Life: Defining the Beginning by the End," *First Things*, May 2003.
[14]Stephen Schwarz, *The Moral Question of Abortion* (Chicago: Loyola University Press, 1990), 52.

be persons," writes Ramesh Ponnuru. "We treat them as dead because they are no longer organisms, no longer capable of directing their own internal functioning."[15]

IS HUMAN EXCEPTIONALISM THE ROOT OF EVIL?

An animal rights activist once confronted me with this question: "So, if you are pro-life, why do you value animals less than humans? That belief has resulted in untold suffering for animals."

I agreed we shouldn't unjustly harm animals but then asked if she really believed the rest of what she'd just said. "Absolutely, I do."

"Then should we hold animals morally responsible for the crimes they commit? If your dog eats a hamster, what should the consequences be?"

We were out of time for that particular discussion, but I might have asked next, "With all due respect, if animals are no different than humans, is a man who kills his dog to feed his starving son no different morally than one who kills his son to feed the dog?"

Radical animal rights activists are mistaken. A robust belief in human exceptionalism does not exploit animals; it protects them from unjust harm. Consider the case of suspended Atlanta Falcons quarterback Michael Vick, sentenced to jail for dog fighting and gratuitous cruelty to animals. According to one report, "the 52 pit bulls found on Vick's estate were mostly emaciated" and kept "ravenously hungry so that they would eagerly assail the flesh of the dogs they met in the ring." The losing animals, the report said, "were sometimes executed if they didn't die in the fight. One dog, the grand jury reported, was hosed down after a loss and then electrocuted."[16]

When a raging Michael Vick clubs his pit bull to death for losing a fight, we're justifiably outraged at his inhumane and beastly behavior. But why are we outraged? Isn't it because we demand better of him *as a man?* Our revulsion of Vick makes no sense unless humans are exceptional. After all, prosecutors and critics are not blaming the dogs in this case; they are blaming humans who ought to behave better than animals. When dogs or rhinos tear each other up or kill unsuspecting prey, there's a reason we don't slap them with jail time. They don't have consciences, and they don't know better. They're just doing what comes naturally.

---

[15]Ramesh Ponnuru posted this on the National Review website The Corner, August 9, 2005.
[16]Gwen Knapp, "Gruesome Details of NFL Star's Dogfighting Indictment Causes Outcry," *San Francisco Chronicle*, July 19, 2007.

If you keep telling humans they are no different than animals, don't be surprised when they act that way. Give Vick back his football.

THE RELIGION THING

What makes human beings valuable? If you reply that all humans have value simply because they are human, someone's going to accuse you of making a controversial religious claim, one that has no place in the public square.

Whenever I hear this, my first question is, "What do you mean by *religion?*"

On college campuses, I'm usually told that religion involves metaphysics—that is, comprehensive doctrines about ultimate reality that can't be proved empirically or argued for rationally. You must accept them on faith. I then ask, "What do you mean by *faith?*" Most often I hear that faith means believing something in spite of the evidence; it's what you fall back on when the facts are against you.

After asking his reasons for believing that, I say, "Tell me why you think anything has value and a right to life." The answer inevitably is grounded in metaphysics, some comprehensive doctrine about the nature of human beings and their place in the world that can't be proved empirically. I then explain that although the pro-life view is implicitly religious, it is no more religious than alternative explanations about human value and human rights. Everyone is asking the same exact question: what makes humans valuable in the first place? Science can't answer that question because science deals only with things we can measure empirically through the senses. If you want an answer, you'll have to do metaphysics.

I deal with alleged metaphysical neutrality in Chapter 6 and give rational support for Christian theism in Chapter 7, but I'll give several reasons here why dismissing pro-life arguments as "religious" just won't work.

First, a non-believer can recognize that human embryos have value in virtue of the kind of thing they are rather than some function they perform. True, it will be difficult to ground that recognition outside a transcendent starting point for human rights and human dignity, but there's no reason a person must first embrace theism before grasping it.

Second, just because the pro-life view is consistent with a particular religious viewpoint (such as Christian theism, Conservative Judaism, or Islam) does not mean it can only be defended with arguments exclusive to that viewpoint. Nearly all Americans would agree it's wrong to kill toddlers for fun, and they don't need a course in church doctrine to apprehend that truth. At the same time, few people can present a completely secular argument detailing why abusing toddlers is objectively wrong. But that hardly stops them from recognizing this moral truth, even if they can't articulate their reasons in strictly secular terms.

Third, the claim that an embryo has value is no more religious than saying an infant or toddler does. Ramesh Ponnuru writes:

> The pro-life argument on abortion is that eight-week-old fetuses do not differ from ten-day-old babies in any way that would justify killing the former. A lot of people believe that God forbids the killing of ten-day-old babies, and many would be unable, if pressed, to give a persuasive account of non-theological reasons for holding such a killing to be wrong.[17]

Indeed, can a thoroughly materialistic (secular) worldview tell us why *anything* has value or a right to life? According to materialism, everything in the universe—including human beings and their capacity for rational inquiry—came about by blind physical processes and random chance. The universe came from nothing and was caused by nothing. At best, human beings are cosmic accidents. In the face of this devastating news, secularists simply presuppose the dignity of human beings, human rights, and moral obligations. But on what naturalistic basis can human rights and human dignity be affirmed?[18]

Fourth, even if we assume the pro-life view is essentially religious (though pro-life advocates can defend their views with reasons accessible to non-believers), why should anyone suppose that religious truth claims don't count as real knowledge?[19] The Declaration of Independence, Abraham Lincoln's Second Inaugural Address, and Martin Luther King's "Letter from the Birmingham Jail" all have their metaphysical roots in the biblical concept of *imago dei* (i.e., humans bearing the image of God). If pro-lifers are irrational for grounding basic human rights in the concept of a transcendent Creator, these important historical documents—all of which advanced our national understanding of equality—are irrational as well.

---

[17]Ramesh Ponnuru, *The Party of Death: The Democrats, the Media, the Courts, and the Disregard for Human Life* (Washington, DC: Regnery, 2006), 82.

[18]Paul Copan explores this problem with atheism in "The Moral Argument for God's Existence," http://www.4truth.net/site/apps/nl/content3.asp?c=hiKXLbPNLrF&b=778665&ct=1264233.

[19]Francis J. Beckwith deals with theology as knowledge in "Taking Theology Seriously: The Status of the Religious Beliefs of Judicial Nominees for the Federal Bench," *Notre Dame Journal of Law, Ethics, & Public Policy*, 20.1 (2006): 455–471.

Fifth, not all faith is blind. Christianity, for example, teaches trust (knowledge) based on evidence.[20] We see this throughout the New Testament:

- Acts 2:32, 36—This Jesus God raised up, and of that we all are witnesses. . . . Let all the house of Israel therefore *know for certain* that God has made him both Lord and Christ, this Jesus whom you crucified.
- Acts 17:2–4—And Paul went in, as was his custom, and on three Sabbath days *he reasoned with them from the Scriptures*, explaining and proving that it was necessary for the Christ to suffer and to rise from the dead, and saying, "This Jesus, whom I proclaim to you, is the Christ." And some of them were persuaded and joined Paul and Silas, as did a great many of the devout Greeks and not a few of the leading women.
- Acts 1:3—He presented himself alive to them after his sufferings *by many proofs*, appearing to them during forty days and speaking about the kingdom of God.
- Mark 2:10–11—"But that you may *know* that the Son of Man has authority on earth to forgive sins"—he said to the paralytic—"I say to you, rise, pick up your bed, and go home."
- Hebrews 11:1—Now faith is the *assurance* of things hoped for, the *conviction* of things not seen.

In short, the Christian faith is historical and places a high value on realism and on claims that are historically verifiable. The apostle Paul says it well: If Christ did not rise from the dead bodily and historically, we are dead in our sins, we are without hope, and our faith is one big ugly joke (cf. 1 Cor. 15:1–15). Of course, it's possible that Christian theism is mistaken in part or in whole (though I think that's highly unlikely), but there are no grounds for saying that biblical teaching promotes blind faith.

Sixth, the "imposing religion" objection is not really an argument, but a ramrod used to silence opposition to abortion. Law professor Mary Ann Glendon rightfully asks why citizens should have to withhold their moral views on abortion but not on other issues where they do not hesitate to advance religiously grounded moral viewpoints—such as the Vietnam War, capital punishment, civil rights, and relief of poverty.[21] Strange though it may seem to liberal elites, most religious conservatives I know don't want a theocracy or "Christian" nation that imposes theological doctrines. What they want is a more just nation, one where no human being regardless of reli-

---

[20]Gregory Koukl develops this at length in his audio CD, "Faith Is Not Wishing, Truth Is Not Ice Cream." Order from Stand to Reason, www.str.org.
[21]Mary Ann Glendon, "The Women of Roe v. Wade," *First Things*, June/July 2003.

gion, gender, size, level of development, location, or dependency is denied basic human rights. They also want judges who respect the rule of law rather than legislate from the bench. Given a choice between a "Christian" President who works against justice for the unborn or an agnostic one who promotes basic human rights for all, including the unborn, religious conservatives will opt in mass for the agnostic. In other words, religious conservatives care more about a candidate's worldview and judicial philosophy than they do his theology and doctrine.[22]

Finally, I could turn the tables on my secular critic and say, "Show me an argument for abortion rights that doesn't assume some transcendent grounding point." Here's the problem for the strict secularist: where does the right to an abortion come from? If it comes from the state, he really can't cry foul if the state decides to revoke that right. After all, the same government that grants rights can take them away. However, most abortion-choice advocates think the right to abortion is fundamental, meaning women have that right *even if* it's not respected by the state. Yet how can fundamental rights of any kind exist without a transcendent source of authority that grants them? Thomas Jefferson recognized this problem and promptly grounded human rights and human equality in the concept of a transcendent Creator. Of course, this by itself does not prove that Christianity, Judaism, or any other world religion is true, but it does make them consistent with the idea of human rights. Can atheism offer an equally plausible starting point for basic human rights? In short, I doubt my secular critic can get his own claim for fundamental abortion rights off the ground without borrowing from the very theistic worldview he so despises.

WHAT DO YOU MEAN BY "CAPACITY"?

Even though the sanctity of human life ultimately has religious origins, I think it's important to provide a line of thinking that pro-lifers can use to connect with those who reject religion but embrace human equality.

In theory, this shouldn't be difficult, given that most people claim to believe that all humans are equal. If they truly believe that, we need only use

---

[22]For example, Albert Mohler of the Southern Baptist Seminary said in 2007 that although Republican candidate Mitt Romney's Mormonism was theologically troubling, Romney nevertheless scored awfully high on family values and morality. "There are circumstances in which I might well vote for Mitt Romney as president of the United States," Mohler said. "In the right political context, there could be a lot of evangelicals voting for a Mormon candidate." Barbara Bradley Hagerty, "Romney Faces Uphill Battle for Evangelical Voters," NPR, *All Things Considered,* July 5, 2007; http://www.npr.org/templates/story/story.php?storyId=11762390. Bob Jones III, chancellor of the ultra-conservative Bob Jones University, even endorsed Romney for President.

science to show the unborn is a human being and their belief about equality should compel them to accept the pro-life view.

Others need more convincing. To the secularist who replies that humans are valuable because we have a capacity for self-awareness, the pro-lifer can expand on two points covered above. First, fetuses have that same natural capacity in virtue of the kind of thing they are. It just so happens that due to their age, they cannot yet immediately exercise it. Second, the essential nature of a thing, not its capacity for certain functions, determines its value. True, the capacities we observe help us know what *kind* of being we're dealing with, but they don't have value in themselves.

Here's how I work both points into my discussions with college students:

Student: I agree the fetus is biologically a human organism, but it has no capacity for self-awareness. Do you agree that the right to life is related to our capacity for self-awareness?

Me: What do you mean by "capacity"? Do you mean a natural one or one that is immediately exercisable?

Student: I'm not sure. I just mean that fetuses are not self-aware, and until they are, they don't have a right to life.

Me: So it's one's ability to immediately exercise a capacity for self-awareness that makes us valuable?

Student: Yes. That's what I'm saying.

Me: Why is the immediate capacity for self-awareness the thing that gives us value and not something else?

Student (pausing): Most people think it does.

Me: I take a different view. I say that our value as human beings is grounded in our common human nature that gives rise to certain capacities in the first place. Even if we fail to fully express these capacities, we remain valuable because of the kind of thing we are. If you deny this, it's difficult to say why human equality applies to anyone.

Student: I'm not sure I follow your distinction between immediate capacities and human nature.

Me: Here's the point I'm trying to make: the rights of individuals in our society are not based on their immediately exercisable capacities but on their common human nature that gives rise to certain natural capacities. This sounds complex, but we make this distinction all the time. People who are temporarily unconscious cannot presently function as self-aware human beings, but they still have value in virtue of their humanity. That is why we do not kill them. From the moment of conception, the unborn has a human nature. That he cannot yet speak, reason, or perform personal acts means only that he cannot yet function to the degree we can, not that he lacks the essential nature that makes those functions possible in the first place.

FROM WHERE DO RIGHTS COME?

Pro-life advocates, echoing Lincoln, argue that we must distinguish between *natural* rights and *legal* ones. Natural rights are those rights that you have simply because you are human. They are grounded in your human nature, or more precisely, on the fact that you are a personal being with a rational nature. You have these rights from the moment you begin to exist.[23] For example, you have a natural right not to be harmed without justification as well as a natural right not to be convicted of a crime without a fair trial. Government does not grant these basic rights. Rather, government's role is to protect them. In contrast, legal (or positive) rights are those rights you can only acquire through accomplishment or maturity. These rights originate from the government and include the right to vote at your eighteenth birthday and a right to drive on your sixteenth. But your *natural* right to live was there all along. It comes to be when you come to be.

To cash this out further, I do not have a legal (positive) right to vote in the next Canadian election for the simple reason that I am not a Canadian citizen. But just because I lack the right to vote in Canada does not mean I lack the right to basic protections whenever I visit that country. Likewise, just because a fetus may not have the positive right to drive a car or vote in the next election does not mean he lacks the *natural* right not to be harmed without justification. Hadley Arkes writes:

> No one would suggest that a fetus could have a claim to fill the Chair of Logic at one of our universities; and we would not wish quite yet to seek its advice on anything important; and we should probably not regard him as eligible to exercise the vote in any state other than Massachusetts. All of these rights or privileges would be inappropriate to the condition or attributes of the fetus. But nothing that renders him unqualified for these

---

[23]Hadley Arkes, *Natural Rights and the Right to Choose* (Cambridge: Cambridge University Press, 2002), 13–14. Of course, angels, God, and extraterrestrial beings also have personal natures and thus are intrinsically valuable.

special rights would diminish in any way the most elementary right that could be claimed for any human being, *or even for an animal*: the right not to be injured or killed without the rendering of reasons that satisfy the strict standards of a "justification."[24]

AN AMUSING PARADOX

Secular liberals insist that abortion is a fundamental human right upon which the state should not infringe. In reply, I once again ask, where did that right to an abortion come from? In other words, is it a *natural* right that springs from our nature as human beings, or is it a positive (legal) right granted by government? If the latter, the abortion-choice advocate cannot really complain that she is wronged if the state does not permit her to abort. As stated above, the same government that grants rights can take them away. On the other hand, if the right to an abortion is a natural right—a right one has in virtue of being human—then the abortion-choice advocate had that right from the moment she came to be, that is, from conception![25] Thus, we are left with this amusing paradox: According to the logic of many abortion-choice advocates, unborn women do not have a right to life but they do have a right to an abortion! Absurd! In short, secular liberals have difficulty telling us where rights come from or why anyone should have them. As Hadley Arkes points out, they have talked themselves out of the very natural rights upon which their own freedoms are built.

IS HUMAN VALUE JUST A CONSTRUCT OF JURISTIC THINKING?

The traditional view of American law, grounded in the Declaration of Independence, held natural rights in high esteem. Government was not an absolute sovereign whose fiat creates rights. Rather, human beings exist prior to the state and have certain basic rights simply because they are human. It was the government's job to protect those basic human rights.

For example, in *Pierce v. Society of Sisters* (1925) the U.S. Supreme Court declared unconstitutional an Oregon law requiring that children be sent to public school. "The child," wrote Justice McReynolds, "is not the mere

---

[24]Hadley Arkes, *First Things: An Inquiry into the First Principles of Morals and Justice* (Princeton, NJ: Princeton University Press, 1986), 366.
[25]Hadley Arkes develops this paradox in detail in *Natural Rights and the Right to Choose*. I owe the observation to his excellent analysis.

creature of the state." The parents had an inherent right to determine their child's education, and that right was not a mere creation of the state.[26]

Later, in *Loving v. Virginia* (1967), the Court declared unconstitutional a Virginia statute forbidding interracial marriage. Chief Justice Warren wrote, "Under our Constitution, the freedom to marry, or not to marry, a person of another race resides with the individual and cannot be infringed on by the State." The right to marry exists prior to the state and is not dependent on it.[27]

Judge John T. Noonan writes that the traditional model is nearly dead, replaced now by the thinking of Austrian jurist Hans Kelsen (1881–1973). For Kelsen, the legal order is the source of all rights. "The physical person is, thus, no natural reality, but a construction of juristic thinking."[28] That is, the state defines who is and is not a person, who does and does not have rights. If the state says you are not a subject with rights, you don't exist.

According to Noonan, Kelsen's thinking has dominated court decisions on abortion since the early 1970s. In a New York state case—*Bryn v. New York City Health and Hospitals Corp.* (1972)—Judge Charles Breitel wrote that although the unborn in the womb were "human" and "unquestionably alive, it is not true that the legal order corresponds to the natural order." Who counted as a legally protected "person" was for the law, not biology, to say. Justice Adrian Burke, dissenting, invoked the Declaration of Independence to argue that all men are created equal with fundamental liberties that precede the state and arise from a source superior to it.[29] Few listened.

Next came *Roe v. Wade*, when Justice Harry Blackmun ignored biological evidence and simply declared that the unborn were not persons in the whole sense (i.e., they were merely potential life). Membership in the human community was not a question of fact but fiat, and only the Court's counted.

Noonan summarizes the danger this way: Your rights flow from your human nature. Yet not one of those rights is secure if power rests with nine men and women to simply define you out of existence.[30]

---

[26]Cited in John T. Noonan, *A Private Choice: Abortion in America in the Seventies* (New York: Free Press, 1979), 13–19.

[27]Cited in ibid.

[28]Hans Kelsen, *The Pure Theory of Law*, trans. Max Knight, 2nd ed. (Berkeley, CA: University of California Press, 1967), 95. Cited in Noonan, *A Private Choice*, 13–14.

[29]Cited in Noonan, *A Private Choice*, 16.

[30]Ibid., 19.

RIGHTS WITHOUT HUMANS

For many on the academic and secular left, natural rights are nothing but an oppressive ideology because for them human nature is nothing but a fiction. "In the understanding of the post-modernists," writes Hadley Arkes, "there is no objective nature of human beings, and no settled truths that arise from that nature: What we call human nature is socially constructed from one place to another according to the vagaries of local culture."[31]

Arkes contends that the very people who profess there can be no moral truths that hold across cultures (in part because there is no human nature that holds from one place to the next) nevertheless cast moral judgments across cultures. Radical feminists condemn wrongs done to women in foreign countries and simply take for granted that there really must be "women" out there, that is, beings with a certain ontological nature. "When we sum up these things," says Arkes, "we arrive, as I say, at the most curious result: In the world of the Left on the campuses, there are 'human rights' to be vindicated all over the globe, but strictly speaking, there are no 'humans,' for there is no such thing as human nature. And because there are no moral truths, there are no 'rights' that are truly meaningful."[32]

Judges soon followed the lead of academic elites and removed from our law any fixed notion of what constitutes a man or human being. Power, raw political power, now determines who is and is not a human being with rights. For example, in *Planned Parenthood v. Casey* (1992), Justices Sandra Day O'Connor, Anthony M. Kennedy, and David Souter announced (in their famous "mystery passage"), "At the heart of liberty is the right to define one's own concept of existence, of meaning, of the universe, and of the mystery of human life."[33] That is, human nature is not fixed but is determined subjectively. But if that is true, there can be no fixed rights that arise from that nature, including a fixed right to an abortion. So why can't a future Court just arbitrarily decide that women *don't* have a right to an abortion? The Court didn't say.

So what are we left with? The Court has affirmed the right of a person to define his own concept of existence, the meaning of the universe, and the meaning of human life. But, writes Arkes, "was there any reality or truth attaching to *him*? And what was there about him that commanded the rest

---

[31]Arkes, *Natural Rights and the Right to Choose*, 18–19.
[32]Ibid.
[33]*Planned Parenthood vs. Casey*, 505 U.S. 833, at 851 (1992). Cited in ibid., 43.

of us to respect these decisions he reached about himself and the universe?"[34] Why can't we just make up such a person to be someone who has no rights if that fits our own concept of meaning and human life? In short, the Court's infamous "mystery passage" assumes the very thing it denies. By demanding that we respect a person's judgment about human life and the meaning of the universe, the Court assumes that the human being in question actually exists, whether my own concept of the universe admits him or not.

To sum up our current legal environment, modern jurists have forgotten two foundational truths understood by their early forefathers. First, the purpose of government is not to create rights but to secure ones that we already have by nature. Second, one cannot speak seriously of things that are truly rightful or of human rights in general without assuming moral realism—that is, the belief that right and wrong are real things, not merely constructs of human opinion or culture. Put simply, if moral truths do not exist as a foundation for law, then law itself becomes merely a system of raw political power accountable to no one.

WIDE-OPEN TO ALL

Opponents of the pro-life view believe that human beings who are in a different location or have a different level of development do not deserve the protection of law. They assert, without justification, the belief that strong and independent humans have basic human rights while small and dependent ones do not. This view is elitist. It violates the principle that once made political liberalism great, a commitment to protect the most vulnerable members of the human community.

We can do better than that. In the past, we used to discriminate on the basis of skin color and gender (and still do at times), but now, with elective abortion, we discriminate on the basis of size, level of development, location, and degree of dependency. We've simply swapped one form of bigotry for another.

In sharp contrast, pro-life advocates contend that no human being, regardless of size, level of development, environment, degree of dependency, race, gender, or place of residence, should be excluded from the human family. In other words, our view of humanity is inclusive, indeed wide-open to all, especially those who are small, vulnerable, and defenseless.[35]

---

[34]Arkes, *Natural Rights and the Right to Choose*, 43. Emphasis in the original.
[35]I'm indebted to Frank Beckwith for the wording of this paragraph (private correspondence).

My colleague Steve Wagner, who serves at Justice for All, describes how he starts discussions about human equality on college campuses. His strategy is simple and effective: He moves the conversation from debate to dialogue by asking the right questions. Each step of the way, he's establishing common ground with his listener:

> Look around this campus at all of the born people. Would you agree that each person has the same basic rights, that each should be treated equally?

Why does Steve begin this way? Because he knows almost everyone he talks to believes in the basic human rights of all born people, regardless of differences or disabilities. He then asks his listener to explain *why* equal human rights exist for anyone:

> But if all of us should be treated equally, there must be some quality we all have equally that justifies that equal treatment, right? What is that characteristic? (Pause) It can't be that all of us look human, because some have been disfigured. It can't be that all of us have functional brains, because some are in reversible comas. It can't be one's ability to think or feel pain, for some think better than others and some don't feel any pain. It can't be something we can gain or lose, or something of which we can have more or less. If something like that grounds rights, equal rights don't exist. And if we look at the whole population of America, almost 300 million people, there is only one quality we all have equally—we're all human. We have a human nature and we all have it equally. You either have it . . . or you don't.

After establishing common ground, Steve gently presses the pro-life argument upon his listener:

> Why are sexism and racism wrong? Isn't it because they pick out a surface difference (gender or skin color) and ignore the underlying similarity all of us share? We should treat women and men, African-Americans and Whites, as equals and protect them from discrimination. Why? Because they all have a human nature. But if the unborn also has that same human nature, shouldn't we protect her as well?[36]

---

[36]From *Common Ground and Uncommon Conversation*, Steve's December 2005 newsletter (see www.str.org). For more, see his book *Common Ground Without Compromise: 25 Questions to Create Dialogue on Abortion* (Signal Hill, CA: Stand to Reason Press, 2008).

REVIEW QUESTIONS

1. What is the substance view of human persons? How does it apply to the pro-life case?

2. When someone asserts that the unborn are human beings but not persons, what question should you ask? Who bears the burden of proof in this case?

3. Mary Anne Warren asserts that a person is a living entity with feelings, self-awareness, consciousness, and the ability to interact with his or her environment. She claims that because a human fetus has none of these capabilities, it cannot be a person with rights. What has Warren failed to tell us?

4. How does the argument of Paul D. Simmons prove too much? In what way does it undermine claims for human equality?

5. How does the embryo differ from the brain-dead person? Why is this significant?

6. Define *religion*.

7. Why is the pro-life view no more religious than the abortion-choice one?

8. List seven reasons why the "religion" objection fails to undermine the pro-life case.

9. How do natural rights differ from legal ones?

10. What is government's role in relationship to natural human rights?

11. How does Hans Kelsen's jurisprudence differ from the traditional American model?

12. What happens to basic human rights when government is free to define who does and does not exist as a person?

13. How successful are human rights claims in the postmodern culture of the university campus? That is, why do claims for either the right to life or the right to an abortion ultimately fail in this environment?

14. What questions does Steve Wagner ask to establish common ground? How do these questions set the stage for the pro-life argument he will present?

HELPFUL RESOURCES

Hadley Arkes. *Natural Rights and the Right to Choose*. Cambridge: Cambridge University Press, 2002.

Francis J. Beckwith. *Defending Life: A Moral and Legal Case Against Abortion Choice.* New York: Cambridge University Press, 2007.

Robert P. George and Christopher Tollefsen. *Embryo: A Defense of Human Life.* New York: Doubleday, 2008.

Timothy Keller. *The Reason for God: Belief in an Age of Skepticism.* New York: Dutton, 2008.

4

IS EMBRYONIC STEM CELL RESEARCH MORALLY COMPLEX?

Research that destroys one human being so that another may benefit is wrong. We can pursue the treatment of disease in morally acceptable ways.

WHEN CELEBRITIES LIKE Mary Tyler Moore and Michael J. Fox say that we have a moral obligation to save lives and promote cures with stem cell treatments, what they mean is that human embryos should be cloned and killed for medical research. And you, the taxpayer, should pay for it.

Pro-life advocates agree that we should save lives. We also support funding stem cell research. But we're opposed to one kind of stem cell research that requires destroying defenseless human embryos so that other humans may (allegedly) benefit. That's immoral.

WHAT ARE STEM CELLS?

Stem cells are fast-growing, unspecialized cells that can reproduce themselves and grow new organs for the body. All 210 different types of human tissue originate from these primitive cells. Because they have the potential to grow into almost any kind of tissue including nerves, bones, and muscle, scientists believe that the introduction of healthy stem cells into a patient may restore lost function to damaged organs, especially the brain. Human embryos have an abundant supply of stem cells that scientists are eager to harvest in hopes of treating Parkinson's disease, Alzheimer's disease, and other illnesses. The practice of securing these early cells is known as *embryonic stem cell research* (ESCR). The problem is, you have to destroy the embryo to secure its stem cells.

Closely related to ESCR is the cloning process known as *somatic cell nuclear transfer* (SCNT), which involves creating an embryo that is a genetic clone of the patient and then using that embryo as a source for stem cells. Advocates of ESCR euphemistically call this "therapeutic cloning," which they hope to distinguish from "reproductive" cloning. But the distinction is totally misleading because *all cloning is reproductive.* So-called "reproductive" cloning means allowing the cloned human to live. "Therapeutic" cloning means creating him for research, but killing him before birth. *In either case, the act of cloning is exactly the same* and results in a living human embryo. Bioethicist Wesley J. Smith describes how this cloning procedure works:

> Let's assume for our discussion that I wanted to clone myself:
> • A mature human egg is obtained from a woman of child-bearing age.
> • In a dish, its nucleus is removed.
> • One of my somatic cells is selected—let's say a skin cell. (All body cells are somatic except for germ cells, e.g., testes and ova.)
> • The skin cell's nucleus is removed.
> • The nucleus from my skin cell is then inserted into the empty space where the nucleus of the egg used to be.
> • The genetically modified egg has the full complement of 46 chromosomes, namely those from my skin cell's nucleus.
> • The modified egg is then stimulated with an electrical current or chemical.
> • If the SCNT takes, the modified egg begins embryonic development. This creates a new cloned human embryo.
> • Theoretically, if implanted in a woman's womb and gestated, the result will be a born cloned baby.[1]

Originally, ESCR advocates told us they only wanted "leftover" IVF (in vitro fertilization) embryos (that is, embryos fertilized in a test tube, then put on ice), but that's no longer the case. They now want federal funding for cloning research.

There are two reasons why. First, the human body is prone to reject cells from outside sources, a problem known as autoimmune rejection. To get around this obstacle without subjecting the patient to a lifetime of powerful drugs, researchers hope to clone customized embryos that genetically match (or nearly match) the patient. Second, there simply aren't enough spare IVF

---

[1]Wesley J. Smith, *A Consumer's Guide to a Brave New World* (San Francisco: Encounter Books, 2004), 16.

embryos to go around. Contrary to media reports, the number of embryos available for research is quite small. That leaves one option: cloning.

STEM CELL GYMNASTICS

The U.S. government began its own quest to fund embryo research in August 1993. At that time, the National Institutes for Health (NIH), under direction from then President Clinton, requested panel discussions for the purpose of issuing ethically and legally appropriate guidelines for the controversial research.

In a bizarre twist of logic, the panel concluded that embryos are entitled to "profound respect, but this does not necessarily encompass the legal and moral rights attributed to persons."[2] Translation: We should respect human embryos, but we may kill them to benefit others. To hedge its incoherent position, the NIH panel condemned human cloning techniques like those eventually legalized in Britain and proposed instead that destructive harvesting of stem cells be limited to so-called "spare embryos" left over from fertility clinics (or, as the NIH euphemistically called them, "embryos in excess of clinical need"). Daniel Callahan of the Hastings Institute writes, "I have always felt a nagging uneasiness at trying to rationalize killing something for which I have profound respect."[3]

Not to be outdone, President Clinton condemned human cloning techniques, but his objection fared no better than the panel's. "Each human life is unique, born of a miracle that reaches beyond laboratory science. I believe we must respect this profound gift and resist the temptation to replicate ourselves."[4] However, if the embryos in question are not human beings, why not destroy them to benefit others? And if it's wrong to clone human embryos because it shows disrespect for the gift of life, why did Clinton think it morally permissible to kill these same embryos (and later, fetuses) through legal abortion up until the moment of birth? It's beyond ironic that the President would trouble himself with the treatment of cloned embryos while wholeheartedly sanctioning the destruction of third-trimester fetuses through partial-birth abortion. His political posturing on the matter was incoherent at best.

In response to the panel's convoluted logic, Congress outlawed federal

---

[2] *Report of the Human Embryo Research Panel* (Washington, DC: National Institutes for Health), September 27, 1994.
[3] Daniel Callahan, "The Puzzle of Profound Respect," *Hastings Center Report* 25, January 1995.
[4] Commencement address by President Clinton at Morgan State University, May 18, 1997.

funding for harmful embryo research in 1996. The ban, known as the Dickey Amendment, was broad-based and specific: Funds could not be used for "research in which a human embryo or embryos are destroyed, discarded, or knowingly subjected to risk of injury or death." The intent of Congress is clear: If a research project requires the destruction of human embryos, it is illegal to use federal funds for the project.

In clear defiance of the law, the Clinton Administration, working through the National Institutes of Health (NIH), authorized federal funds for destructive research on leftover embryos. The NIH argued that public funds would not be used to destroy the embryos, only to conduct research *after* the embryos are killed. The reasoning here was baffling. The deliberate killing of a human embryo is an essential component of the proposed federal research. "If we had a law that barred research in which porpoises were killed, no one would entertain for five seconds that a federal agency could arrange for someone else to kill the porpoises and then proceed to use them in research," writes Douglas Johnson, legislative director for National Right to Life.[5] Clearly, the NIH's determination to pursue human embryo research showed contempt for and defiance of the legislative will of the U.S. Congress.[6]

Clinton, however, never got around to implementing his policy on stem cells taken from human embryos. Thus, when George W. Bush took office in 2001, he inherited both a no-funding policy and a proposal to allow funding. After taking several months to converse with experts on both sides of the funding issue, Bush announced his decision in a televised address to the nation on August 9, 2001. Contrary to popular belief, President Bush did not ban ESCR. In fact, he funded it, but only on stem cells taken from embryos killed before his August 9 speech. If researchers wanted to destroy more human embryos for research, they could do so, but not with federal dollars. In short, the Bush policy neither bans nor funds the destruction of human embryos for medical research.[7]

HYPE VERSUS REALITY

The moment President Bush announced his stem cell policy, secular critics denounced it as anti-science and devastating to the hopes of millions of Americans needing cures. Years later, their sound bite remains the same.

---

[5]National Right to Life Committee press release, August 23, 2000.
[6]Sam Brownback, "The Embryo-cell Battleground," *Philadelphia Inquirer*, August 27, 2000.
[7]The facts in this paragraph are taken from Ramesh Ponnuru, "The Case Against Federal Funding of Stem-Cell Research," *Hoover Digest*, No. 4, 2004.

Yet for all their talk about promised cures, the problems with embryo cell treatments are numerous.

First, embryonic stem cells, though allegedly more flexible than their adult counterparts, are hard to control once implanted. They sometimes form tumors instead of usable tissue.[8] Second, the cloning procedures needed to produce embryos for research are hugely expensive. As Wesley Smith points out, The National Academy of Sciences claims "it could take about 100 human eggs per patient—at a cost of $1,000 to $2,000 apiece— just to derive one cloned embryonic-stem-cell line for use in regenerative therapy."[9] If true, it would be next to impossible to secure the billions of human eggs needed for widespread therapeutic cloning. And even if the biotechnology could be developed, "it would either be available only to the super rich or so costly that it would have to be stringently rationed."[10] Third, noncontroversial adult stem cells are currently treating well over seventy-five known diseases while their embryonic counterparts are treating none, leading some scientists to wonder if embryo cells have any therapeutic value whatsoever.[11] Fourth, prospective investors have so far failed to pony up the cash for highly speculative research that might not cure anyone for years to come, if at all. Finally, there's good reason to suppose that cloning technology may never yield substantial treatments unless cloned humans are developed well past the embryonic stage.[12]

"Despite the clear progress we have made, we are nowhere near the point of having a 'recipe book' for cooking up cellular repair kits to treat human disease and injury," writes Dr. Maureen Condic, associate professor of neurobiology and anatomy at the University of Utah. "Immune rejection, tumor formation, and embryonic development have proved themselves to be profoundly serious scientific challenges, and they are likely to remain so for decades into the future."[13]

Condic notes that researchers have completely unrestricted funding to conduct research on animal embryonic stem cells (before moving to human

[8]Rick Weiss, "Embryonic Stem Cells Found to Acquire Mutations," *Washington Post*, September 5, 2005.
[9]Wesley J. Smith, "Cell Wars: The Reagans' Suffering and Hyped Promises," *National Review*, June 8, 2004; http://www.nationalreview.com/comment/smith200406081105.asp.
[10]Ibid.
[11]"Benefits of Stem Cells to Human Patients: Adult Stem Cells v. Embryonic Stem Cells," *Do No Harm*, http://www.stemcellresearch.org/facts/treatments.htm.
[12]Robert Lanza et al, "Long-Term Bovine Hematopoietic Engraftment with Clone-derived Stem Cells," *Cloning and Stem Cells* 7, 2 (June 2005): 95–106, cited in "Research Cloning and Fetus Farming: The Slippery Slope in Action," a report by the United States Conference of Catholic Bishops, http://www.usccb.org/prolife/issues/bioethic/cloning/farmfact31805.shtml.
[13]Maureen Condic, "What We Know About Stem Cells," *First Things*, January 2007.

trials), and yet they can't get around these serious scientific problems. "Millions of dollars have been consumed, and hundreds of scientific papers published, and yet the problems still remain. The promised miraculous cures have not materialized even for mice, much less for men."[14]

There are problems with egg donation as well. In 2005, Korean scientist Hwang Woo-Suk fraudulently claimed to have derived eleven stem cell lines from cloned human embryos. Within one year the whole project was exposed as fake. There were no stem cell lines from cloned human embryos, and to this day no one has successfully demonstrated that it's possible to clone a surviving embryo in the first place. But greater horrors awaited investigators. Hwang pressured junior female colleagues to donate their eggs for his research, despite the potential risks for sterility and death that accompanies egg donation procedures. Condic asks a devastating question: "Given that thousands of human eggs from more than a hundred women were used by Hwang and not even a single viable cloned embryo resulted from this research, how can the medical risks to women entailed by this research possibly be justified?"[15]

IS ESCR COMPLEX?

Despite claims to the contrary, ESCR is not morally complicated. It comes down to just one question: Is the embryo a member of the human family? If so, killing it to benefit others is a serious moral wrong. It treats the embryonic human being as a commodity we trade to enhance our own well-being. If, however, the embryos in question are not human, why not put them in the crosshairs of scientists?

We've already established (Chapter 2) that from the earliest stages of development, the embryos in question are distinct, living, and whole human beings capable of directing their own internal development. Although they have yet to mature, they are whole human beings nonetheless.

Advocates of ESCR reply that fertility clinics have large numbers of "excess" embryos—up to five hundred thousand of them—that could be harvested for their stem cells if only the restrictions on federal funding were lifted. Since these embryos will go to waste and die anyway, so the claim goes, there are no good reasons to delay using them.

Sure, there are. First, there may be five hundred thousand embryos in

[14]Ibid.
[15]Ibid.

storage, but "excess" does not mean "available." A 2004 study shows that most of these embryos are still wanted by their parents (who pay high fees to store them), and unless Congress wants to override parental rights, few are truly available for research.[16] Although parents have the option of donating their embryos for research, less than 3 percent are donated, and only 5 percent are left unclaimed.

Second, moral considerations call the "they're going to die anyway" argument into question. Suppose you oversee a Cambodian orphanage with two hundred abandoned toddlers. The facility cannot care for them any longer. Water levels are critically low, and food supplies are exhausted. It's only a matter of time before starvation and disease will set in. A scientist has offered to take the toddlers off your hands and use them for grisly medical research designed to cure cancer. He confronts you with the hard facts: Many of these children will die soon, and there's nothing you can do to prevent it, so why let all those organs go to waste? Nonetheless, you refuse. You could never, even for a moment, consider turning the kids over to the scientist on grounds that "these kids are going to die anyway, so let's put them to good use." True, given your impoverished circumstances, you are powerless to save them, but you would never be complicit in actively killing vulnerable human beings, which is what ESCR does.

Of course, there are many other examples to consider. Prisoners on death row are going to die anyway, but no one (especially liberals) suggests that we use them for destructive medical research. And we don't slit the throats of mortally wounded soldiers to recover their organs.

In short, unless one begins with the assumption that the embryos in question are not human beings, the "they're going to die anyway" claim doesn't work. All of us are going to die sometime. Do those of us who will die later have the right to kill and exploit those who will die sooner? So once again we're back to the question we started with: What are these "excess" embryos? If they are human beings, I see only one morally acceptable option: Wait for adoptive parents.[17]

SCIENCE VERSUS MORALITY

Regrettably, moral concerns with embryonic stem cell research are often dismissed (rather than refuted) as anti-science and anti-progress, much like the persecution of Galileo. "Our conviction about what is natural or right

---

[16]Arthur Caplan, Andrea Gurmankin, and Dominic Sisti, "Embryo Disposal Practices in IVF Clinics in the United States," *Politics and the Life Sciences*, Vol. 22, No. 2, 2004.
[17]The Snowflakes program specializes in embryo adoption; http://www.nightlight.org/snowflakeadoption.htm.

should not inhibit the role of science in discovering the truth," Tony Blair told critics of Britain's plan to clone human embryos for research. "[We will] not stand by as successful British science once more ends ups being manufactured abroad."[18] Echoing these same sentiments, U.S. Senator Orrin Hatch remarked, "It would be terrible to say because of an ethical concept, we can't do anything for patients."[19] Ron Reagan, son of the late pro-life President, told the 2004 Democratic National Convention that "many opponents to the research are well-meaning and sincere, but their beliefs are just that—an article of faith. . . . The theology of a few should not be allowed to forestall the health and well-being of many."[20]

However, if Blair, Hatch, and Reagan are correct that scientific progress trumps morality, one can hardly condemn Hitler for grisly medical experiments on Jews. Nor can one criticize the Tuskegee experiments of the 1930s in which black men suffering from syphilis were promised treatment, only to have it denied so scientists could study the disease.

Ramesh Ponnuru writes that pro-cloning polemics frequently frame the debate in terms that obscure the point at issue. "A cloning ban is said to be an attempt to ban research, its supporters are said to fear knowledge, and it is opposed on that basis. It is, of course, true that a ban would bar certain types of research and could prevent certain knowledge from being discovered—but because the research to get the knowledge involves homicide, not because it is research."[21]

ETHICAL RESEARCH WORKS

Not only is embryonic stem cell research immoral, it may be unnecessary. First, numerous peer-reviewed studies indicate that adult stem cells are more effective at treating disease than previously thought.[22] Unlike embryonic stem cell research, we can extract these adult cells without harming the donor. Critics of the pro-life view, like the late actor Christopher Reeve, insist that these adult cells won't work. However, the evidence suggests just the opposite. So far adult stem cells are outperforming their embryonic counterparts. Here are just a few examples:

---

[18]"Don't Turn Against Science, Blair Warns Protesters," *London Daily Telegraph*, November 18, 2000.
[19]Cited in "Clone Wars, Part II," *National Review Online*, July 1, 2002; http://www.nationalreview.com/01july02/ponnuru070102.asp.
[20]Roger Pedersen and Julia Polak, "A U.S.-U.K. Stem-Cell Connection," *San Francisco Chronicle*, December 6, 2004; http://www.sfgate.com/cgi-bin/article.cgi?f=/c/a/2004/12/06/EDGD99EP5J1.DTL.
[21]Ramesh Ponnuru, "Lapse of Reason," *National Review*, February 11, 2002; http://www.nationalreview.com/11feb02/ponnuruprint021102.html.
[22]For a complete summary of adult treatments, go to www.stemcellresearch.org.

- Adult stem cells found in the bone marrow can be coaxed into functioning as nerve cells for the brain. This confirms earlier studies suggesting that adult stem cells are not restricted but are more flexible than previously thought (i.e., able to develop into other types of tissue). Because these stem cells come from the patient's own bone marrow, there is no risk of rejection.
- Cadavers can supply versatile brain stem cells that can turn into different kinds of nerve cells. And skin, bones, and just about every other tissue can be coaxed into producing brain cells.
- Body fat contains a virtually limitless source of adult stem cells needed for people with damaged joints and organs.
- Stem cells taken from cord blood treat leukemia, repair damage from strokes, and may reverse damage from certain neurological disorders.
- Adult stem cells can also treat degenerative diseases of the eye. Evidence suggests that adult corneal stem cells restore useful vision to patients who are legally blind.
- Adult stem cells repair liver damage and may reverse diabetes. Meanwhile, cells from the patient's own transplanted bone marrow can turn into liver tissue.

Second, new research suggests we can pursue embryo cell treatments in morally acceptable ways. Altered Nuclear Transfer (or ANT) is one new technology that seeks a morally acceptable means of producing pluripotent stem cells (the functional equivalent of embryonic stem cells) without the creation and destruction of human embryos.[23] Instead, researchers will use biological entities that have some of the properties of embryos but are not living organisms.[24]

In 2007, the news got even better. Researchers in Japan and the United States, using slightly different methods, successfully coaxed ordinary adult skin cells to function just like pluripotent embryonic ones. This remarkable breakthrough demonstrated that pluripotent cells can be obtained without destroying human embryos. True, the serious scientific problems associated with embryo cell treatments remain, but the moral quandary over how we get them shows promise of resolution.[25]

This should come as thrilling news for everyone in the cloning debate

[23]A. Meissner and R. Jaenisch, "Generation of nuclear transfer-derived pluripotent ES cells from cloned Cdx2-deficient Blastocysts," *Nature*, October 16, 2005. Cited in Clementine Wallace, "Controversy-Free Stem Cells," *The Scientist*, October 17, 2005.
[24]Kathryn Jean Lopez, "One Small Island of Unity in a Sea of Controversy," *National Review Online*, December 6, 2005.
[25]Gina Kolata, "Scientists Bypass Need for Embryos to Get Stem Cells," *The New York Times*, November 21, 2007.

intent on using embryo cells. But it hasn't. Cloning advocates are after much bigger game.

BETTING THE FARM

For years now, advocates of embryonic stem cell research have flatly denied any intention of implanting cloned embryos in order to harvest tissues or organs from later-term fetuses, a practice known as fetus farming. But researchers are growing impatient. Stem cells from early embryos have yet to deliver one promised cure, and their tendency to form dangerous tumors could render them therapeutically useless. Indeed, there's growing concern among scientists that usable cells will not be obtained unless cloned humans can be gestated well past the embryonic stage.[26]

Anyone who thinks they are kidding should revisit January 4, 2004.

On that date, then New Jersey Governor James McGreevey signed into law the most permissive stem cell legislation in the United States, Senate Bill 1909. Ironically, Garden State residents were told they were getting an anti-cloning bill. It was anything but that.

The new law makes it legal to create a cloned embryo, implant it in a woman's womb, then gestate it through the ninth month of pregnancy— so long as you kill the embryo before birth, the point at which it magically becomes "a new human individual."[27] Thanks to the new law, there's nothing to stop researchers from cultivating late-term (cloned) fetuses for spare parts, fetus farming. In short, New Jersey's alleged anti-cloning bill not only fails to ban cloning, it sets the stage for fetal harvesting at taxpayers' expense.

"S-1909 has blown the cover off of the true agenda of the biotechnology industry," says Wesley J. Smith, author of *The Culture of Death* and *The Consumer's Guide to a Brave New World*. "Rather than restricting therapeutic cloning to the harvesting of stem cells from early embryos, as the industry often pretends in the media, the Biotechnology Industry Organization's (BIO) enthusiastic support of the New Jersey bill proves that [pro-cloning types] want an unlimited license to harvest cloned human life from inception through the ninth month."[28]

Leading pro-life advocates share Smith's concern. "The New Jersey legislation expressly encourages human cloning for, among other things, the

---

[26]Lanza et al, "Long-Term Bovine Hematopoietic Engraftment with Clone-derived Stem Cells," cited in "Research Cloning and Fetus Farming: The Slippery Slope in Action."
[27]Kathryn Jean Lopez, "The State of Cloning," *National Review Online*, January 5, 2004.
[28]Cited in Ibid.

harvesting of 'cadaveric fetal tissue,'" writes Robert P. George of Princeton University and a member of the President's Council on Bioethics. "The bodies in question are those of fetuses created by cloning specifically to be gestated and killed as sources of tissues and organs."[29] New Jersey Right to Life's Marie Tasy says, "This law will allow human lives to be treated as a commodity, creating classes of lesser humans to be created and sacrificed for the good of humanity."[30]

At the same time, the legislation expressly permits "reasonable payment" for "removal, processing, disposal, preservation, quality control, storage, transplantation, or implantation of embryonic or cadaveric fetal tissue." Put simply, nothing in the legislation prevents cloning entrepreneurs from paying women a "reasonable" fee to gestate later-term fetuses that will be killed for their body parts.

Other states are considering similar laws.

Douglas Johnson, legislative director for National Right to Life, says we're headed toward using fetuses for spare parts. "Elements of the biotech industry are definitely moving toward fetus farming and Congress must act to prevent that before it's too late."[31]

Indeed, experiments are already underway in which cloned cow embryos are implanted, gestated to the early or late fetal stage, then killed so their organ tissues can be harvested.[32] Among the many benefits, cells extracted from later-term fetuses are stable, allowing researchers to get around the tumor problem associated with embryo cells. "We hope to use this technology in the future to treat patients with diverse diseases," said Robert Lanza, who coauthored one of the cow studies.[33] Legally, he has a green light: The New Jersey law—and others soon to be styled after it—permit this same cloned organ farming in humans.

STEALTH CLONING AND PHONY BANS

The relationship between fetus farming and cloning is clear. First, cloning (theoretically) provides a rich supply of embryos that can be grown to the

[29] Robert P. George, "Fetal Attraction: What the Stem Cell Scientists Really Want," *The Weekly Standard*, October 3, 2005.
[30] Cited in Lopez, "The State of Cloning."
[31] Cited in "Fetal Farming Is on the Horizon," *Citizen Link*, September 27, 2005.
[32] Lanza et al, "Long-Term Bovine Hematopoietic Engraftment with Clone-Derived Stem Cells," cited in "Research Cloning and Fetus Farming: The Slippery Slope in Action."
[33] Advanced Cell Technology, "Somatic Cell Nuclear Transfer Gives Old Animals Youthful Immune Cells," June 29, 2005; www.advancedcell.com/press-release/somatic-cell-nuclear-transfer-gives-old-animals-youthful-immune-cells.

fetal stage where organs can be harvested. Second, cloning allows research-ers to derive these organs from a fetus that's a genetic match of the patient, thus minimizing the potential for organ rejection. Bottom line: You can't pursue fetus farming if you don't first sell the public on embryo cloning. The problem is, when asked directly if tax dollars should be used to clone human embryos for destructive research, a majority of the public says, *"Yuck!"*[34]

Fearing public backlash, big biotech is trying to legalize cloning on the sly with a series of phony bans. Known more accurately as "clone and kill" laws, these alleged "bans" allow human embryos to be cloned provided they are destroyed for medical research prior to birth.

Shocking though it may seem, some "pro-life" advocates support these bills.

In Missouri, former GOP Senator John Danforth is honorary co-chair for the Missouri Stem Cell Research and Cures Initiative (sponsored by the Missouri Coalition for Lifesaving Cures), a ballot measure that would amend the state's constitution to permanently allow embryonic stem cell research. Danforth assures us that he is solidly "pro-life" and has "always voted pro-life" and that the initiative "respects the sanctity of life." But mis-leading cloning language is all over the group's "Setting the Record Straight" fact sheet and other website documents.

We're told in the fact sheet, for example, that the initiative "clearly and strictly bans human cloning."[35] But in the "Frequently Asked Questions" section, we get this baffling statement:

> We believe that ALL types of stem cell research should be pursued in the effort to find lifesaving cures, including research involving adult stem cells, Somatic Cell Nuclear Transfer (SCNT) and stem cells from excess fertility clinic embryos (also called blastocysts or pre-embryos) that would otherwise be discarded. We also believe that human cloning should be banned.[36]

Several paragraphs later, SCNT is defined as "a process that uses a patient's own cell and an empty, unfertilized egg to create ES [embryonic stem] cells."

The deception here is breathtaking.

---

[34] Wilson Research Strategies did a poll for the National Right to Life Committee (August 2004) that found 53 percent oppose using tax dollars for destructive embryo research, while 38 percent support funding. The complete poll can be viewed at http://www.nrlc.org/Killing_Embryos/NRLCStemCellPoll.pdf.
[35] "Setting the Record Straight," http://www.missouricures.com/settingtherecord.php.
[36] "Frequently Asked Questions," http://www.missouricures.com/faq.php.

First, Somatic Cell Nuclear Transfer (SCNT) *is* cloning, and Danforth knows it. A decade ago, this exact same technique gave us Dolly, the first cloned sheep. What Danforth's Missouri Cures proposal rejects is the birth of a cloned human being, not its destruction for medical research.

Second, there is no such thing as a "pre-embryo." As pro-cloning advocate Lee Silver points out, the term is scientifically misleading and is used to deliberately fool the public into accepting destructive embryo research and cloning. "I'll let you in on a secret. The term pre-embryo has been embraced wholeheartedly by IVF practitioners for reasons that are political, not scientific."[37] Ronan O'Rahilly and Fabiola Müller, in their textbook *Human Embryology and Teratology*, write that the term is "ill-defined," "inaccurate," "unjustified," and "equivocal."[38] Even during the Clinton Presidency, both the Human Embryo Research Panel (sponsored by the National Institutes for Health at Clinton's direction) and the National Bioethics Advisory Commission rejected the term.[39] The report from the Advisory Commission describes the human embryo from its earliest stages as a living organism and a "developing form of human life."[40] The highly respected 1995 Ramsey Colloquium statement on embryo research acknowledges:

> The [embryo] is human; it will not articulate itself into some other kind of animal. Any being that is human is a human being. If it is objected that, at five days or fifteen days, the embryo does not look like a human being, it must be pointed out that this is precisely what a human being looks like—and what each of us looked like—at five or fifteen days of development.[41]

The term "fertilized egg" is also misleading because once fertilization takes place, sperm and egg (or, in the case of cloning, the female egg and the donor cell) cease to exist. That is, they surrender their constituents into the

---

[37]Lee Silver, *Remaking Eden: Cloning and Beyond in a Brave New World* (New York: Avon Books, 1997), 39. Silver is a Princeton University biology professor.

[38]Ronan O'Rahilly and Fabiola Müller, *Human Embryology and Teratology*, 2nd ed. (New York: Wiley-Liss, 1992), 55, 81.

[39]*Report of the Human Embryo Research Panel* (Bethesda, MD: National Institutes of Health), November 1994; see also *Cloning Human Beings* (Rockville, MD: National Bioethics Advisory Commission), June 1997. Both are cited in "On Human Embryos and Stem Cell Research: An Appeal for Ethically Responsible Science and Public Policy," The Center for Bioethics and Human Dignity (CBHD), http://www.cbhd.org/resources/stemcells/position_statement.htm.

[40]*Cloning Human Beings*. Cited in "On Human Embryos and Stem Cell Research."

[41]The Ramsey Colloquium, which is sponsored by the Institute on Religion and Public Life, is a group of Jewish and Christian theologians, philosophers, and scholars that meets periodically to consider questions of ethics, religion, and public life. Cited in "On Human Embryos and Stem Cell Research."

makeup of a new human organism. Danforth and his colleagues at Missouri Cures know this, but they insist on deceptive language anyway.

Third, SCNT does not make embryonic stem cells from unfertilized eggs. It creates living human embryos that will be destroyed so researchers can *get* stem cells. And just when you thought the deception couldn't get worse, we're told that the Missouri Cures initiative "resolves concerns about human cloning by strictly banning human *reproductive* cloning to create babies."[42]

Let's be clear: Cloning is cloning—period! As mentioned above, the alleged distinction between "therapeutic" cloning and "reproductive" cloning is totally misleading because all cloning is reproductive. In each case, what's banned is the *birth* of cloned human beings, not their creation for destructive research. For example, New Jersey's own clone bill (S-1909) was sold to the public as a strict prohibition on human cloning, but with a hidden lethal twist: That so-called strict prohibition was simply that all cloned embryos and fetuses *must* be killed before they have a chance to develop into more mature human beings. Meanwhile, California law bans initiating a pregnancy with a cloned embryo, but only if that pregnancy "could result in the *birth* of a human being."[43] In other words, human lives may be created with cloning technology if and only if technicians agree—under threat of law—to destroy any clones *prior to birth*. That's the proposed ethical safeguard that allegedly bans cloning. It's a sham.[44]

Moreover, pro-lifers don't oppose the destruction of cloned human embryos because it kills "babies"—we oppose it because it unjustly takes the life of a defenseless human being, regardless of his or her stage of development. For Danforth and a sympathetic press to pretend otherwise is shameful but not surprising.

"The mainstream media still discusses these issues as if scientists only want to use embryos left over from IVF procedures," writes Smith. "But those days are long gone. It is now undeniable that Big Biotech and its politician and university allies do not even intend to restrict biotechnological research to early embryos situated in petri dishes." As bills in New Jersey and these other states clearly demonstrate, "the ground is being plowed already to allow cloned fetal farming, the next, but certainly not last, step intended to lead us to a Brave New World."[45]

---

[42]Press release, October 11, 2005; http://www.missouricures.com/rel_101105.php. Emphasis mine.
[43]California Health and Safety Code ß125300. Cited in Catholic Bishops, "Research Cloning and Fetus Farming: The Slippery Slope in Action," emphasis mine.
[44]Wesley J. Smith, "Stealth Cloning," *National Review Online*, February 15, 2005.
[45]Ibid.

PERSONHOOD ETHICS

Writing in the *New York Times*, Michael Gazzaniga attacks President Bush's anti-cloning policy as follows:

> The president's view is consistent with the reductive idea that there is an equivalence between a bunch of molecules in a lab and a beautifully nurtured and loved human who has been shaped by a lifetime of experiences and discovery. . . . DNA must undergo thousands if not millions of interactions at both the molecular and experiential level to grow and develop a brain and become a person.[46]

Notice the unsupported claims here. Why should we suppose that brain development bestows value on a person? As usual with pro-cloning advocates, Gazzaniga does not tell us why development matters, nor does he say why certain value-giving properties are value-giving in the first place. True, he later appeals to one's immediate capacity to experience memories, loves, and hopes, but isn't that just question-begging since the issue is whether one is a human subject even if one does not have memories, loves, and hopes? Newborns lack all of these qualities—does it follow that they are fitting subjects for destructive research? Once society accepts that human beings have value only because of some acquired property like self-awareness, there remains no logical reason to exclude only embryos. Fetuses and newborns will also lose their right to life.

Gazzaniga then says that it squares with our basic intuitions to accept that adults and children are people while clumps of cells in a petri dish are not:

> Look around you. Look at your loved ones. Do you see a hunk of cells or do you see something else? . . . We do not see cells, simple or complex— we see people, human life. That thing in a petri dish is something else. It doesn't yet have the memories and loves and hopes that accumulate over the years.[47]

Setting aside Gazzaniga's sloppy science (embryos are not mere hunks of cells but are living human organisms—see Chapter 2), there are troubling philosophical problems with the idea of personhood coming into existence only after some degree of bodily development. One is that you end up saying

---

[46]Michael Gazzaniga, "All Clones Are Not the Same," *New York Times*, February 16, 2006.
[47]Ibid.

things like "my body existed before I did" or "my body was an embryo before my conscious self showed up." Yet nowhere in his essay does Gazzaniga defend his metaphysical assumption that personhood is an accidental property rather than something intrinsic to the human subject.

Meanwhile, Gazzaniga's appeal to our intuitions—"these embryos don't look like your relatives" (my paraphrase)—is naive, though I agree that some people will not be impressed with a two-week-old human embryo. For them, it's counterintuitive to suggest that something the size of a dot is a human being. But as Richard Stith said earlier, if it were possible to view a photograph of a relative shortly after he was conceived, a very different intuition would kick in. We'd naturally say, "Look, Uncle Jim, that's you!" That intuition squares nicely with the science of embryology, which says we each began as embryonic beings.[48] In short, intuitions are not infallible (some whites thought it counterintuitive to say blacks were human), though we're justified believing them until presented with superior evidence. In this case, Gazzaniga's appeal to intuition does not refute the strongly evidenced claim for the humanity of the embryo; it merely sidesteps it.

STAY FOCUSED

Debates over ESCR and cloning are riddled with misinformation and euphemistic language. If you are not careful, you'll lose sight of your main objective, which is to clarify the moral issue. Stay focused on these key points:

- Pro-lifers are not opposed to stem cell research. But we're opposed to one kind of stem cell research that requires killing defenseless human beings so that others may (allegedly) benefit. That's immoral.
- When ESCR advocates say they only want to find cures for disease and can't understand why religious conservatives would oppose that, what they usually mean is that human embryos should be cloned and killed for medical research.
- Somatic Cell Nuclear Transfer (SCNT) is cloning and reduces human life to a commodity.
- Cloning is cloning—period! Advocates of ESCR seek to distinguish "therapeutic" cloning from "reproductive" cloning. But the distinction is totally misleading because all cloning is reproductive. So-called "reproductive" cloning means allowing the cloned human to be born alive. "Therapeutic" cloning means creating him for research but killing

---

[48]Stith, "Does Making Babies Make Sense?"

him before birth. In either case, the act of cloning is exactly the same and results in a living human embryo.

* Embryos don't come from stem cells; they are living human beings who have stem cells. And extracting these cells is lethal for the tiny human subject.

Hadley Arkes provides the question that pro-life advocates should put to their critics: "Given a choice between a therapy that happens to be lethal for human subjects and one that is not, wouldn't we be inclined to favor the therapy that is not lethal? Wouldn't that be even more the case if that non-lethal therapy turns out to be vastly more promising, and far less speculative, than the lethal therapy?"[49]

Stem cells drawn from adults have already yielded some striking achievements, and they do not require the killing of the human being from whom they are drawn.[50] The extraction of stem cells from human embryos does, however, result in the destruction of defenseless human beings. Therefore, it is morally wrong. There's nothing complex about it.

REVIEW QUESTIONS

1. What are stem cells, and how do they differ from embryos?

2. What is Somatic Cell Nuclear Transfer, and how does the process work?

3. When critics say that President Bush banned ESCR, what are they leaving out?

4. Why do ESCR advocates need cloning?

5. Why is the debate over embryonic stem cell research not morally complex? What is the crux of the debate?

6. Why are Tony Blair's comments about the relationship between science and morality so disturbing? What historical examples point out this danger?

7. Why is adult stem cell research morally permissible? How effective is it when compared to its embryonic counterpart?

8. Define *fetus farming*. How does it differ from embryonic stem cell research?

9. Why is New Jersey's cloning bill the most permissive in the country? What does it prohibit, and what does it permit?

10. List five current problems with ESCR that must be overcome before it has any hope of working.

---

[49]Hadley Arkes, "Senseless on Stem Cells," *National Review Online*, August 23, 2004.
[50]For a complete summary of these adult stem cell treatments, go to www.stemcellresearch.org.

11. Why are some researchers looking to harvest older fetal tissue instead of embryonic cells?

12. The Missouri Cures initiative claims to strictly ban human cloning, yet it specifically promotes somatic cell nuclear transfer. Why is this claim breathtakingly deceptive?

13. Why are the terms *pre-embryo* and *fertilized egg* misleading?

14. What's wrong with saying personhood comes into existence only after some degree of bodily development?

PART TWO

Pro-Life Christians Establish a Foundation for the Debate

5

THE GROUND RULES, PART 1: CAN YOU NAME MY CLAIM?

When pro-life advocates claim that elective abortion unjustly takes the life of a defenseless human being, they are not saying they dislike abortion. They are saying it's objectively wrong, regardless of how one feels about it.

LET'S REVISIT THE CONVERSATION between Emily and Pam in Chapter 1. Emily argued that elective abortion was wrong and could never be justified to solve a difficult life problem. Her friend Pam replied that she, too, disliked abortion and was personally opposed to it. Nevertheless, Pam insisted that each woman must decide for herself. "If you and I don't like abortion, we don't need to have one," she told Emily. "But we shouldn't force our views on others who might feel differently."

In case you didn't notice, Pam subtly changed the entire nature of the exchange with a single word—*like*.

CLAIMS ABOUT ICE CREAM VERSUS CLAIMS ABOUT TRUTH

There are two kinds of truth relevant to our present discussion. *Objective truths* are true propositions that correspond to reality. They are true whether I recognize them as such or not. These objective truths transcend human subjects. That is, I don't create them through language or perception. I *discover* them through the proper use of my mental faculties. For instance, the statement "The Dodgers won the World Series in 1988" is objectively true.

Notice that my *accepting* it as true did not *make* it true. It was true already, and my job was to get in line with reality.[1]

Conversely, *subjective truths* are personal in nature, preferences if you will. They apply to the individual subject but may not apply to anyone else. Suppose I said, "Chocolate ice cream is better than vanilla." You might well reply (rightly), "Ha! That's true for you and your tastes, but I like vanilla better." In this case, I'm really telling you what I *prefer or feel*, not what's right or wrong, true or false.[2] The problem is, many people today confuse claims about ice cream with claims about truth. When it comes to morality, they simply don't know (or choose to ignore) the difference between subjective and objective truth claims.[3]

Consider the popular bumper sticker, "Don't like abortion? Don't have one!" Notice what's going on here. The pro-life advocate makes a moral claim that he believes is objectively true—namely, that elective abortion unjustly takes the life of a defenseless human being. The abortion-choice advocate responds by changing that objective truth claim into a preference he likes better, as if the pro-lifer were talking about what she *likes* rather than what's true. But this misses the point entirely. Pro-life advocates don't oppose abortion because they find it distasteful; they oppose it because it violates rational moral principles. The negative emotional response follows from the moral wrongness of the act.

Francis J. Beckwith writes:

> Imagine if I said, "Don't like slavery, then don't own one." If I said that, you would immediately realize that I did not truly grasp why people believe that slavery is wrong. It is not wrong because I don't like it. It's wrong because slaves are intrinsically valuable human beings who are not by nature property. Whether I like slavery or not is not relevant to the question of whether slavery is wrong. Imagine another example, "Don't like spousal abuse, then don't beat your spouse." Again, the wrongness of spousal abuse does not depend on my preferences or tastes. In fact, if someone liked spousal abuse, we would say that that he or she is evil or sick. We would not adjust our view of the matter and I [sic] say, "I guess spousal abuse is right for you, but not for me."[4]

---

[1] For a complete discussion of objective truth claims, see R. Scott Smith, *Truth and the New Kind of Christian: The Emerging Effects of Postmodernism in the Church* (Wheaton, IL: Crossway Books, 2005).
[2] The "emotivists" held that ethical sentences were not statements at all but expressions of emotion, like "ouch" or "ahh."
[3] I owe the ice cream example to Gregory Koukl, who develops this theme in his audio CD "Truth Is Not Ice Cream/Faith Is Not Wishing." (Order from Stand to Reason at www.str.org.)
[4] Carl E. Olson, "The Case Against Abortion: An Interview with Dr. Francis Beckwith, Author of *Defending Life*," *Ignatius Insight*, January 21, 2008; http://www.ignatiusinsight.com/features2007/beckwith_defendlife_dec07.asp.

In short, when the abortion-choice advocate tells the pro-life advocate, "Don't like abortion; don't have one," he fails to grasp what the latter is truly claiming. The pro-lifer isn't stating his preferences; he's stating what's right and wrong regardless of his likes and dislikes. Most people find rape and murder personally offensive, but it doesn't follow that there are no moral reasons for making them illegal.[5] Of course, it's possible that the pro-life advocate is wrong about the humanity of the unborn and the inhumanity of abortion (the pro-life advocate must still argue his case), but no one should mistake the *type* of claim he is making.

"DICTATORSHIP OF RELATIVISM"

When Pam changed Emily's moral claim into a preference (likes and dislikes), she unwittingly espoused ethical relativism, the belief that right and wrong are up to us to decide. Pope Benedict XVI (formerly Joseph Cardinal Ratzinger) writes that relativism is so pervasive in Western culture that dissent is hardly tolerated:

> Having a clear faith, based on the Creed of the Church, is often labeled today as a fundamentalism. Whereas, relativism, which is letting oneself be tossed and "swept along by every wind of teaching" looks like the only attitude (acceptable) to today's standards. We are moving towards a dictatorship of relativism which does not recognize anything as for certain and which has as its highest goal one's own ego and one's own desires.[6]

I deal more fully with relativism in a later chapter, but here's my quick take on where this kind of thinking comes from and how to respond.[7]

Ethical relativism comes in two primary forms. *Cultural relativism* states that right and wrong are determined by one's own culture. That is to say, because cultures disagree on important moral issues, objective moral truths either do not exist or if they do exist we cannot know them. At best, our sense of morality is socially constructed. Hence, each culture must determine its own moral codes and refrain from judging other societies that might hold to different moral standards. *Individual relativism* asserts that right and wrong begin with each human being. What's wrong for one

---

[5]For more, see Edward Fesser, "On Legislating Morality: The Anti-Conservative Fallacy," *Tech Central Daily*, May 31, 2005.
[6]Homily at the Mass for the Election of the Roman Pontiff, St. Peter's Basilica, April 18, 2005.
[7]For a complete treatment of relativism, see Francis J. Beckwith and Gregory Koukl, *Relativism: Feet Firmly Planted in Mid-Air* (Grand Rapids, MI: Baker, 1998). I owe my thoughts here to this excellent book.

person may be fine for another. Morality is reduced to personal preferences and tastes, meaning we shouldn't push our morality on others or pass judgment on individual choices.

Neither form of relativism is persuasive. First, cultures may not differ as much as we think. Sometimes the differences are factual, not moral. For example, I once heard a talk show host say that humans have intrinsic value, yet early abortion is morally permissible. He said that because he thinks the unborn is not a human entity until later in pregnancy. He's factually mistaken on this point (see Chapter 2), but he holds to the same moral principle the pro-lifer does—namely, that humans have intrinsic value in virtue of the kind of thing they are, not some function they perform. This is not a moral difference; it's a factual one.

Second, even if cultures do in fact differ, it does not follow that nobody is correct. As Hadley Arkes points out, the absence of consensus does not mean an absence of truth. "It is not uncommon for mathematicians to disagree over proofs and conclusions," he writes, "yet nothing in their disagreement seems to inspire anyone to challenge the foundations of mathematics or to call into question the possibility of knowing mathematical truths."[8] The relativist is guilty of the is/ought fallacy: While people and cultures may in fact differ, we shouldn't assume there are no right answers. People once disagreed on slavery and equal rights for women, but that didn't mean moral truth was out of reach.

Third, if morals are relative to culture or the individual, there is no ethical difference between Adolf Hitler and Mother Teresa; they just had different preferences. The latter liked to help people, while the former liked to kill them. Who are we to judge? But such a view is counterintuitive.

Fourth, relativism, in any form, cannot say why I *ought* to be tolerant of other cultures. Suppose my culture decides not to tolerate minorities. Now what? Moreover, if right and wrong are relative to one's particular society, moral reformers like Martin Luther King and Gandhi are by definition evil. After all, they challenged their own society's moral codes.

Finally, relativism can be judgmental. For example, if the relativist thinks it's wrong to judge, how can he say that pro-lifers are mistaken in the first place? Isn't he judging the pro-lifer?

---

[8]Hadley Arkes, *First Things: Inquiry into the First Principles of Morals and Justice* (Princeton, NJ: Princeton University Press, 1986), 6.

DO MORALS COUNT AS TRUE KNOWLEDGE?

Pro-life arguments are sometimes dismissed a priori because of their alleged ties to the metaphysics of religion, and more specifically, Christian theism. Throughout the media and academia, the reigning secular orthodoxy dictates that we allow for objective truth in science but never in religion or ethics. If we can't measure something empirically through the five senses (so the argument goes), it's simply a matter of personal taste. Science, and science alone, counts as real knowledge. Everything else—philosophy, metaphysics, morals, and religion, to name a few—cannot be measured empirically. Therefore, they're nothing more than subjective opinions.

Despite the self-refuting nature of the claim (i.e., the assertion that science is the only truth *is itself* a metaphysical claim, not a scientific one), examples of this secular orthodoxy abound.

HOW DID WE GET HERE? THE SHIFT FROM MORAL REALISM TO MORAL NON-REALISM

Western culture has undergone a dramatic shift from *moral realism* (the conviction that objective morals exist even if I don't recognize or acknowledge them) to moral *non-realism* (the belief that morals are merely subjective opinions). The following sketch of moral knowledge from the ancients until now, though by no means complete, highlights this shift.[9]

We begin our history with the moral realism of the Old Testament, where moral truth is both real (objective) and knowable. From Moses forward, biblical texts point to objective moral truths that exist independent of my thinking that they exist. That is, my believing them to be real does not make them real. Instead, moral truths are grounded in the character of God and are accessible to all his people. (See Deuteronomy 30:11—"For this commandment that I command you today is not too hard for you, neither is it far off.") At times these objective moral standards take on a utilitarian application, as in Deuteronomy 30:19—"Choose life, that you and your offspring may live." However, this utilitarian application does not cheapen the objective truth standards but instead shows their practical benefits.

Even secular thinkers like Plato and Aristotle recognized these objective moral truths. For Plato, universal morals are grounded in the world of ideas

---

[9]For a more complete analysis of this shift, see R. Scott Smith, *Truth and the New Kind of Christian*, 23–33; see also Smith's lecture notes "Ethics and the Search for Moral Knowledge" (Biola University, March 2004). I owe much of my insights here to Smith's work.

(forms) but are nonetheless real. For Aristotle, objective morals are rooted in the nature of man, namely, his immaterial soul or essence. Moreover, man can know what's right and wrong through the rational faculties of the soul. Man's duty, then, is to cultivate virtuous habits so that he acts and behaves in a manner consistent with (and proper for) his nature as a human being. Both man's nature and the standards he is obliged to obey exist objectively.

Moral realism continues with the New Testament writers but with one significant addition. Not only is moral truth real and knowable, it is also transforming. That is, while ethics are deontological in their foundation, they do not end with duty for duty's sake. Rather, through the transforming power of the Holy Spirit, God's objective truth radically changes the Christian disciple more and more into the image of his Master. However, even the nonbeliever can know certain objective moral truths and act upon them without the aid of special revelation. The moral law, rooted in God's general revelation, is something all men know intuitively. True, that intuitive knowledge is not sufficient to save nonbelieving men from their sins, but it doesn't follow from this that they can't recognize right and wrong, even if they work overtime to suppress that recognition. (See Romans 1:18–32.)

During the Middle Ages, Thomas Aquinas combined Aristotle's ethics with Christian theology, preserving the moral realism of the biblical writers. However, there's a slight twist. While the biblical writers grounded objective morals in the character of God, Aquinas grounds it more or less in man's unique nature as a rational being, a substance made in God's image with both a body and a soul. Unlike the Protestant Reformers who come later, Aquinas is confident that human reason, unaided by special revelation, can know moral truth (an idea known as natural law).

Then comes the decisive empirical (modern) shift of the seventeenth and eighteenth centuries. For empiricists like Thomas Hobbes (1588–1679) and David Hume (1711–1776), all true knowledge is restricted to what we can observe through the five senses. Since morals are immaterial things that cannot be observed empirically (i.e., we cannot taste, smell, feel, hear, or see them), they are not items of true knowledge. Instead, they are passions and feelings, mere preferences if you will. Human nature is also diminished. Hobbes, for example, disputes that man possesses a unique immaterial nature (soul) that bears God's image. Instead, human beings are just heaps of physical parts. Morals are reduced to self-interest, and only a dominant ruler (a *Leviathan*) can keep self-interested humans from tearing each other apart.

Immanuel Kant (1724–1804) attempts to rescue objective moral truth from empiricism, but his solution is problematic. For Kant, we cannot know things as they truly are (the *noumena*), but only as we perceive them through our senses (the *phenomena*). We are trapped behind our sense perceptions. However—and here Kant takes a bizarre leap—we must act as if an objective moral lawgiver exists (i.e., God) and trust our transcendent minds (or universal ego) to get at the truth. While morals themselves may not be objectively knowable, at least our transcendent minds are universally so. Problem is, does Kant really know this, or is he trapped behind his own sense perceptions?

The influence of Hobbes, Hume, and Kant is still felt today. If morals are not real and knowable, who are you to push your views on me or anyone else? Morality is reduced to mere preference, like opting for chocolate ice cream over vanilla.

For the most part, Christians in the eighteenth and nineteenth centuries did not respond to these empiricist attacks with anything like a vigorous intellectual counterpunch. At first, they simply surrendered. The father of Protestant liberalism, Friedrich Schleiermacher (1768–1834), proposed a strict dichotomy between faith and what's really true. The historical reliability of the Christian faith, along with its doctrines, could be set aside. What mattered was individual religious experience. Thus, even if the resurrection and other doctrines were disproved scientifically, faith could survive as feeling.[10]

Later those believers who resisted liberalism grew suspicious of intellectual ideas altogether, retreating first into revivalism—where emotional, simplistic preaching produced converts with no real grasp of Christian ideas—and then into fundamentalism, where evangelicals committed to biblical truth withdrew from the universities to form their own Bible colleges and seminaries. While evangelical fidelity to theological orthodoxy was truly commendable, the retreat from the marketplace of ideas further marginalized Christians.[11]

Finally, we arrive at the postmodern turn of the twentieth century and its leading analytical philosopher, Ludwig Wittgenstein (1889–1951). The preceding modern view (Kant) said that we are trapped behind our sense

---

[10]See Norman L. Geisler, *Baker Encyclopedia of Christian Apologetics* (Grand Rapids, MI: Baker, 1999), 687–689.

[11]For more on the Christian retreat from the marketplace of ideas, see J. P. Moreland, *Love Your God with All Your Mind* (Colorado Springs: NavPress, 1997), 22–40; Nancy Pearcey, *Total Truth: Liberating Christianity from Its Cultural Captivity* (Wheaton, IL: Crossway Books, 2004).

perceptions and therefore can't get at the truth. For Wittgenstein, truth can't be known because we are trapped behind language. Sure, we can talk about truth all day long, but there is no correspondence between what we *say* is real and what actually *is* real. We must therefore construct morals and religion through our various language communities, just as we do law.

Postmodern thinking had a near-catastrophic impact on religion and ethics. If there is no truth in religion, why should anyone take seriously a worldview that's just a construct of the Christian language community (or any other community)? If the postmodern view is correct, it follows that the gospel can make no real truth claims whatsoever on a Muslim or Hindu who comes from a different faith (or language) community. Privately, gospel teaching may enhance the Christian's personal life, but we should never think of it as genuine knowledge.

Ironically, that hasn't stopped Christian postmodernists from making sweeping (universal) knowledge claims of their own. According to Brad Kallenberg, we are indeed trapped behind language and can't get out to the real world. Thus, language does not represent reality; it constitutes reality.[12] The question is, how can Kallenberg know this given his claim that no one has privileged access to what is real? Is it true that we are trapped behind language, or is that just the view of *his* community? If it's just the view of his particular language community, why should I accept it? Attempts to ground the truth of Christianity in postmodernism are bound to fail. Again, why should anyone take the Christian worldview seriously if it's just a construct of our own language?

Meanwhile, the postmodern turn fractured the concept of moral truth in many ways. We're now told that the Christian language community socially constructs Christian morality while Islamic and Jewish communities socially construct their respective moral rules (and so on and so on). What's true according to one community's article of faith may not be true for anyone else. Hence, one community should not impose its moral views on another.

ASK THE WHY QUESTION

Next time you hear "I personally oppose abortion, but think it should remain legal," ask this simple question: *Why do you personally oppose abor-*

---

[12]Brad Kallenberg, *Ethics as Grammar: Changing the Postmodern Subject* (Notre Dame, IN: University of Notre Dame Press, 2001), 221, 227. Cited in Scott Smith, *Virtue Ethics and Moral Knowledge: Philosophy of Language after MacIntyre and Hauerwas* (Aldershot, UK: Ashgate, 2003), 109.

tion? I mean, if elective abortion does not take the life of a defenseless human being without justification, why oppose it at all?

If your critic is still confused about the kind of claim you are making, consider applying his personally opposed logic to something you both agree is objectively wrong. Robert George, like me, condemns abortion-related violence. But to show how untenable the "personally opposed" logic is when applied to moral claims, he provides a satirical example:

> I am personally opposed to killing abortionists. However, inasmuch as my personal opposition to this practice is rooted in a sectarian (Catholic) religious belief in the sanctity of human life, I am unwilling to impose it on others who may, as a matter of conscience, take a different view. Of course, I am entirely in favor of policies aimed at removing the root causes of violence against abortionists. Indeed, I would go so far as to support mandatory one-week waiting periods, and even nonjudgmental counseling, for people who are contemplating the choice of killing an abortionist. I believe in policies that reduce the urgent need some people feel to kill abortionists while, at the same time, respecting the rights of conscience of my fellow citizens who believe that the killing of abortionists is sometimes a tragic necessity—not a good, but a lesser evil. In short, I am moderately pro-choice.[13]

Again, I condemn all abortion-related violence. But notice that in saying so, I'm not saying I merely *dislike* it. I'm telling you I think it's *wrong*. That's the difference between a moral claim and a mere claim of preference. That's the most important distinction in the entire abortion debate.

REVIEW QUESTIONS

1. What are the two types of truth claims? How do they differ?
2. What word did Pam use to change the kind of claim Emily was making?
3. Consider the popular bumper sticker, "Don't Like Abortion? Don't Have One." What is the abortion-choice advocate failing to grasp?
4. Describe the two kinds of relativism summarized in this chapter.
5. List four reasons why relativism is not persuasive.
6. How did the empirical shift of the eighteenth and nineteenth centuries impact debates over morality? How did Christians respond to the challenges from empiricism?

---

[13]Taken from Robert P. George's remarks in "Killing Abortionists: A Symposium," *First Things*, December 1994.

7. Describe the postmodern turn. How has it impacted ethics?

8. Why is postmodernism self-refuting?

9. When someone says he personally opposes abortion, what question should you ask?

HELPFUL RESOURCES

Hadley Arkes. *First Things: An Inquiry into the First Principles of Morals and Justice.* Princeton, NJ: Princeton University Press, 1986.

Francis J. Beckwith and Gregory Koukl. *Relativism: Feet Firmly Planted in Mid-Air.* Grand Rapids, MI: Baker, 1998.

Paul Copan. *True for You but Not for Me.* Minneapolis: Bethany, 1998.

Edward Feser. "On Legislating Morality: The Anti-Conservative Fallacy." *Tech Central Station Daily,* May 31, 2005.

Peter Kreeft. *A Refutation of Moral Relativism: Interviews with an Absolutist.* San Francisco: Ignatius, 1999.

J. P. Moreland. "Truth, Contemporary Philosophy, and the Postmodern Turn," paper delivered at the Evangelical Theological Society, November 18, 2004.

———. *Love Your God with All Your Mind: The Role of Reason in the Life of the Soul.* Colorado Springs: NavPress, 2007.

Nancy Pearcey. *Total Truth: Liberating Christianity from Its Cultural Captivity.* Wheaton, IL: Crossway Books, 2004.

R. Scott Smith. *Truth and the New Kind of Christian: The Emerging Effects of Postmodernism in the Church.* Wheaton, IL: Crossway Books, 2005.

6

THE GROUND RULES, PART 2: IS MORAL NEUTRALITY POSSIBLE?

Moral neutrality is impossible. Both sides of the abortion controversy bring prior metaphysical commitments to the debate. Why, then, is it okay for liberals to legislate their metaphysical views on the status of the unborn but not okay for pro-lifers to legislate theirs?

METAPHYSICS (literally, "beyond the physical") is not about New Age thinking or Eastern herbal remedies for the common cold, though many people mistakenly think of the term that way. Though difficult to define precisely, metaphysics generally has to do with being (ontology), or if you will, the nature of reality. Metaphysics asks questions such as: What's ultimately real, and is that reality one or many, material or immaterial? Do living things have specific natures that define the kinds of things they are? Do human beings have minds as well as bodies? And what makes those humans valuable in the first place?[1] As we shall see, all sides in the abortion controversy bring metaphysical assumptions to the debate, though some pretend otherwise. *Epistemology* is about how we know things. Questions like, are my beliefs justified? and how do we know what's real? are epistemological in nature.[2] Both of these philosophical disciplines play key roles in determining what's true in disputes over abortion and embryonic stem cell research.

---

[1]Space will not allow a lengthy discussion of metaphysics here. For a detailed discussion, see J. P. Moreland and William Lane Craig, *Philosophical Foundations for a Christian Worldview* (Downers Grove, IL: InterVarsity Press, 2003), 171–303.
[2]Ibid., 69–170.

NO FREE LUNCH: EVERYONE DOES METAPHYSICS

As stated in Chapter 3, metaphysical presuppositions lurk beneath every public policy debate. The controversy over embryonic stem cell research (ESCR) is a case in point.

As stated in Chapter 4, stem cells are fast-growing, unspecialized cells that can reproduce themselves and grow new organs for the body. Human embryos have an abundant supply of stem cells (so we are told) that scientists are eager to harvest in hopes of treating disease. The practice of securing these early cells is known as embryonic stem cell research. There's only one problem: Unlike noncontroversial adult stem cell research, which in no way harms the adult donor, you must kill the embryo to secure its stem cells. (I say more about both types of stem cell research in Chapter 4.)

In a 2005 *New York Times* editorial, former U.S. Senator John Danforth writes that government restrictions on ESCR wrongly impose a particular religious view (that of the "religious right") on a pluralistic society. "It is not evident to many of us that cells in a petri dish are equivalent to identifiable people suffering from terrible diseases . . . the only explanation for legislators comparing cells in a petri dish to babies in the womb is the extension of religious doctrine into statutory law."[3]

This is not at all persuasive. First, Danforth is just plain wrong that pro-life advocates opposed to ESCR provide no rational defense for their position. Sure, they do. The problem is, he takes no time to actually engage the sophisticated case that pro-life philosophers present in support of the embryo's humanity.[4] Even at the popular level, he can't bring himself to answer a basic pro-life argument based on science and philosophy. As stated earlier, pro-lifers contend that from the earliest stages of development, the embryos in question are not mere clumps of cells in a petri dish but distinct, living, and whole human beings. True, they have yet to grow and mature, but they are whole human beings nonetheless. The facts of science confirm this.[5] Philosophically, pro-lifers argue that there is no morally significant difference between the embryo you once were and the adult you are today. Differences of size, level of development, environment, and degree of dependency are not relevant in the way that ESCR advocates need them to be to

---

[3]John Danforth, "In the Name of Politics," *New York Times*, March 30, 2005.
[4]See, for example, Francis J. Beckwith, "The Explanatory Power of the Substance View of Persons," *Christian Bioethics* 10.1 (2004): 33–54.
[5]Maureen Condic, "Life: Defining the Beginning by the End," *First Things*, May 2003.

say it was okay to kill you then but not now. Pro-lifers don't need Scripture or church doctrine to tell them these things. They are truths that even secular libertarians can, and sometimes do, recognize.[6] Yet nowhere in his piece does Danforth present a principled argument explaining why pro-life advocates are mistaken on these points.

Second, Danforth's own position, like the pro-lifer's, is grounded in prior metaphysical commitments. As Francis J. Beckwith explains, the nature of the ESCR debate is such that all positions presuppose a metaphysical view of human value, and for this reason the pro-research position that Danforth defends is not entitled to win by default.[7] At issue is not which view of ESCR has metaphysical underpinnings and which does not, but which metaphysical view of human value does a better job of accounting for human rights and human dignity, pro-life or pro-destructive research.

The pro-life view on ESCR is that humans are intrinsically valuable in virtue of the kind of thing they are. True, they differ immensely with respect to talents, accomplishments, and degrees of development, but they are nonetheless equal because they share a common human nature. Their right to life comes to be when they come to be, either at conception or at the completion of a cloning process. Danforth's own view is that humans have value (and hence rights) not in virtue of the kind of thing they are, members of a natural kind, but only because of an acquired property that comes to be later in the life of the human organism. Because the early embryo does not appear (to him) as a human being with rights, destructive research is permissible.

Notice that Danforth is doing the abstract work of metaphysics. That is, he is using philosophical reflection to defend a disputed view of human value in his quest to defend ESCR. In short, Danforth's attempt to disqualify the pro-life view from public policy based on its alleged metaphysical underpinnings works equally well to disqualify his own view.

Now maybe Danforth, echoing political philosopher John Rawls, meant to convey a more sophisticated claim—namely, that society should confer a large degree of liberty by not legislating on controversial moral issues for which there is no consensus, especially if those issues involve comprehensive moral doctrines based on prior metaphysical commitments. Embryonic

---

[6]See Libertarians for Life (http://l4l.org) and Godless Pro-lifers (http://godlessprolifers.org). Although secularists can recognize moral truths, I do think they ultimately have trouble grounding moral claims.

[7]Francis J. Beckwith, "Law, Religion, and the Metaphysics of Abortion: A Reply to Simmons," *Journal of Church and State* 43.1 (Winter 2001): 19–33. Beckwith is speaking principally to the issue of abortion and is not addressing Danforth, but his thoughts apply to the ESCR debate as well. I owe my thoughts in this section to his excellent analysis.

stem cell research, so the argument goes, is a divisive and controversial issue. Therefore, government should not restrict it.[8]

But as discussed in Chapter 3, this view is self-refuting. To say government should remain neutral on metaphysical questions is itself a metaphysical claim, a comprehensive moral doctrine about how government *should* function.[9] It's also controversial: Do we have a consensus that we should not legislate on divisive matters like ESCR? Moreover, slavery and racism were controversial issues that involved prior worldview commitments. Are we to conclude that it was wrong to legislate against them? The fact that people disagree is no reason to suppose that nobody is correct.

Third, the "religious" sword in this case cuts both ways. The overwhelming majority of mainline Protestant denominations (including Danforth's own Episcopal Church) hold to the same metaphysical view he does regarding the embryo—namely, that developing humans are *not* valuable in virtue of the kind of thing they are (substances with a particular nature) but only because of some accidental property acquired sometime after the early human comes to be.[10] Many of these left-leaning groups specifically cite Scripture to make the case that embryos and fetuses are not human beings.[11] The bottom line is, if the pro-life view opposing ESCR is suspect because of its alleged connection to the metaphysics of religion, so is the pro-destructive research one.

Fourth, the claim that "an embryo is a human subject with rights" is no more religious than claiming it's not. Both claims involve prior metaphysical commitments. Our job is to see which claim better explains human dignity and equality. So far Danforth contents himself with calling his opponents names from a distance rather than engaging the substance of their ideas.

Finally, state neutrality is impossible. The law either recognizes the unborn as valuable human beings and thus protects them or it does not and permits killing them.[12] By agreeing that human embryos are fitting subjects for destructive research, Danforth is taking a public policy position that embryos do not deserve the same protections owed to toddlers or other human beings. This is hardly a neutral position; it's an extremely controversial one with deep metaphysical underpinnings. Why, then, is it okay for

---

[8]See John Rawls, *Political Liberalism* (New York: Columbia University Press, 1995).

[9]For more on this, see Edward Feser, "The Myth of Libertarian Neutrality," *Tech Central Station*, August 3, 2004.

[10]See, for example, The Religious Coalition for Reproductive Choice website, http://www.rcrc.org.

[11]I deal with this question in detail in Chapter 8.

[12]Here I summarize Ryan T. Anderson, "For Humanity," *National Review*, October 8, 2007, 68–70.

Danforth to legislate his own view on the status of human embryos but not okay for pro-lifers to legislate theirs?

EVERYONE TAKES A POSITION

Here's another example of alleged neutrality that really isn't. The March of Dimes (MOD) supports federal funding for embryonic stem cell research,[13] yet declares itself neutral on the philosophical questions surrounding the abortion controversy.[14]

However, the moral permissibility of ESCR and abortion come down to the same basic question: Is the unborn a member of the human family? If so, research on human embryos should be conducted within the same guidelines we use for other children who, because of immaturity, cannot consent to treatment themselves. That is to say, the research must personally benefit the embryo and place it at no significant risk. If the embryos in question are not human, destroying them for any reason requires no further justification.

When the MOD officially condoned destroying human embryos for medical research, it took the position that embryos do not deserve the same protections we give to other children. For example, the organization would never fund destructive medical research on two-year-olds scheduled for execution by a totalitarian regime, even if doing so would cure millions of disease. Thus, the MOD, in supporting destructive research on human embryos, is taking a position that embryos are not the moral equivalent of other children. This is hardly a neutral position.

Suppose a nineteenth-century medical school delivered this opinion on the issue of slavery: "We take no position on the morality of owning slaves. We are neutral. However, in our quest to cure many diseases, we fund many groups that conduct medical experiments on those African-American slaves scheduled for execution. Rest assured: We do not pay money for these groups to kill slaves. They must use private funds for that. We pay only for the beneficial research they conduct after the slave is killed. In fact, we think slaves deserve profound respect. However, they do not carry the same moral status as white people. Once the slaves are executed, it would be morally wrong to let all that tissue go to waste. Remember this: These slaves are

---

[13]Stem Cell Letter to House and Senate Appropriations Committees, July 29, 1999. The MOD signed this letter, which requests federal funds for ESCR.
[14]For MOD's statement on abortion neutrality, see http://www.marchofdimes.com/professionals/691_2160.asp.

going to die anyway, and we don't pay people to kill them. We simply fund the research after the fact."

Would anyone in America today consider this a neutral position on slavery? Clearly, the medical school would be complicit in the deaths of executed slaves. By funding the research, it would be taking a position that black slaves are the sorts of beings that can be killed and treated as property. The message would be clear: Blacks are not full-fledged members of the human community.

Reasonable persons should commend the March of Dimes for its laudable work in improving the health of babies, preventing birth defects, and reducing infant mortality. These are good and noble actions.

But good deeds do not atone for bad ones. By embracing destructive embryo research, the March of Dimes has violated the principle that once made it great—its basic commitment to assist the small, weak, and defenseless. It's regrettable that this great organization would treat the most vulnerable members of the human community, the unborn, as nothing more than disposable instruments to be used for someone else's benefit.

TAKING THEOLOGY SERIOUSLY

In review, both positions—pro-life and pro-ESCR—are attempting to answer the exact same question: What makes humans valuable in the first place? Science cannot answer that question; only metaphysics can. So why is only the pro-life position disqualified from the public square (for its alleged ties to the metaphysics of religion) while the pro-ESCR view gets a free pass?

During a nationally televised speech at the 2004 Democratic Convention, Ron Reagan (son of President Ronald Reagan) said the following about those who oppose ESCR:

> Now, there are those who would stand in the way of this remarkable future, who would deny the federal funding so crucial to basic research. They argue that interference with the development of even the earliest stage embryo, even one that will never be implanted in a womb and will never develop into an actual fetus, is tantamount to murder. . . . [M]any are well-intentioned and sincere. Their belief is just that, an article of faith, and they are entitled to it. But it does not follow that the theology of a few should be allowed to forestall the health and well-being of the many.[15]

[15]Cited in Francis J. Beckwith, "Taking Theology Seriously," *Notre Dame Journal of Law, Ethics & Public Policy*, 20:1 (2006): 455–471.

Reagan goes on to say that early embryos "are not, in and of themselves, human beings" because they "have no fingers and toes, no brain or spinal cord. They have no thoughts, no fears. They feel no pain."

With that single statement, Reagan has injected his own "article of faith" into the debate, as Beckwith explains:

> Ironically, by classifying early embryos as morally outside the circle of legal protection, Ron Reagan enters an area of theological exploration on a question of philosophical anthropology. He chooses to answer a question of scholarly interest to theologians and philosophers ("What is man?") in order to justify a particular act (the killing of embryos). He refers to the position of his adversaries as "an article of faith," even though he chooses to answer the same exact question ("What is man?") his adversaries answer.[16]

As stated before, the claim that an embryo has value is indeed a claim with theological underpinnings, but it's no more a religious claim than saying a ten-year-old has value. Can a truly secular ethic tell us why anything has a right to life? At the same time, pro-life advocates do not rely on theology alone. They do, after all, offer reasoned arguments in support of their position, arguments that can be understood by skeptics. Why won't Reagan admit this? According to Beckwith, the problem is intellectual dishonesty:

> In my opinion, it is only because the younger Reagan and his allies do not consider theological beliefs as belonging to a knowledge tradition that they can dismiss, a priori, theologically informed policy proposals as de facto epistemically inferior to so-called secular ones, even when secular ones answer precisely the same questions as do the so-called "article of faith." The younger Reagan and his allies offer no reasons for the epistemological apartheid, since they know that convincing their peers that a view is or may be "religious" relieves them of their epistemic duty to rationally assess that view as a serious contender to the deliverance of so-called secular reason.[17]

Admittedly, many secularists reject any presupposition that smells of theism. However, debates over God's existence are no different in kind from other philosophical arguments, for example, current controversies over

---

[16]Ibid.
[17]Ibid.

abortion, ESCR, and same-sex marriage. They are controversial questions about which thoughtful people often disagree. So why the double standard with religiously informed views? Edward Feser writes:

> Do secularists demand that those in favor of legalized abortion and same-sex marriage refrain from advocating their positions in the public square simply because their arguments are nowhere near universally accepted? Of course not, nor should they. So why do they demand that religion and politics be separated not just in the constitutional sense that no one ought to be forced to belong to a particular denomination or to accept a particular creed, but also in the stronger sense that religious considerations, however well supported by rational arguments, ought to get no hearing in the public square and have no influence on public policy? Why the constant harping about the separation of church and state, but not, say, the separation of naturalistic metaphysics and the state, the separation of feminist theory and the state, or the separation of Rawlsian liberalism and the state?[18]

A FINAL CHALLENGE: LET'S DO SCIENCE

Nevertheless, I'm prepared to take Senator Danforth at his word and remove religion from the starting point for the ESCR debate. Let's use science, and science alone, to settle the question, is the embryo a human being? Robert P. George, member of the President's Council on Bioethics, suggests the following methodology for resolving the issue with critics of the pro-life view who affirm human equality but deny it applies to embryos used for destructive research:

> There are three positions that can be defended without quickly falling into logical inconsistency. The first is that human beings are in no morally relevant way different from other creatures and therefore have no special dignity. The second is that human beings have an inherent and equal dignity; each and every human being possesses it simply by virtue of his or her humanity. The third is that some, but not all, human beings have dignity; those who have it possess it by virtue of some quality or set of qualities that they happen to possess that other human beings do not possess (or do not yet possess, or no longer possess).
>
> Anyone who believes that stepping on an ant is not a grave moral wrong but murdering your grandmother to prevent her spending down your inheritance is one, has already rejected the first position. Anyone who

---

[18]Edward Feser, "How to Mix Religion and Politics," *Tech Central Station Daily*, March 29, 2005.

accepts the third position will, in fairly short order, find himself driven by the force of logical argumentation into the [infanticide] positions infamously defended by Peter Singer. (We can go through this exercise, if you like.)

Assuming one doesn't want to embrace Singerism, that leaves the second position. Now, once one adopts that position, the key question in the debate over embryo-destructive research is "When does the life of a human being begin?" To answer this question is to decide whether or not human embryos are, in fact, human beings and, as such, possessors of inherent human dignity. Where do we go to find the answer? Not to the Catechism of the Catholic Church. If the Catechism takes a position, it must do so derivatively. That is to say, its position will be derived from another source. (I'll identify that source in a moment.) Not to the Bible, which says nothing about human embryos. Not to the Talmud, which (like the Bible) was composed centuries before the discovery of the ovum—a time when almost nothing was known about embryogenesis. Not to the Koran. Not to our "moral intuitions."

Rather, we go to the standard texts of modern human embryology and developmental biology—for example, the texts by Keith Moore and T.V.N. Persaud; Bruce M. Carlson; Ronan O'Rahilly and Fabiola Mueller; and William J. Larsen.[19] When we consult these works, we find little or nothing in the way of scientific mystery or dispute. The texts tell the same story and answer the key question in the same way. Anyone who wishes to know when he or she as a distinct living member of the species Homo sapiens came into existence need only open any of these books and look up the answer.

So I have a proposal for people of goodwill who wish to affirm the inherent and equal dignity of all human beings but disagree with those of us who are opposed on moral grounds to embryo-destructive research. Let's leave religion out of this. Let's agree to resolve our difference of opinion strictly on the basis of the best available scientific evidence as to when the life of a new human being begins. Any takers?[20]

How about it, Senator?

REVIEW QUESTIONS

1. What is metaphysics, and how does it differ from epistemology?

---

[19]For some of the sources George lists here, see Keith L. Moore and T. V. N. Persaud, *The Developing Human: Clinically Oriented Embryology* (Toronto: B.C. Decker, 1988); Ronand O'Rahilly and Fabiola Müller, *Human Embryology and Teratology*, 2nd ed. (New York: Wiley-Liss, 1996).
[20]Robert P. George posted this on the *National Review* website, http://corner.nationalreview.com/post/?q=NjQy YmY5NmU3MjY3MDc4MjY3OTUwMGY5MzgzODY4YjA=. Paragraph breaks were inserted for clarity.

2. In what way is Senator Danforth's alleged moral neutrality anything but neutral? Contrast his own metaphysical views about the embryo with those of the pro-life advocate.

3. Why is state neutrality in general impossible on abortion and ESCR?

4. What does Ron Reagan assume about theology when making his case for ESCR?

5. Robert P. George outlines three metaphysical views of human value. What are they? And how does science fit into his own proposal?

6. Edward Feser writes about a double standard that's often applied to religious truth claims. What does he mean by this?

HELPFUL RESOURCES

Francis J. Beckwith. "Law, Religion, and the Metaphysics of Abortion: A Reply to Simmons." *Journal of Church and State* 43.1 (Winter 2001): 19–33.

———. "Taking Theology Seriously: The Status of Religious Beliefs of Judicial Nominees for the Federal Bench." *Notre Dame Journal of Law, Ethics & Public Policy*, 20:1 (2006): 455–471.

Robert P. George. *The Clash of Orthodoxies: Law, Religion, and Morality in Crisis.* Wilmington, DE: ISI Books, 2001.

Esther Lightcap Meek. *Longing to Know: The Philosophy of Knowledge for Ordinary People.* Grand Rapids, MI: Brazos Press, 2003.

Edward Feser. "How to Mix Religion and Politics." *Tech Central Station Daily*, March 29, 2005.

———. "The Myth of Libertarian Neutrality." *Tech Central Station Daily*, August 3, 2004.

Joseph Cardinal Ratzinger (now Pope Benedict XVI). *Truth and Tolerance: Christian Belief in World Religions.* San Francisco: Ignatius Press, 2004.

7

FOUNDATIONS: DOES GOD MATTER? (OR AM I JUST MATTER?)

Even if the pro-life view cannot be fully explained without explicit reference to Christian faith, it does not follow that the pro-life view is inherently irrational. Christian theists make rational arguments for their position, and it's wrong for materialists to simply presume the truth of their position.

WHEN MY SON JEFFREY WAS TEN, he broke his hand after a nasty fall on a Razor Scooter. While awaiting treatment at the local emergency room, he noticed a woman in a wheelchair—she had no legs. Wiping aside his own tears, he said, "Dad, that lady has no legs, but she's still a human being." This was indeed comforting to me as a parent (even though I was about to shell out big bucks for medical expenses) because he articulated a truth that my wife and I had taught him since he was little—namely, that although humans differ in their respective degrees of development, they are nonetheless equal because they share a common human nature made in the image of their Creator.

Secularism rejects the transcendent grounding point for human dignity that we've taught to our sons. As one abortion-choice blogger writes, "It's not so much that the anti-abortion view is suspect because it is endorsed by religions—it's that the view itself seems to be based solely, or at least heavily, on religion. . . . What I'm skeptical of is that there exists a totally non-religious argument against abortion."[1]

---

[1] This was posted by a blogger named Dadahead at http://dadahead.blogspot.com/2005/08/wingnut-metaphysics-revisited.html.

And I'm skeptical that there exists one *for* it. (See Chapter 3.)

Nevertheless, there's no denying that a majority of pro-life advocates do, in fact, embrace some form of Christian theism and are motivated by it to defend the weak and defenseless. Are their beliefs rationally defensible?

In its broadest theological sense, Christian theism is a cosmological explanation about the nature and origin of the universe, as well as man's place in it. The story line has four parts: 1) God's creation, 2) man's rebellion through the sin of Adam, 3) God's redemption through the death and resurrection of Jesus Christ, and 4) creation's restoration.

What follows is by no means an exhaustive defense of Christian theism.[2] My goal here is really quite modest. I simply hope to show that *even if* the pro-life view cannot be explained without ultimately grounding it in the Christian faith, it does not follow that the pro-life view is inherently irrational: Christian theists make rational arguments in defense of their position. Admittedly, some critics may not be persuaded by these arguments, but it's grossly inaccurate to claim that Christianity has no rational basis.

At the same time, I'm not suggesting that theism (or atheism) can be proved beyond all doubt. However, certitude is not required in order to hold that theism is rational. The theist merely needs to show that his explanation for the universe as we know it is superior to rival explanations. By that standard, Christian theism in particular fares very well.

To summarize the case I'll present, the real conflict over cosmology is not between religion and science—it's between religion and materialism, between those who think that religious truth is both real and knowable and those who think that science explains everything. But as Stephen Barr points out, *materialism* is not science; it's a presupposed philosophical worldview dressed up as science.[3] *Its central philosophic claim is that matter alone constitutes ultimate reality and that everything that exists is the product of strict physical laws and blind random chance.* However, there's nothing about science in general that assumes, much less demands, a materialistic view of the universe. In fact, the actual scientific data, once stripped of its materialistic presuppositions, points toward a universe uniquely designed to sustain life. Meanwhile, materialism cannot adequately explain many things we know to be true such as non-material minds, the existence of

---

[2]For a more exhaustive defense of Christian theism, see J. P. Moreland and William Lane Craig, *Philosophical Foundations for a Christian Worldview* (Downers Grove, IL: InterVarsity Press, 2003); William Lane Craig, *Reasonable Faith: Christian Truth in Apologetics* (Wheaton, IL: Crossway Books, 1984, 2008).
[3]Stephen Barr, *Modern Physics and Ancient Faith* (Notre Dame, IN: University of Notre Dame Press, 2003), 6.

moral and rational oughts, and basic human rights, to name a few. Finally, the evidence for Christian theism in particular is compelling. Multiple lines of argument affirm the New Testament documents as historically reliable and trustworthy. Christ's followers didn't fabricate stories of his death and resurrection—they recorded them.

THE PRESUMPTION OF MATERIALISM

Let's begin by determining the ground rules for the debate. Should our interpretation of the facts be restricted to what materialism will allow or be open to free inquiry?

According to Barr, scientists with a prior commitment to materialism simply rule out anything that smells like teleology (i.e., purpose through religion), fearing that people will somehow be led astray from the high road of science into "the barren wastelands of fruitless metaphysical speculation."[4] He writes that most arguments for materialism beg the question and boil down to this: Materialism is true because it *must* be true. The alternative, special creation, is simply unacceptable. Darwinist Richard Lewontin concedes this very point:

> We take the side of science in spite of the patent absurdity of some of its constructs, in spite of its failure to fulfill many of its extravagant promises of health and life, in spite of the tolerance of the scientific community for unsubstantiated just-so stories, because we have a prior commitment, a commitment to materialism. It is not that the methods and institutions of science somehow compel us to accept a material explanation of the phenomenal world, but, on the contrary, that we are forced by our a priori adherence to material causes to create an apparatus of investigation and a set of concepts that produce material explanations, no matter how counter-intuitive, no matter how mystifying to the uninitiated. Moreover, that materialism is an absolute, for we cannot allow a Divine Foot in the door.[5]

For other Darwinists, the presumption of materialism is justified because claims for design are "extraordinary" and therefore require extraordinary proof. In the absence of extraordinary proof, we're told we should presume atheism. The charge typically goes something like this: "You theists

---

[4]Ibid., 138.
[5]Richard Lewontin, "Billions and Billions of Demons," *The New York Review of Books*, January 9, 1997, 31. Cited in Benjamin Winker, *Moral Darwinism: How We Became Hedonists* (Downers Grove, IL: InterVarsity Press, 2003), 294–295.

claim that God supernaturally created the universe out of nothing. That's an extraordinary assertion. Extraordinary statements require extraordinary proof."

This is false. The claim "God does not exist" is just as much a claim to know something as saying "God does exist," meaning the atheist needs just as much substantiation for his claim as the theist does for his.[6] And who says that extraordinary claims demand extraordinary proofs? As Bob and Gretchen Passantino point out, that's an extraordinary claim, a claim that seems to be universal, absolute, and invariant. What extraordinary proof do atheists have that their claim is true and valid? Moreover, the Passantinos illustrate how the charge can be thrown back at the atheist:

> It is an extraordinary claim to say this vast and complex universe came from nothing and was caused by nothing. It's an extraordinary claim to tell us the incredible order we see throughout the universe was caused by blind chance. It's an extraordinary claim to argue that the innate sense of right and wrong that all of us share—even when it condemns our own actions—came about by non-moral mindlessness or mere human consensus. It's certainly an extraordinary claim to say that a man who has all of the character and credentials to back up his claim to be the Son of God—and who rises from the dead to prove it—is really a self-deluded fool or, worse yet, a deceiver. In conclusion, no, the evidence is far too weak to believe the extraordinary claim of atheism that there is no God behind these things.[7]

CAN SCIENCE EXPLAIN EVERYTHING?

For the materialist, scientism reigns supreme. *Scientism* asserts that all metaphysical claims, especially those tied to organized religion, are simply beyond the pale of rational thought. Only science counts as true knowledge. But such a claim is hugely problematic. First, it's self-refuting. To say that science is the measure of all true knowledge is *not* a scientific truth but a *philosophic* claim about science. It's scientism posing as science. In fact, Barr and other critics of materialism point out that you can't even do the work of science without assuming several metaphysical truths, meaning that metaphysics is conceptually prior to science, not vice versa:[8]

---

[6]For more on this, see Paul Copan, "The Presumptuousness of Atheism," http://www.paulcopan.com/articles/pdf/Presumptuousness-of-Atheism.pdf.
[7]Bob and Gretchen Passantino, "The 2002 Great Debate: Atheism vs. Christianity—Testing the Case: Which View Prevailed?"; http://www.answers.org/atheism/debate.html.
[8]Barr, *Modern Physics and Ancient Faith*, 14. See also Moreland and Craig, *Philosophical Foundations for a*

• You must assume that your questions about the natural world have rational and intelligible answers.
• You must assume that the external world can be known.
• You must assume that our cognitive and sensory faculties are reliable enough to provide us with justified true belief on a given proposition.
• You must assume that the laws of logic exist and can be known by the scientist.
• You must assume that language is adequate to describe the world as it really is.
• You must assume that the scientist has a moral duty to report his findings honestly and to go no further with his conclusions than the evidence allows.

Second, we know many things to be true outside of science. To expand upon Barr's thesis, we are rationally justified in believing that it's wrong to torture toddlers for fun, but the physical world did not tell us that. Our moral (non-physical) intuitions did. Yet if objective morals truly exist and if they aren't physical things, materialism is false. Moreover, if raw scientism trumps metaphysics, how can we condemn doctors who use prisoners for horrific medical experiments, as happened in the Soviet Gulags?

Third, there is no good reason to suppose that religious claims are inherently irrational. Indeed, Christian thinkers like St. Augustine and Thomas Aquinas insisted that no interpretation of Scripture should willingly conflict with reason and experience.[9] Even today, most Christian apologists reject an exclusive (non-overlapping) model that says science and theology have nothing to say to each other, ever. True, the Bible does not speak to all issues (for example, where did AIDS come from?), and science says little about doctrine (for example, is the doctrine of the Trinity true?), but it does not follow from this that there can be no overlap. Instead, Christian theists resolve the alleged conflict between science and faith by conceding that while the Bible is infallible, science and theology are not. Both disciplines are subject to correction by the other.

Again, there is no conflict between science and faith if *science* means an objective investigation of the facts and *faith* means knowledge based on evidence. Conversely, if *science* means ruling out scientific facts in order to

---

Christian Worldview, 178, 348.
[9]See, for example, St. Augustine, "On the Literal Meaning of Genesis," in *Ancient Christian Writers: The Works of the Fathers in Translation*, trans. John Hammond Taylor, No. 41 (New York: Newman Press, 1982), 42–43; Thomas Aquinas, *Summa Theologiae*, Ia, 68,1. Both sources are cited in Barr, *Modern Physics and Ancient Faith*, 7.

assert one's philosophic worldview (i.e., materialism), then science and faith collide dramatically in a manner that harms both.

IS THE DESIGN THESIS REASONABLE?

The crux of the debate over cosmology comes down to this: Is it rational to suppose that all reality can be reduced to blind physical processes, or is there evidence of design? According to the rules imposed by materialism, there's no room for debate: Strict physical necessity and blind random chance *must* explain everything in the universe, including human minds and their capacity for rational inquiry. The universe came from nothing and was caused by nothing.

In 2004, distinguished atheistic philosopher Antony Flew made worldwide news when he repudiated his lifelong commitment to atheism and affirmed theism. Though his support for theism was minimal (his current position resembles Deism), Flew made one thing very clear: The evidence of intelligent design in DNA and the arguments of American intelligent design theorists played an important role in his shift. In Flew's words, he simply "had to go where the evidence leads."[10]

Proponents of Intelligent Design (ID) contend that materialism's presuppositions do not adequately explain the scientific data as we know it.[11] Their challenge to Darwin is not merely religious but empirical and philosophical. They contend that the science needed to sustain Darwin's materialism just isn't there.

First, Big Bang cosmology refutes the materialist claim that the universe always existed, a claim popularized by Carl Sagan's mantra, "The cosmos is all there is, all there ever was, and all there ever will be."[12] As Barr points out, the claim for an eternal cosmos does not square with the evidence, most notably Hubble's 1929 discovery of an expanding physical universe, one flying apart from some primeval explosion. If the universe had a beginning, as Hubble's discovery suggests, it's reasonable to conclude that it was caused.[13]

---

[10]See Flew's interview with Gary Habermas at http://www.biola.edu/antonyflew/flew-interview.pdf.

[11]Barr, *Modern Physics and Ancient Faith*, 1–35. See also Phillip Johnson, *Reason in the Balance: The Case Against Naturalism in Science, Law, and Education* (Downers Grove, IL: InterVarsity Press, 1995), 51–70; William Dembski, *Intelligent Design: The Bridge Between Science and Theology* (Downers Grove, IL: InterVarsity Press, 1999), 122–152.

[12]Sagan said this in the award-winning 1980 television series *Cosmos: A Personal Voyage*, which has been seen by more than six hundred million people in over sixty countries, making it the most widely watched PBS program in history.

[13]Hugh Ross, *The Creator and the Cosmos* (Colorado Springs: NavPress, 2001), 32–33.

Second, the finely-tuned Big Bang we observe presents challenging questions for the materialist. Why was there a universe in the first place? It hardly seems this universe was a necessity. And why this particular (life-sustaining) universe rather than another? Barr argues that the initial probability of there being such a universe is quite small. Slight increase in the gravitational force would leave us with stars too large (and too hot) to sustain any kind of life. Slight reductions in the nuclear force would convert all matter to hydrogen. Meanwhile, the cosmological constant (which tells us how much gravitational pull is exerted by empty space) must remain at nearly zero (to 120 decimal places!) or life is impossible. According to Barr, this is one of the most precise fine-tunings in all of physics.[14] Similarly, astrophysicist Hugh Ross notes that if the universe were to expand too slowly or too rapidly, the resulting fusing of nucleons would produce elements either too heavy or too light to sustain biological life.[15] Occurrences like these suggest that from the earliest moments of existence, the universe was uniquely fitted to sustain life. Skeptics say the universe came from the roll of the dice, but J. P. Moreland replies, "it sure looks like those dice were rigged in advance for life to appear."[16]

Third, even the simplest life-forms show evidence of design. There is information in the cell that can't be explained by chance alone. According to scientist Robert Gange, the amount of information found in the DNA of an amoeba exceeds what is contained in great libraries.[17] Yet, to date, materialists have been unable to explain the origin of the digital information needed to build the first living cell.

Biochemist Michael Behe, observing the mechanics of a bacterial flagellum, writes that the flagellum is not only complex, it's *irreducibly complex*. A system is irreducibly complex if it consists of several interrelated parts that must be in place *simultaneously* for it to function. Removing even one part will render it useless. Behe uses the common mousetrap as an illustration. To function, a mousetrap needs a platform, a spring, a killing wire, and a safety catch. The trap is irreducibly complex because each of these parts must be in place as a whole before it can function. An evolving mousetrap with only a spring and a platform will not catch any mice. Behe then argues that even

---

[14]Barr, *Modern Physics and Ancient Faith*, 129–130.
[15]Ibid. See also Ross, *The Creator and the Cosmos*, 34.
[16]Cited by J. P. Moreland in his interview with Lee Strobel, "Is the Supernatural Real?"; http://www.leestrobel.com/videoserver/video.php?clip=strobelT1011.
[17]Robert Gange, *Origins and Destiny* (Waco, TX: Word Books, 1986), 71–73. Cited in Gary Habermas, *The Risen Jesus and Future Hope* (Lanham, MD: Rowman and Littlefield, 2003), 58.

a simple bacteria cell has a number of interrelated parts, and subtracting any one would destroy the cell's function. In short, the cell cannot develop over time through chance mutations since all the elements must work together as a whole. To function, Behe concludes, the cell "would have to arise as an integrated unit, in one fell swoop."[18]

Fourth, the design thesis fits our basic intuitions. Atheist (and Darwinist) Richard Dawkins admits in his book *The Blind Watchmaker* that living things give the appearance of having been designed for a purpose; yet he rejects design as simply unthinkable.[19] But if the universe looks designed, why is it implausible to think that it *is* designed? As William Dembski points out, the information found in the universe, even with simple life-forms, is both *specified* and *complex*, and this suggests design.[20] Imagine a group of pencils on the floor that reads, "Hello My Good Friend." It's possible the arrangement is random (perhaps the wind did it), but you don't buy that explanation for a second. The information is both too complex *and* too specified to happen by accident. The most plausible explanation is that somebody did the arranging.

THE PROBLEM OF MINDS, IDEAS, AND MORALS

Materialism can be questioned philosophically as well as scientifically. First, materialists cannot account for the emergence of non-material minds from purely physical processes. That is to say, they must show how consciousness arises from unconscious brain matter. John Searle writes that "the leading problem in the biological sciences is the problem of explaining how neurobiological processes cause conscious experience."[21] If that were not challenging enough, materialism must also explain how these non-material minds cohere with the physical states of the brain. The interaction between non-material minds and physical bodies suggests design.[22]

Second, materialism cannot account for rational or moral oughtness. That is, it suffers from an *idea* problem that renders it self-refuting. "If ideas are just patterns of nerve impulses," writes Barr, "then how can one say that any idea (including the idea of materialism itself) is superior to any other?

[18]See Michael Behe, *Darwin's Black Box: The Biochemical Challenge to Evolution* (New York: Free Press, 1998), 39–45, 69–72.
[19]Richard Dawkins, *The Blind Watchmaker* (New York: Norton, 1986), 1.
[20]Dembski, *Intelligent Design: The Bridge Between Science and Theology*, 17–18.
[21]John Searle, "The Mystery of Consciousness: Part II," *New York Review of Books* (November 16, 1995), 61. Cited in Paul Copan, "Can Michael Martin Be a Moral Realist?" *Philosophia Christi*, Vol. 1, No. 2, 1999.
[22]J. P. Moreland develops this theme in his article, "Searle's Biological Naturalism and the Argument from Consciousness," *Faith and Philosophy*, 15, 1 (January 1998), 68–91.

One pattern of nerve impulses cannot be truer or less true than another pattern, any more than a toothache can be truer or less true than another toothache."[23] Robin Collins underscores the significance of this—namely, that human judgment and evaluation, needed to determine truth and error (including the truth or error of materialism), presuppose a world of moral meaning that transcends the physical-material world. In short, the very effort to argue for materialism ends up refuting it.[24]

At the same time, how can we trust our minds to think rationally about anything, including materialism, if they are the products of blind, non-rational forces? The mechanism of evolution does not promote rational thought. It promotes survival. Gary Habermas writes:

> Naturalism holds that the human mind developed by chance. From this scenario, it follows that our thinking may be simply the motion of atoms, and we have no reason to believe we can think rationally. Further, naturalistic arguments aimed at disputing this position must assume the very point it opposes, namely, the reality of rational thought.[25]

Third, materialism cannot account for the rise of intrinsically valuable moral agents. According to materialism, we start from nothing and, through a series of chance happenings, end up with a world of individuals who feel obligated to act a certain way.[26] How did we get from *is* to *ought*? And what gives our moral intuitions their oughtness? Gregory Ganssle writes that what's striking about our universe is not only that it sustains life (which is improbable enough), but that it sustains the sort of life to which moral truths apply. Materialism has no plausible explanations for this. Indeed, if the universe is the product of blind chance, we end up with "a set of necessary moral truths that are, so to speak, waiting around. There is nothing at all to which these truths apply and there is no guarantee that they will ever apply to anything." Somehow (luckily) a totally accidental process lasting twenty billion years or so produces moral creatures, "creatures that exactly match the moral truths that have been waiting in the wings throughout the whole show."[27] Such a claim is highly suspect.

---

[23]Barr, *Modern Physics and Ancient Faith*, 197.
[24]Robin Collins, "Religion and Science Revisited," *First Things*, November 2003.
[25]Habermas, *The Risen Jesus and Future Hope*, 54.
[26]Paul Copan addresses this problem at length in "Can Michael Martin be a Moral Realist?" *Philosophia Christi*, 1999.
[27]Gregory Ganssle, "Necessary Moral Truths and Their Need for Explanation," *Philosophia Christi*, Vol. 2, No. 1, 2000.

Paul Copan writes, "Just think about it. Intrinsically-valuable, thinking persons do not come from impersonal, non-conscious, unguided, valueless processes over time. A personal, self-aware, purposeful, good God provides the natural and necessary context for the existence of valuable, rights-bearing, morally responsible human persons."[28]

Fourth, it's difficult to see how materialists can ground the moral claims they inevitably end up making. To cite one example, atheist Peter Singer equates moral decency with a series of universal shoulds and oughts: Americans ought to renounce material wealth and give liberally to the poor in developing countries. We ought to increase pleasure and minimize pain for animals as well as humans. We should treat all sentient beings equally, regardless of species membership.[29]

Yet how can Singer account for any of these moral obligations given his materialistic worldview? "When we reject belief in a god," he writes, "we must give up the idea that life on this planet has some preordained meaning. Life as a whole has no meaning. Life began [in] a chance combination of molecules; it then evolved through chance mutations and natural selection. All this just happened; it did not happen for any overall purpose."[30] That single statement undermines Singer's attempt to ground any moral claim, including one that says we should treat animals fairly. How can he account for objective, universally binding morals in a universe that admits no objective, moral lawgiver?

If his atheistic premise is correct, then asking me to put other species on equal footing with my own is ridiculous. To the contrary, nothing makes more sense in a Darwinian "survival of the fittest" universe then subjugating other species to *my* use. Ayn Rand is correct: If there is no God, we should live selfishly.[31]

To be clear, Singer can certainly *recognize* moral obligations and *act* according to them. His concern for the world's poor is proof he can be good without God! But Singer's job is not done. He must still explain how a mindless universe furnished us with a set of objective moral truths we are *obliged* to obey. Where did these moral truths come from? If they are the product of blind random chance, why should I obey them? For example,

---

[28]Paul Copan, "The Moral Argument for God's Existence," http://www.4truth.net/site/apps/nl/content3.asp?c=hiKXLbPNLrF&b=778665&ct=1264233.
[29]See Singer's interview on the Princeton University website, http://www.princeton.edu/~psinger/faq.html.
[30]Peter Singer, *Practical Ethics* (Cambridge: Cambridge University Press, 1993), 331.
[31]For an excellent discussion on this problem for atheists, see Copan, "Can Michael Martin Be a Moral Realist?" See also Bill Weaks, "Practically Nonsense," www.firstgen.org.

if I'm playing the board game Scrabble and I see the phrase "go home," am I obliged to obey?[32] I am not. There's no authority behind the accidental arrangement of the letters. For morals to have force, they need grounding in some kind of authority. Evolution can't supply that authority. Only a transcendent moral lawgiver can. In short, Singer provides no ontological foundation for his strong moral claims.

Fifth, materialists have difficulty grounding their rights claims. Singer is well known for his animal rights advocacy. He writes that sentient animals (apes, cats, pigs, etc.) deserve the same moral standing as sentient human beings. Before making this claim, however, he must answer a prior question: From where do rights come? Do they come from the state, in which case government is free to grant or withdraw rights (including those for animals), or are they transcendent? The problem for Singer is this: If there is no God, how can there be transcendent, universal rights that apply to animals? Singer replies with a half answer: If God does not exist, there is no justification for treating humans as inherently more valuable than other sentient beings. Perhaps so, but neither is there any justification for treating animals humanely. If the government rejects animal rights, to what can the atheist Singer appeal? Certainly not to fundamental moral rights, which by necessity are grounded in the concept of a transcendent Creator who grants them. Singer's claim for animal rights therefore exists in a vacuum.

MUST DESIGN ADVOCATES EXPLAIN EVERYTHING?

Nevertheless, atheist Theodore Drange rejects design explanations on grounds that the Genesis account of creation is hopelessly vague. We don't know how God created the universe, why he did it (his motive), or how this particular universe compares to the rest of his alleged creation. For Drange, this is a fatal flaw. Why posit ID when the designer in question fails to explain himself? "For the [design] explanation to be complete," writes Drange, "we still need to know what the attributes of the designers are, and how and why they did what they did."[33] If those things are not made clear, he maintains, the ID hypothesis is grossly flawed.

But why should anyone accept the claim that we must know *why* God

[32]Greg Koukl uses this example in his talk "The New Atheists: Old Arguments, New Attitude," available from Stand to Reason, www.str.org.
[33]Theodore Drange, "A Response to Parrish on the Fine-Tuning Argument," *Philosophia Christi*, Vol. 2, No. 1, 2000.

created before we can know *that* he created? And why should we suppose that just because ID advocates can't explain everything, they therefore can't explain anything? While it's true that God's motives are sometimes mysterious, he has still left evidence of design. That is to say, the design inference can still be the most plausible explanation for the evidence even if we're unclear on a divine motive. For example, a hiker who discovers an arrangement of stones reading "Walk this way" would logically infer design even if he knew nothing about the motive, context, or history of the designer. Was it the work of a Boy Scout troop? An Aerosmith fan? We may never get a complete explanation, but given the specified complexity of the arrangement, who among us would question design? Likewise, theists contend that ID explanations are rationally superior to their materialistic rivals even if we understand little about the designer in question.[34]

J. P. Moreland sums up the case for Intelligent Design this way: "Big bangs need a banger. Rigged dice need a rigger. And information has an informer."[35]

GOD IS NOT GREAT?

A lawyer friend once disclosed his courtroom strategy: "When you have the facts, pound the facts. When you don't have the facts, pound the table—and do it loudly."

The so-called "new" atheism is loud and nasty. Religion, we are told, is not only foolish, it's dangerous, vile, hateful, and cruel and should hardly be tolerated, even in the home. Given all the evil that religion has brought us, God can't plausibly exist. Richard Dawkins, for example, calls religion a "virus" responsible for wars, persecution, torture, and suffering of every kind—we'd be better off without it.[36] Christopher Hitchens writes that religion poisons everything and devotes an entire book to chronicling the evils done in its name.[37] What we have here is atheism with attitude, but it's really more than that. The goal is to drive anything that smells of religious metaphysics from the public square. The field of bioethics is not immune from the influences of this new atheism. According to atheist Sam Harris,

---

[34]Stephen Parrish develops this theme in his reply to Theodore Drange, *Philosophia Christi*, Vol. 2, No. 1, 2000.
[35]Moreland said this in his interview with Lee Strobel, which can be viewed at http://www.leestrobel.com/videoserver/video.php?clip=strobelT1011.
[36]Richard Dawkins, *A Devil's Chaplain: Reflections on Hope, Lies, Science, and Love* (New York: Houghton Mifflin, 2004).
[37]Christopher Hitchens, *God Is Not Great: How Religion Spoils Everything* (New York: Hachette Book Group, 2007).

the case against destructive embryo research is an attempt to force irrational and intolerant religious absolutism on an unsuspecting public.[38] Thus, it must be squashed.

Although the new atheism is loud and sells books, it fails to knock out theism intellectually. First, religion isn't false just because it's cruel. "Even if every one of Hitchens's accusations were accurate, they don't disprove the truth of religion," writes Melinda Penner. "God might be a cruel being who does delight in manipulating man. In that case, Hitchens's claim that 'religion poisons everything' might be true, but his real claim is that God doesn't exist. And that just doesn't follow from every evil example of religion."[39]

Second, just because religious people do bad things does not mean religion itself is evil or that we should banish it. Without sex, for example, we would not have rape, sex crimes, or sexually transmitted diseases. Shall we live without it? As Stephen Barr points out, every natural and necessary thing can be perverted, even reason.

> Religion has led to hateful ideas, but has any Christian writer ever published ideas as hateful as the social Darwinism of H.G. Wells? Religion has led to persecutions, but none even nearly as massive as those produced by militant irreligion. More people were killed by the "scientific atheism" of communism on an average day than the Spanish Inquisition killed in an average decade. And largely responsible for this fact was the teaching of a contempt for religion of exactly the kind that Dawkins propagates.[40]

Indeed, the crimes of religion pale in comparison to those of secular regimes. This doesn't justify wrongs done in the name of Christianity, but it does undermine unchecked enthusiasm for a godless utopia. "In the 20th century alone," writes Dennis Prager, "more innocent people have been murdered, tortured, and enslaved by secular ideologies—Nazism and communism—than by all religions in history."[41] The numbers are staggering: over sixty-six million wiped out under Communist regimes in the former Soviet Union; between thirty-two million and sixty-one million killed in Communist China; roughly 2.7 million killed by the Khmer Rouge.

---

[38]Sam Harris, "Response to My Fellow 'Atheists,'" http://www.samharris.org/site/full_text/response-to-my-fellow-atheists.

[39]Melinda Penner, "Hitchens Doesn't Have the Goods," Stand to Reason blog, May 25, 2007; http://str.typepad.com/weblog/2007/05/hitchens_docsnt.html.

[40]Stephen Barr, "The Devil's Chaplain Confounded," *First Things*, August/September 2004.

[41]Dennis Prager, *Ultimate Issues*, July-September 1989. Cited in Gregory Koukl, "Just the Facts, Ma'am," *Solid Ground*, March/April 2008.

Institutionalized atheism, not religion, is responsible for the carnage.[42] Alister McGrath sums up the twentieth century as one of the most distressing paradoxes in human history: "The greatest intolerance and violence of that century were practiced by those who believed that religion caused intolerance and violence."[43]

Third, Dawkins and Hitchens must cheat to get their own claims against religion off the ground. Each says that religion is truly evil, and each uses moral language to condemn it, but neither explains how, as materialists who believe only in a world that science alone can explain, they can lay claim to non-physical moral truths. In a strictly material universe, where do these morally binding truths that religion is guilty of transgressing come from?

At the same time, their impassioned pleas for rationality as the antidote to religion make no sense whatsoever. If man is purely material, as each author believes, he's nothing more than a machine programmed by blind natural forces. He's hardwired to think a certain way, meaning his thoughts and beliefs—including his thoughts and beliefs about religion—are strictly predetermined. How can rationality exist in such a world? Thus, there's no point in Dawkins or Hitchens trying to convince religious people they're wrong, since none of us are free to think any differently than we do.[44]

Finally, the claim that religion poisons everything only makes sense if "everything" has intrinsic purposes. Where do these intrinsic purposes come from? For example, when Hitchens writes that religion ruins human beings, he assumes that these same humans have particular natures that, thanks to religion, they're failing to fulfill. Yet how can Hitchens say this, given he rejects design in the universe? Religion can't poison anything unless there's a way things ought to be.

Richard Dawkins fares no better. For example, when President Bush vetoed federal funding for ESCR in 2007, Dawkins spoke of a presidential mind "massively infected with the disease of religion."[45] It was unforgivable for a "pro-life" President to value non-sentient embryos "that are no bigger than a pinhead" while ignoring innocent civilians killed in Iraq. Clearly he thinks Bush *ought* to do better both morally and rationally. However, in a

[42]Donald Mcfarlan, ed., *Guinness Book of World Records 1992* (New York: Facts on File, Inc., 1991), 92. Cited in Gregory Koukl, "Just the Facts, Ma'am."

[43]Alister McGrath, *The Twilight of Atheism: The Rise and Fall of Disbelief in the Modern World* (Oxford: Oxford University Press, 2004), 230. Cited in Timothy Keller, *Reason for God* (New York: Dutton, 2008), 5.

[44]Penner, "Hitchens Doesn't Have the Goods."

[45]Richard Dawkins, "Collateral Damage 1: Embryos and Stem Cell Research," blogpost at http://www.richard dawkins.net/mainPage.php?bodyPage=article_body.php&id=157. See also Sam Harris, "Response to my Fellow 'Atheists.'"

naturalistic universe there are no moral or rational oughts; there is only what *is*. Real oughts exist only in a place that has been designed for a purpose, something Dawkins's own worldview flatly rejects.

RESURRECTION: FACT OR FICTION?

The truth of Christian theism in particular stands or falls on the resurrection of Jesus Christ. Paul tell us in 1 Corinthians 15 that if Christ did not rise bodily from the dead, the Christian faith is one cruel joke.

Liberal critics claim that Christ's disciples made the whole story up. Conservative critics point to the trustworthiness of the New Testament documents. Who's right?

By any reasonable standard, the New Testament shines brighter than any other document of antiquity. For example, the earliest biographical accounts of Alexander the Great were written nearly four hundred years after his death; yet historians consider them generally reliable. The Gospels, meanwhile, were written during the lifetime of the original eyewitnesses, long before there was time enough for legends to appear. In short, it would not have been easy to invent or distort the historical events of Christ's life when hostile (and living) eyewitnesses could easily refute the story.

Unlike legendary sightings of JFK or Elvis, which always transpire in far-away places with virtually no reliable eyewitnesses, the disciples proclaimed the resurrection of Jesus in the very city, Jerusalem, where he was crucified. And they did it in front of the same Jewish and Roman leaders who ordered his death (and who could also order theirs)! It's hard to imagine anyone taking risks like that unless the tomb truly was empty.

And what are we to make of the disciples' transformation? Remember, on the eve of Christ's crucifixion, they fled in terror. Peter even denied knowing Jesus. Yet just a few weeks later, here they are boldly preaching a resurrected Jesus. How do we account for this remarkable change? The best explanation is that the disciples truly believed they saw the risen Jesus.

Some critics reply that the disciples stole the body of Jesus and created a resurrection hoax. But why should anyone think the disciples capable of pulling off such a stunt? Given they fled when Jesus was arrested, it's difficult to imagine them gathering the courage to subdue or bypass the Roman guards posted at the tomb. And what motivation would they have for taking that risk in the first place? They had nothing to gain and everything to lose. Creating a hoax would bring them persecution and death, not to mention theological damnation for blaspheming their Jewish faith. The evidence for a stolen body simply isn't there.

Other critics assert that Jesus never died, that he was merely in a coma and the cool environment of the tomb revived him. This is extremely unlikely. First, the Romans were experts at killing prisoners with crucifixion. They had to be. If a soldier failed to kill the prisoner, the penalty was death! Second, a mere man could not survive torture, crucifixion, and three days in a tomb with no medical attention. Third, how could a semi-comatose Jesus, badly in need of medical attention, roll away the heavy stone and overcome the Roman guards? Fourth, even if he did escape the tomb and overwhelm the guards, would the sight of a Jesus badly in need of medical attention convince his disciples that he had gloriously and triumphantly conquered death?

MANUSCRIPT EVIDENCE

The Gospel accounts fare extremely well when compared to other ancient documents. For Alexander the Great, we have three hundred or so manuscript fragments. For the New Testament Gospels, we have over five thousand pieces of manuscript evidence—some partial, some complete— showing remarkable similarity to each other. Discrepancies that do occur involve obvious spelling and grammatical errors or perhaps incomplete narratives, but not conflicts in doctrine or historical events.

Nevertheless, critics influenced by theological liberalism insist that the Gospels are not reliable because Christ's disciples later reconstructed and embellished the events surrounding his life and death.

However, the fact that Christ's closest followers recorded his words and deeds does not mean they freely made things up about him. In fact, there is no real evidence that the New Testament writers took any liberty with the text. Rather, as Michael Wilkins and J. P. Moreland point out, liberal and secular critics simply *assume* that because the Gospel accounts contain supernatural elements, they were later embellished.[46] But this reply is question begging, as it rules out the evidence a priori. Rather than investigate the evidence for the supernatural on its merits, critics simply dismiss it because their naturalistic worldview will not allow it. This is intellectually dishonest.

---

[46]Michael Wilkins and J. P. Moreland, general editors, "Introduction: The Furor Surrounding Jesus," in *Jesus Under Fire: Modern Scholarship Reinvents the Historical Jesus* (Grand Rapids, MI: Zondervan, 1995), 1–10.

Craig Blomberg makes an excellent point. Jewish scholars are the foremost authorities on Hitler's holocaust against the Jews. It is Jewish researchers, after all, who create museums, gather eyewitness testimony, etc. about the Holocaust. They clearly have an ideological purpose, but they have also been most faithful and objective in reporting the facts. Only anti-Semite racists question their scholarship. Why should the New Testament writers be treated any differently? Is it fair to assume, as the Jesus Seminar does, that because the disciples followed Christ, they freely reconstructed him?[47]

COPYCAT JESUS?

The central theme of the New Testament is the death and resurrection of Jesus Christ. But some critics say the story was borrowed from earlier Greek and Roman beliefs about the afterlife. Others point to similarities found in Jewish legends and various mystery religions. How do Christian accounts of resurrection compare to these other traditions?

(1) Christian resurrection differs radically from Greek thought about the afterlife. New Testament scholar N. T. Wright has exhaustively studied the resurrection accounts and compared them to the Greek and Roman thought of the day. He concludes that the borrowing thesis is problematic.

The Christian claim was that Christ rose *bodily* from the dead. Not only did he rise bodily, he rose with a radically transformed and perfected body, one no longer subject to weakness, aging, or death. In 1 Corinthians 15 Paul makes clear that Christ's bodily resurrection was not an isolated event but a foretaste of what Christians everywhere can expect when the imperfect is made perfect. Just how similar, then, are these other pagan traditions to the Christian understanding of resurrection?

As Wright points out, the ancient Greek worldview allowed for the soul to survive the death of the body, but never bodily resurrection.[48] Once people die, they do not return. They may continue to exist as spirits in the underworld, but they do not reappear with resurrected bodies. Not even in drama or myth was resurrection permitted. When Apollo tries to bring a child back from the dead, Zeus punishes both of them with a thunderbolt. "Once a man has died, and the dust has soaked up his blood, there is no resurrection," states Apollo in Aeschylus' *Eumenides.*

Every Greek knew that dead people do not return. Culturally, resurrec-

---

[47]See Lee Strobel, *The Case for Christ* (Grand Rapids, MI: Zondervan, 1998), 32.
[48]N. T. Wright, *The Resurrection of the Son of God* (Minneapolis: Augsburg Fortress Publishers, 2003), 32–309. I am deeply indebted to Wright's analysis here.

tion of the body was a startling, distasteful idea that was completely unacceptable to the educated classes of the day. The best anyone could hope for was a legendary name and a beautiful image.

For Homer and his followers, the body is the real self (essence), while the spirit (soul) exists as a kind of half-life. Upon death, the real you—that is, your body—ceases to exist, while your half-life (soul) proceeds immediately to Hades. Hence, dead men may in fact exist after death, but only as subhuman shadows of their former selves, spirits with no hope of return. Homer refers to the dead as ghosts, shades, and phantoms. In no way are they fully human, though they may look that way to us. This dark Homeric view of disembodied souls remained a powerful cultural force up through the time of Christ.

With Plato, the Greek picture changes, but not in ways that bring it closer to a Christian concept of resurrection. For Plato, the non-material soul is the real, genuine self, while the body is the ghost. In fact, the body is a prison, a place from which to escape. The separation of body and soul was desired precisely because it would allow the soul to flourish. The reason people do not return from Hades is because life is good there. There were exceptions, but again none with relevant parallels to Christianity. The mythical Hercules, for example, escapes Hades, but he's not resurrected bodily. Rather, he is admitted to the company of the gods. In short, neither the Homeric nor the Platonic view of the afterlife bore any resemblance to the resurrection of the body proclaimed by the early church. To the contrary, Christianity broke into a world where its central claim of bodily resurrection was thought absurd. Homer's Greeks couldn't return; Plato's Greeks wouldn't want to.[49]

(2) Christian resurrection builds on Jewish traditions but differs from them. When the Jews spoke of resurrection, it was not something they expected to happen to their own God or in the middle of history to one man. Instead, it would happen to *all* men at the *end* of history. This Jewish understanding possessed by the disciples explains their obvious confusion when Christ foretells his own resurrection in John 11. True, there were examples of people coming back to life in both the Old and New Testaments (i.e., the widow's son and Lazarus), but not with transformed bodies that would never again taste death.[50]

(3) Christian resurrection differs significantly from the dying and rising

---

[49]Ibid., 32–83.
[50]Ibid.

gods (cyclical) of ancient mystery religions. These icons of mystery religions are not analogous to a historical Jesus. Many times they are not real people, and most postdate Christianity. Thus, the comparisons to Christianity are unfair. As for those accounts that do involve real people, the most famous is Apollonius of Tyana, who allegedly rivaled Christ not only in his claims of deity but in resurrection as well. However, there are serious historical and theological reasons to contest this. First, the author of the story, writing a hundred and twenty years after Apollonius dies, has the alleged messiah figure visiting Nineveh and Babylon, cities that were destroyed hundreds of years earlier. Second, what we get with Appollonius is apotheosis—that is, a man who is elevated to a godlike figure after death—not bodily resurrection as early Christians understood and proclaimed it. Third, the Appollonius story is backwards to the Christian one. Appollonius the man dies, then becomes godlike. Christ, meanwhile, first exists as God, eventually takes on an additional human nature, dies, gains a resurrected and transformed body, then finally returns to the Father. Hence, the alleged parallels between Apollonius and Christ are far from compelling.[51]

(4) *Christian resurrection differs from the alleged resurrection stories about Alexander the Great.* Critics sometimes argue that Christ's alleged miracles and subsequent resurrection are foreshadowed in the life of Alexander the Great. On this account, the earliest Christians borrowed liberally from the miracles attributed to Alexander, including his superhuman, death-defying feats. However, this argument is not persuasive. Unlike the early Gospels where miracle claims are recorded early while eyewitnesses were still living, the stories of Alexander's miracles are embellishments that evolved over a thousand-year period. Early accounts of his life contain almost no miraculous events. In fact, the completed accounting of his legendary behavior actually dates later than Christ, which leads the reader to question who truly influenced whom. Moreover, the Gospels were written within the context of Jewish monotheism, which held that under no circumstances could mere humans become gods. The stories of Alexander, meanwhile, were composed within a pagan, polytheistic worldview where it was believed that humans could, and often did, become gods. There simply is no meaningful parallel between the two worldviews that would lead a rational person to conclude that New Testament accounts of resurrection were borrowed from this Greek tradition.[52]

---

[51]Norman Geisler, *Baker Encyclopedia of Christian Apologetics* (Grand Rapids, MI: Baker, 1999), 44–45. See also Wright, *The Resurrection of the Son of God*, 74–76.
[52]Geisler, *Baker Encyclopedia of Christian Apologetics*, 45–46.

THE MINIMAL FACTS POINT TO RESURRECTION

The Christian theist can follow the lead of Gary Habermas, William Lane Craig, N. T. Wright, and others and argue that the resurrection thesis posited by the New Testament writers best explains the evidence as we know it. That is, whatever the similarities between classical/pagan mythology and early Christian teaching might be, they are not similar in the way that liberal critics need them to be in order to discount the resurrection. Gary Habermas, for example, posits a minimal facts argument that renders the debate over origins largely moot, allowing defenders of a historical resurrection to argue from a position of strength.[53]

The minimal facts generally accepted by a majority of both liberal and conservative scholars include: 1) Jesus died due to crucifixion. 2) Jesus was buried. 3) The disciples despaired after the crucifixion. 4) Jesus' tomb was found empty. 5) The disciples had real experiences that convinced them of a risen Jesus. 6) As a result of these real experiences, the disciples were completely transformed, to the point of being willing to die for their belief. 7) The disciples proclaimed the resurrection of Jesus early, in the very city where he was crucified. 8) The early gospel message centered on the death and resurrection of Jesus. 9) Paul and James, initially skeptics, became Christians based on what they thought were real experiences of the resurrected Jesus. Given that the majority of scholars accept these minimal facts (though a small minority disputes #4), it's difficult to see why the question of origins is even relevant. The better question is, given these facts, all with multiple attestation, what's the best explanation for them? Habermas concludes that the resurrection best explains these minimal facts.

Christian resurrection is unique. Neither the pagan world nor the Jewish one anticipated bodily resurrection as proclaimed by the apostles. The early Greeks thought it absurd, later Greeks found it distasteful, and the Jews simply couldn't imagine it. In short, there is no reason to suppose that the New Testament authors made up the story from borrowed sources. If critics aim to prove the resurrection false because of its alleged parallels to the ancient world, they would do well to consult that world before discounting the claims of the New Testament writers.

---

[53]Gary Habermas, *The Risen Jesus and Future Hope*, 9–10, 26–31.

THEISM IS RATIONAL

To review, my purpose here was not to present a comprehensive defense of Christian theism. I'll leave that to other, more qualified individuals. I simply want to show that even if the pro-life view has religious underpinnings grounded in Christian theism, it does not follow that the pro-life position is inherently irrational. Theists make reasonable arguments that scholars should debate, not dismiss. Given that neither Christian theism nor materialism can claim certitude, both sides must draw inferences to the best explanation. The question is not which side is religious and which is rational, but which side better explains the evidence as we know it.

We should also remember that science has limitations. Some atheists claim that science proves there is no God. But as Gregory Koukl points out, this is completely false. Science operates on induction and can only draw conclusions based on what scientists find, not what they cannot find. If scientists cannot prove that extraterrestrials do not exist, how can they prove that God doesn't? More generally, critics of theism should distinguish between materialism as a philosophic worldview and materialism as science.[54] Intellectual honesty requires us to consider all of the relevant evidence, not just that which squares with our presupposed worldview.

GODLESS PRO-LIFERS?

Yes, they exist, and I'm glad to have their help fighting abortion. But their metaphysics are deeply problematic. As Paul Copan pointed out earlier, atheists have difficulty offering a substantive ontological foundation for human dignity, human rights, or moral obligations. They simply presuppose these things. But on what naturalistic basis can human rights and human dignity be affirmed? Aren't we all just accidents of nature? True, atheists can recognize moral truth epistemologically, but they can't *ground* their moral claims ontologically. They can't really tell us why we *ought* to behave rightly on abortion or any other moral issue.[55]

A theistic universe better explains human rights and human dignity. Humans have value in virtue of the kind of thing they are, creatures who bear the image of their Maker. At the same time, objective morals make sense because they are grounded in the character of an objective, moral lawgiver.

---

[54]Gregory Koukl, "What Science Can't Prove," http://www.str.org/site/News2?page=NewsArticle&id=5559.
[55]See Copan, "Can Michael Martin be a Moral Realist?," 45–72.

REVIEW QUESTIONS

1. Describe in a couple of sentences the worldview known as Christian theism. How does it differ from materialism?

2. What's really at issue in the conflict over cosmology?

3. Materialists simply presuppose the truth of their position. What reasons do they give for doing that, and are those reasons persuasive?

4. What standard of proof must the theist meet? Why is certainty not the correct standard of proof?

5. Stephen Barr writes that most arguments for materialism beg the question. What does he mean by this? Give examples.

6. Define scientism. Why is it not truly science?

7. What metaphysical truths must you assume before you can even do science?

8. While Christian pro-lifers are right to oppose scientism, what should they not become? What steps should they take to avoid the label anti-science?

9. List several ways Big Bang cosmology presents problems for the materialist.

10. William Dembski points out that the information found in the universe, even in simple life-forms, "is both specified and complex," and this suggests design. What does he mean by this? Give examples.

11. Materialism suffers philosophically in five ways. What are they?

12. Throughout his book *Practical Ethics*, atheist Peter Singer equates moral decency with a series of universal shoulds and oughts: We *ought* to renounce material goods and give our excess wealth to the poor. We *ought* to increase pleasure and minimize pain. We *should* treat all sentient beings equally and allow infanticide if it will make room for a healthy, happier child. Given his materialistic worldview, what problems does Singer have saying any of this?

13. According to Paul in 1 Corinthians 15, if Jesus did not rise bodily and historically, Christians are toast. Why does he say this?

14. The earliest manuscripts about Alexander the Great were written four hundred years after he died. When were the earliest manuscripts about Jesus written?

15. The disciples proclaimed the resurrection of Jesus in Jerusalem, the very city where Christ was killed. Why is this fact significant? How does it differ from legendary sightings of Elvis or JFK?

16. To disprove the resurrection, all the Jews had to do was:

17. How does the number of manuscripts for Jesus compare to those for Alexander?

18. Secular critics, like those in the so-called Jesus Seminar, rule out the resurrection before looking at the evidence. These same critics insist that since Christ's closest followers wrote the Gospel accounts, they must have made them up. How should we respond? (Hint: use Craig Blomberg's example.)

19. People say that the early Christians borrowed their resurrection accounts from Greek and Roman mythology. Yet anyone who studies the subject knows this isn't true. How does Christian resurrection differ radically from pagan views of resurrection? Give specific examples to back up your claim.

20. How does Christian resurrection differ from Jewish thought?

21. Gary Habermas offers a "minimal facts" argument for the historical reliability of the resurrection accounts found in the Gospels. What are these minimal facts?

22. What key metaphysical problems confront godless pro-lifers?

HELPFUL RESOURCES

Stephen Barr. *Modern Physics and Ancient Faith.* Notre Dame, IN: University of Notre Dame Press, 2003.

Kenneth Boa and Robert Bowman Jr. *20 Compelling Evidences That God Exists: Discover Why Believing in God Makes So Much Sense.* Colorado Springs: Victor, 2005.

Paul Copan. *How Do You Know You're Not Wrong? Responding to Objections That Leave Christians Speechless.* Grand Rapids, MI: Baker, 2005.

William Lane Craig. *Reasonable Faith: Christian Truth and Apologetics.* Wheaton, IL: Crossway Books, 1984, 2008. See also Dr. Craig's numerous debates on God's existence and the resurrection of Jesus at http://reasonablefaith.org

William Dembski. *Intelligent Design: The Bridge Between Science and Philosophy.* Downers Grove, IL: InterVarsity Press, 1999.

Gary Habermas. *The Risen Jesus and Future Hope.* Lanham, MD: Roman and Littlefield, 2003.

Steve Hays. *This Joyful Eastertide: A Critical Review of The Empty Tomb.* See http://www.reformed.plus.com/triablogue/ebooks.html.

Phillip E. Johnson. *Reason in the Balance: The Case Against Naturalism in Science, Law, and Education.* Downers Grove, IL: InterVarsity Press, 1995.

Timothy Keller. *The Reason for God: Belief in an Age of Skepticism.* New York: Dutton, 2008.

Michael Wilkins and J. P. Moreland. *Jesus Under Fire: Modern Scholarship Invents the Historical Jesus.* Grand Rapids, MI: Zondervan, 1995.

N. T. Wright. *The Resurrection of the Son of God.* Minneapolis: Fortress Press, 2003.

8

DEAD SILENCE:
DOES THE BIBLE JUSTIFY
ABORTION?

We don't need Scripture to expressly say that elective abortion is wrong before we can know that it's wrong. The Bible affirms that all humans have value because they bear God's image. The facts of science make clear that from the earliest stages of development, the unborn are unquestionably human. Hence, biblical commands against the unjust taking of human life apply to the unborn just as they do to other human beings.

ABORTION-CHOICE ADVOCATES with the Religious Coalition for Reproductive Choice and Planned Parenthood Federation of America contend that the Bible is silent on abortion and that none of the Scriptures traditionally cited by pro-life advocates establishes the humanity of the unborn. "One thing the Bible does not say is 'Thou shalt not abort,'" writes Roy Bowen Ward, professor emeritus of comparative religion at Miami University of Ohio.[1] His advice to pro-life Jews and Christians is simple: Speak where the Bible speaks, and be silent where it is silent.

Reverend Mark Bigelow, Member of Planned Parenthood's Clergy Advisory Board, writes, "Even as a minister I am careful what I presume Jesus would do if he were alive today, but one thing I know from the Bible is that Jesus was not against women having a choice in continuing a pregnancy. He never said a word about abortion (nor did anyone else

---

[1] Roy Bowen Ward, "Is the Fetus a Person?" *Mission Journal* (January 1986). Article is posted by the Religious Coalition for Reproductive Choice at http://www.rcrc.org/pdf/RCRC_EdSeries_Fetus.pdf.

in the Bible) even though abortion was available and in use in his time."[2] Paul D. Simmons, former professor of Christian ethics at Southern Baptist Theological Seminary, finds the Bible's silence on abortion "profound" and remarks that not once does the subject appear in the apostle Paul's lists of prohibited actions.[3] We can sum up the thinking of all three men this way: If the Bible doesn't condemn abortion, pro-life advocates shouldn't either. We should trust each woman to decide the issue according to her own personal faith.

Suppose we grant that Ward, Bigelow, and Simmons are correct: Scripture is silent on abortion. Let's further suppose that none of the specific passages cited by pro-life advocates (Ps. 51:5; 139:13–15; Luke 1:41–44, to name a few) demonstrates conclusively that the unborn are human. What follows? Are we to conclude from the alleged silence of Scripture that women have a God-given right to abort?

DOES SILENCE EQUAL PERMISSION?

Abortion advocates are correct that the Bible does not specifically mention abortion, but what's the best explanation for its silence?

The hidden (and undefended) premise in the argument advanced by Ward, Bigelow, and Simmons is that whatever the Bible doesn't condemn, it condones. It's easy to see why this premise is flawed. The Bible does not expressly condemn many things including racial discrimination against blacks, killing abortion doctors for fun, and lynching homosexuals, yet few people proclaim these acts to be morally justified. To the contrary, we know they are wrong by inference. For example, Scripture tells us it's wrong to treat human beings unjustly. Lynching homosexuals treats human beings unjustly. Therefore, we know that Scripture condemns this activity even though the topic of lynching is never addressed.

WHAT'S THE REAL ISSUE?

A century ago racists argued from the alleged silence of Scripture that blacks were not human. Some went so far as to deny that black people had souls.[4]

---

[2]Mark Bigelow, letter to Bill O' Reilly of Fox News, November 22, 2002. Cited in Jeff Johnson, "Christ Was Pro-Abortion?" CNS News, December 4, 2002; http://archive.newsmax.com/archives/articles/2002/12/4/70006.shtml.
[3]Paul D. Simmons, "Personhood, the Bible, and the Abortion Debate," the Religious Coalition for Reproductive Choice, http://www.rcrc.org/pdf/RCRC_EdSeries_Personhood.pdf.
[4]Josiah Priest, *Bible Defense of Slavery: Origin, Fortunes and History of the Negro Race*, 5th ed. (Glasgow, KY: W. S. Brown, 1852), 33.

Again, this was hardly persuasive. While Scripture does not mention each specific race and nationality, it does teach that all humans have value because they bear the image of their Creator and were made to have fellowship with him (Gen. 1:26; Gal. 3:28; Col. 3:10–11; Jas. 3:9). Thus, we are never to take human life without justification (Exod. 23:7). The inference from these biblical truths is clear: If blacks are human beings, they are made in God's image, and we should not treat them unjustly. No further proof from Scripture is necessary.

The same is true with the unborn. If embryos and fetuses are human beings, commands that forbid the unjust taking of human life apply to them just as they do to other humans. Appealing to the Bible's alleged silence on abortion misses the point entirely.

When abortion advocates argue their case from the silence of Scripture, I simply ask, "Are you saying that whenever the Bible does not specifically condemn something, it condones it?" When they say no (and they must), I reply, "Then what is your point?"[5]

A BETTER EXPLANATION FOR THE BIBLE'S SILENCE

There are good reasons to suppose that the alleged silence of Scripture does not mean the biblical writers condoned abortion but that prohibitions against it were largely unnecessary. We should remember that the Bible as a whole is not a comprehensive code of ethics but the story of God's redemption of his people. That is, the biblical writers, under guidance from the Holy Spirit, selectively discuss subjects relevant to their intended audiences while leaving many other topics unstated. The bottom line is, if the Hebrews of the Old Testament and the Christians of the New were not inclined to abort their unborn offspring, there's little reason for Scripture to address the matter. Looked at objectively, the biblical and cultural evidence suggests they were not inclined to consider abortion even though it was practiced in the surrounding cultures. Turning first to the Hebrew worldview of the Old Testament, we find that:

- Humans have intrinsic value in virtue of the kind of thing they are— creatures made in the image of God. Hence, the shedding of innocent blood is strictly forbidden (Gen. 1:26; 9:6, Exod. 23:7; Prov. 6:16–17).

---

[5]I'm indebted to Gregory Koukl for this excellent question. See his "Tactics in Defending the Faith" series at www.str.org.

- Children were seldom seen as unwanted or as a nuisance (unless they turn wicked) but as gifts from God, the highest possible blessing (Gen. 17:6; 33:5; Ps. 113:9; 127:3–5).
- Immortality was expressed through one's descendants. God promises Abraham to make of him a great nation, and that promise is passed on to Isaac, Jacob, etc. "Behold, children are a heritage from the LORD, the fruit of the womb a reward," writes the Psalmist (127:3; see also Gen. 48:16). Indeed, the very hope of the nation was tied to the belief that the seed of Abraham, Isaac, and Jacob would multiply and flourish. "To perpetuate not only the nation but one's own individual family line was thus a sacred responsibility, requiring special customs and laws to safeguard it," writes biblical scholar N. T. Wright. "Continuance of the family line was not simply a matter of keeping a family name alive. It was part of the way in which God's promises, for Israel and perhaps even the whole world, would be fulfilled."[6]
- Therefore, it comes as no surprise that sterility and barrenness were a curse, a source of great shame and sorrow. Hence, Peninnah's harsh ridicule of Hannah, the prophet Samuel's mother, because of the latter's initial barrenness (1 Sam. 1:6; see also Gen. 20:17–18; 30:1, 22–23). Likewise, to see one's own offspring suffer premature death was perhaps the greatest parental disaster imaginable.

Germain Grisez sums things up nicely: Among a Hebrew people who saw children as a gift and barrenness as a curse, it was virtually unthinkable that any woman from that culture would desire an abortion.[7] Hence, the Old Testament's silence on abortion suggests that prohibitions against it were largely unnecessary, not that the practice was tacitly approved.

Ward disputes this conclusion, noting it was common for authors of both Testaments to condemn the practices of neighboring nations, "such as idol worship, sacred prostitution, and the like, yet they did not choose to condemn abortion," a practice common in those surrounding cultures.[8]

Ward's rejoinder, however, is not persuasive. Unlike abortion, idolatrous practices were not restricted to foreign cultures but were pervasive among God's *own* people. It's odd that Ward overlooks this. Indeed, Israel and Judah were taken captive on numerous occasions precisely because of their persistent idolatry (Ps. 106:35–43; Jer. 1:16; 2:23; Ezek. 6:1–10). Hence, it's no surprise that the biblical writers mention this sin but not abortion.

---

[6]N. T. Wright, *The Resurrection of the Son of God* (Minneapolis: Fortress Press, 2003), 99–100.
[7]Germain Grisez, *Abortion: The Myths, the Realities, and the Arguments* (New York: Corpus Books, 1970), 123–127.
[8]Ward, "Is the Fetus a Person?"

Moreover, Ward's argument from silence proves too much. The Bible does not mention one of the most heinous practices of the surrounding ancient world, female infanticide. Does it follow that the act is morally justified? Again, the question is not, was abortion practiced in the ancient world by neighboring cultures? (it was), but, was it practiced by the people whom the biblical authors specifically address, in this case the Hebrew culture of that day?

In short, Ward fails to interpret the Old Testament within its own intellectual and cultural framework. His contention that the absence of a direct prohibition meant that women had a God-given right to kill their offspring was utterly foreign to the Hebrew culture of the time for the reasons cited above.

WHY IS THE NEW TESTAMENT SILENT?

Michael Gorman writes that the first Christians, including all but one of the New Testament authors, were Jewish Christians with an essentially Jewish morality.[9] Hence, if a Jewish consensus against abortion existed at the time, the early Christians most certainly would have shared that consensus.

As Gorman points out, early Judaism was in fact quite firmly opposed to abortion. Jewish documents from the period condemn the practice unequivocally, demonstrating a clear anti-abortion consensus among first-century Jews:[10]

- *The Sentences of Pseudo-Phocylides* (written between 50 B.C. and A.D. 50): "A woman should not destroy the unborn babe in her belly, nor after its birth throw it before the dogs and vultures."
- *The Sibyline Oracles* includes among the wicked those who "produce abortions and unlawfully cast their offspring away." Also condemned are sorcerers who dispense abortifacients.
- *First Enoch* (first or second century B.C.) says that an evil angel taught humans how to "smash the embryo in the womb."
- Josephus (first-century Jewish historian) wrote: "The law orders all the offspring be brought up, and forbids women either to cause abortion or to make away with the fetus." A woman who did so was considered to have committed infanticide because she destroyed a "soul" and hence diminished the race.

---

[9]Michael Gorman, "Why Is the New Testament Silent About Abortion?," *Christianity Today*, January 11, 1993.
[10]The following sources are cited in ibid.

These texts, writes Gorman, "bear witness to the general Jewish and Jewish-Christian attitude of the first and second centuries, thus confirming that the earliest Christians shared the anti-abortion position of their Jewish forebears."[11]

Finally, we should remember that theology of the New Testament is primarily task theology written to address specific issues in specific churches. For example, Paul is largely silent on the historical career of Christ (with one notable exception—1 Corinthians 15), but this does not mean that he questioned the facts of Jesus' earthly ministry. Rather, a discussion of those facts never became necessary. To cite New Testament scholar George Eldon Ladd, "We may say that we owe whatever understanding we have of Paul's thought to the 'accidents of history' which required him to deal with various problems, doctrinal and practical, in the life of the churches."[12]

The best explanation, then, for the New Testament's silence on abortion is not that its authors condoned the practice but that a discussion of the issue was unnecessary. As Gorman points out, there was no deviation from the norm inherited from Judaism. Unlike the surrounding pagan cultures, the early Christians to whom the New Testament was written were simply not tempted to kill their children before or after birth.

BACK TO THE ONE QUESTION

So far we've seen that the permissibility of abortion comes down to just one question: Is the unborn a member of the human family? If so, elective abortion is a serious moral wrong that violates biblical commands against the unjust taking of human life. It treats the distinct human being, made in the image of God, as nothing more than a disposable instrument. Conversely, if the unborn are not human, elective abortion is easy to justify.

While Scripture (we will grant) is silent on the humanity of the unborn (as it is on the humanity of whites, blacks, and Asians, to name a few), it's clear that we are not to take human life without justification. Hence, if a positive case can be made for the humanity of the unborn apart from Scripture (as we can make a case for the humanity of the French apart from Scripture), we can logically conclude that biblical commands against the unjust taking of human life apply to the unborn just as they do to other human beings.

At this point science provides an assist to theology. That is to say, science

---

[11]Ibid.
[12]George Eldon Ladd, *A Theology of the New Testament* (Grand Rapids, MI: Eerdmans, 1974), 377–378.

gives us the facts we need to arrive at a theologically sound conclusion. As stated in Chapter 2, the science of embryology is clear that from the earliest stages of development, the unborn are distinct, living, and whole human beings. They are not parts of other human beings (like skin cells are) but whole living organisms able to direct their own internal development. True, they are immature humans, but they are human beings nonetheless.[13]

ARE HUMANS VALUABLE BY NATURE OR BY FUNCTION?

According to Dr. John Swomley, professor emeritus of social ethics at St. Paul School of Theology in Kansas City, the biblically relevant factor isn't biology, it's personhood, and fetuses need not apply. Swomley contends that the image of God resides only in those humans with "abilities to love and to reason" and "the capacity for self-awareness and transcendence" as well as "the freedom to choose, rather than to live by instinct."[14] Given that fetuses lack the brain development necessary to immediately exercise these capacities, they do not bear God's image the way real persons do.

Though Swomley's arguments are dressed up in religious garb, they suffer from the same flaws we saw earlier in Warren, Simmons, and Gazzaniga.

First, the idea that a human becomes a person only after some degree of physical development amounts to saying, "I came to be after my body came to be" or "I inhabit a body that was once an embryo." Absurd.

Second, why should anyone suppose that brain development bestows value on a person? Swomley never presents a biblical case why this is so and, like Warren and Simmons earlier, doesn't say why certain value-giving properties like self-awareness are value-giving in the first place.

Third, newborns lack the immediate capacity for self-awareness and the ability to make choices until several months after birth. Are we to conclude that the Bible permits infanticide? As mentioned earlier, Peter Singer rightly points out that if self-awareness makes one valuable as a person, it follows that fetuses and newborns are both disqualified. You can't draw an arbitrary line at birth and spare the newborn.[15]

---

[13]See T. W. Sadler, *Langman's Embryology*, 5th ed. (Philadelphia: W.B. Saunders, 1993), 3; Keith L. Moore, *The Developing Human: Clinically Oriented Embryology* (Toronto: B.C. Decker, 1988), 2; Ronand O'Rahilly and Fabiola Müller, *Human Embryology and Teratology*, 2nd ed. (New York: Wiley-Liss, 1996), 8, 29.
[14]John Swomley, "Abortion: A Christian Ethical Perspective," http://rcrc.org/pdf/christianperspectives.pdf.
[15]Singer, *Practical Ethics* (Cambridge: Cambridge University Press, 1993), 169–171.

Our immediate capacities for self-awareness, reasoning, and making choices may come and go during the course of our lives. At any given moment, some of us can exercise those capacities better than others can. In what sense then are we equal? Only in this: We share a common human nature because we are all made in the image of our Creator. All other explanations for human equality fail.

DOES EXODUS 21 JUSTIFY ABORTION?

Some abortion advocates appeal directly to Scripture to make their case for elective abortion. Exodus 21:22–25 is one of their favorite references. The passage presents a situation where two men fighting accidentally injure (harm) a pregnant woman. Here's the passage in context, from the New American Standard Bible:

> If men struggle with each other and strike a woman with child so that she gives birth prematurely, yet there is no injury, he shall surely be fined as the woman's husband may demand of him, and he shall pay as the judges decide. But if there is any further injury, then you shall appoint as a penalty life for life, eye for eye, tooth for tooth, hand for hand, foot for foot, burn for burn, wound for wound, bruise for bruise.

Abortion-choice advocates argue that this Scripture passage proves that the unborn are not fully human because the penalty for accidentally killing a fetus is less than that for killing its mother. But this argument is flawed on several counts.

First, assuming that the pro-abortion interpretation of this passage is correct (i.e., that the unborn's death is treated differently than the mother's), it does not follow that the unborn are not fully human. The preceding verses (20–21) present a situation where a master unintentionally kills his slave and escapes with no penalty at all (the lack of intent being proven by the interval between the blow and the death); yet it hardly follows that Scripture considers the slave less than human.

Second, this passage does not even remotely suggest that a woman can *willfully* kill her unborn child through elective abortion. Nothing in the context supports this claim. At best the text assigns a lesser penalty for *accidentally* killing a fetus than for accidentally killing his mother. It simply does not follow that a woman may deliberately abort her own offspring.

Third, the pro-abortion interpretation of this passage (that a lesser penalty applies for accidental fetal death) is highly suspect. When read in the original Hebrew, the passage seems to convey that both the mother and the child are covered by *lex talionis*, the law of retribution. According to Hebrew scholar Gleason Archer, "There is no second class status attached to the fetus under this rule. The fetus is just as valuable as the mother."[16] Furthermore, we should not presume that the child in question is dead, as in the case of elective abortion. Millard Erickson, citing the work of Jack Cottrell, writes that the passage can be reasonably translated "the child comes forth," and if he or she is not injured, the penalty is merely a fine.[17] But if he or she is harmed, the penalty is life for life, tooth for tooth, etc. (Note also that the text calls the expelled fetus a "child," a fact that abortion-choice advocates cannot easily get around.)

NEPHESH

Finally, abortion advocate Roy Bowen Ward argues that humans are uniquely defined as persons by the Hebrew term *nephesh*, which he equates with physical "breath." Adam, Ward argues, did not become a living soul until God breathed into him "the breath of life" through the nostrils (Gen. 2:7). Because the unborn don't yet breathe air through their nostrils, Ward contends that they are not valuable human beings.[18] Ward is wrong on three counts.

First, his argument proves too much. Some newborns do not breathe air through the nostrils until a couple of minutes after birth, which means that immediately upon delivery, the parents would be justified committing infanticide if it suits their preferences.

Second, the unborn do in fact breathe long before birth, but through the umbilical cord rather than the nostrils. At birth, only the *mode* of breathing changes, like switching from AC to DC current.[19]

Third, Ward's breath argument doesn't do the work he needs it to. All it proves is that any adults whom God immediately creates out of dirt are not alive until he breathes air into their nostrils. On that point I quite agree. However, since you and I were not immediately created as adults from raw

---

[16]Cited in John Ankerberg and John Weldon, *When Does Life Begin?* (Brentwood, TN: Wolgemuth & Hyatt, 1989), 195–196. See also Meredith Kline, "Lex Talionis & the Human Fetus," *Simon Greenleaf Law Review* 5 (1985–1986), 73–89.
[17]Millard Erickson, *Christian Theology* (Grand Rapids, MI: Baker Books, 1999), 572. See also Jack Cottrell, "Abortion and the Mosaic Law," *Christianity Today*, March 16, 1973.
[18]Roy Bowen Ward, "Is the Fetus a Person?"
[19]Bernard Nathanson, *Aborting America* (New York: Doubleday, 1979), 210–211.

dirt but began life in the womb, the verse cannot apply to us; it is specific only to Adam.[20]

Finally, Ward's equation of *nephesh* with physical breath is sloppy exegesis. As J. P. Moreland and Scott Rae point out in their book *Body and Soul*, although the Hebrew word *nephesh* ("soul") primarily applies to human beings, "it is also used of animals (Gen. 1:20, 9:10) and God himself (Judges 10:16 [KJV]; Isa. 1:14). When the term is used of God, it certainly cannot mean physical breath or life since God is an immaterial, transcendent self." Furthermore, "there are passages where *nephesh* refers to the continuing locus of personal identity even after death—when breathing has long ceased" (Gen. 35:18; 1 Kings 17:21; Ps. 16:10; 30:3; 49:15; 86:13; 139:8).[21]

CONCLUSION: THE BIBLE IS PRO-LIFE

Taken together, the exegetical, philosophical, and scientific considerations we've examined in this chapter show that the theological case for elective abortion is seriously flawed. Nothing in the Hebrew culture of the Old Testament supports the practice. And given the consensus against abortion by early Jewish Christians, there is no reason to suppose that the New Testament authors approved of it either. Moreover, the facts of science make clear that from the earliest stages of development, the unborn are members of the human family. As such, they bear the image of their Maker, and that alone gives them inestimable value.

REVIEW QUESTIONS

1. Suppose the Bible is silent on abortion. Why is the argument from silence a weak one?

2. When someone says the Bible doesn't expressly condemn abortion, and therefore abortion is permissible, what is the hidden premise in the argument? What question should you ask to expose it?

3. Suppose Scripture says nothing about the humanity of the unborn. Why doesn't this help abortion advocates make their case?

4. What's the best explanation for the Old Testament's silence on abortion? What cultural factors made abortion unlikely?

5. What's the best explanation for the New Testament's silence on abortion?

6. Give three reasons why Exodus 21 does not justify abortion.

---

[20]I owe this observation to Gregory Koukl, who used it in a talk at Biola University in June 2004.
[21]J. P. Moreland, *Body and Soul: Human Nature and the Crisis in Ethics* (Downers Grove, IL: InterVarsity Press, 2000), 27–28.

HELPFUL RESOURCES

Robert Bowman Jr. "Argument for the Silent: A Biblical Case Against Abortion." *Facts for Faith*, Issue 6, 2001; http://www.reasons.org/resources/fff/2001issue06/index.shtml#abortion.

Michael Gorman. *Abortion and the Early Church: Christian, Jewish and Pagan Attitudes in the Greco-Roman World*. Eugene: Wipf & Stock, 1998.

————. *Holy Abortion: A Theological Critique of the Religious Coalition for Reproductive Choice*. Eugene: Wipf & Stock, 2003.

————. "Why Is the New Testament Silent About Abortion?" *Christianity Today*, January 11, 1993; http://www.goodnewsmag.org/library/articles/gorman-mj93.htm.

PART THREE

Pro-Life
Christians Answer
Objections Persuasively

9

FROM DEBATE TO DIALOGUE: ASKING THE RIGHT QUESTIONS

Next time you hit a roadblock in a conversation, ask a good question. The results might just transform the discussion and put you back in the driver's seat, where you belong.

HAVE YOU EVER BEEN on the hot seat? Think back to Chapter 1. Once abortion became the topic of discussion, Pam morphed into a human machine gun, firing assertion after assertion Emily's way. Poor Emily barely got a word in edgewise. No wonder she quit in frustration. Who can blame her?

Thankfully, there's a better way. Three simple questions, graciously asked, can make a world of difference in your next conversation. Gregory Koukl calls them "Columbo Questions," named after the famous TV detective played by actor Peter Falk.[1]

At first glance, Columbo doesn't impress anyone. His wardrobe needs a definite upgrade, and eloquence isn't his strong suit. He comes across bumbling, inept, and completely harmless. The crooks are sure he's too dumb to figure things out. They don't realize he is dumb like a fox. He just keeps asking questions and building a case until he nails them! Vintage Columbo sound bites include:

- "I got a problem. Something about this t'ing bothers me. Maybe you can clear dis up for me."
- "I was talkin' to da wife the other day . . . Do you mind if I ask you a question?"
- "Just one more thing."

---

[1]Gregory Koukl, "Tactics in Defending the Faith," lecture notes. Order from Stand to Reason, www.str.org.

- "Hey, I'm sorry, I'm making a pest of myself. Yes, yes, I am. I know it's because I keep asking these questions. But I'll tell ya, I can't help myself. It's a habit."

Koukl says it's a habit you should get into. He describes the key to the Columbo tactic as follows: "The Christian goes on the offensive in a disarming way with carefully selected questions to productively advance the conversation." The tactic can be used to:

- gain information and keep you out of the hot seat,
- reverse the burden of proof,
- indirectly exploit a weakness or a flaw in someone's views.

There's nothing dirty or tricky about it. The goal is clarity, not domination. So the next time you're in a tight spot, ask a good Columbo question. Here are the three that are most useful:[2]

1. **"What do you mean by that?"** This is a clarification inquiry that tells you what your opponent thinks so you don't misrepresent his view. At the same time, it forces him to think more clearly about his own statements. Your tone should be mild and inquisitive. Consider the following objections, and note the Columbo-type response in parentheses:

- "The Bible's been changed many times." ("Oh? How so?")
- "Pro-lifers force their views on others." ("In what ways?")
- "Embryos are just a mass of cells." ("What does that mean?")
- "Religious views don't belong in the public square." ("What makes a view religious?")
- "Science and faith exclude each other." ("What do you mean by *science*, and what do you mean by *faith*?")
- "Abortion is a fundamental right." ("What do you mean by *fundamental*? And where does that right come from?")

2. **"How did you come to that conclusion?"** This is the most important Columbo question, and it can be asked a number of different ways. "Why do you believe that?" "How do you know that?" "What are your reasons for thinking you're right?" In each case you're reversing the burden of proof and putting it back on the person making the claim, where it belongs:

---

[2]The material in this section is adapted from ibid.

- "The Bible is full of fairy tales." ("Why would you believe a thing like that?")
- "Thousands of women died from illegal abortions." ("How do you know that?")
- "Christians shouldn't claim to be right." ("I'm curious why you think that.")
- "Fetuses are not self-aware." ("Why does self-awareness matter in the first place?")
- "No one can say which beliefs are right or wrong." ("Then why should we believe you?")
- "No single religion or person can see the whole truth. Each sees only a part." ("How could you possibly know that each sees only a part unless you can see the whole, something you just claimed was impossible?")

3. **"Have you considered . . . ?"** Then finish the sentence in a way relevant to the issue at hand. Here you are offering an alternative view that gently dismantles your opponent's case or, at the very least, exposes a serious flaw in his reasoning. It's critically important that your tone remain gracious. Otherwise your opponent will become defensive.

- "Everything is just an illusion." ("Have you considered that if that's true, we could never know it?")
- "Fetuses have no right to life because they are not self-aware." ("Have you considered that newborns aren't self-aware either?")
- "You shouldn't judge people!" ("Have you considered that you just did?")

Let's reconstruct a portion of the conversation between Emily and Pam to see what difference the Columbo tactic can make.

Pam: C'mon, Emily. If abortion is outlawed, women will go to jail. Your view is way too extreme for me.

Emily: Tell me what you mean by *extreme*. (Columbo question #1)

Pam: I mean it's just plain wrong. Think about the consequences for women.

Emily: What's wrong with a law that says you can't kill innocent human beings and if you do, there will be consequences? (Columbo question #2)

Pam: But untold numbers of women will get abortions despite the new law and end up dead or in prison.

Emily: I'm curious how you know that. What's your evidence for it? (Columbo question #2)

Pam: Okay, I'm guessing, but you still haven't said what should happen to a woman who gets an abortion. Should she go to jail?

Emily: That depends. It's hard to discuss actual consequences until we know the specifics of the individual case. That's true of any crime. Motive and intent will undoubtedly play a factor, as will her relationship to those who most influenced her decision. So it's premature to say that we should send anyone to jail without fully considering the circumstances. We're careful to investigate other crimes; so what's your reason for thinking we won't do the same with abortion? (Columbo question #2)

Pam: I haven't thought about it. I just can't get past the idea of prosecuting women.

Emily: Again, my point is very modest. All I've said is that the consequences should fit the nature of the crime. Tell me why you think that's unreasonable. (Columbo question #2)

Pam: I don't know, but won't you have to rewrite the laws of all fifty states?

Emily: Actually, no. Mostly, I'd just like to enforce the ones that we have. A majority of states already have laws stating that if you kill a human fetus, you're guilty of a crime. The only exception is abortion. Do you find that odd? (Columbo question #1)

Pam: That's because abortion is legal.

Emily: Yes, but have you considered the implications of that? (Columbo question #3)

Pam: What do you mean?

Emily: Consider this: A mother who harms her unborn offspring with alcohol or drug abuse will be prosecuted in most states today. But if she chooses to abort her child, we look the other way. That's absurd. If that weren't crazy enough, imagine that same woman on her way to the abortion clinic. Just prior to arrival, the doctor scheduled to perform the abortion accidentally broadsides her car, killing her unborn offspring. Guess what he gets charged with in most states?

Pam: It's homicide, right? Like that guy Scott Peterson who killed his wife Laci and her unborn baby out in California. It was all over the news. Didn't they get him for double murder?

Emily: Yes, exactly. Here's something else to consider [Columbo question #3]: Why is it legally okay for Laci Peterson to kill her unborn child but if Scott does it, he's convicted of murder?

Pam: I don't know about that one. Makes no sense to me.

Notice that Emily is no longer on the hot seat. She's graciously asking questions, but she is in full command of the conversation. Her questions expose Pam's rhetoric as a random compilation of assertions with nothing to back them up. True, Emily doesn't convert Pam on the spot, but she does get her thinking.

ENGAGE WITH QUESTIONS

In one-on-one or small-group discussions, you're better off engaging listeners with questions before stating your own position. Below are some typical objections to the pro-life view and a few Columbo questions you might use to advance the conversation. These dialogues are simplified to illustrate the tactic:

1. Laws can't stop all abortions.

- Do you mean "all" or do you mean "most"?
- How do you know that most women won't obey the law?
- Have you considered that laws against rape don't stop all rape, but they do drastically reduce its frequency? Why would it be any different with abortion?

2. The Bible is silent on abortion, and pro-lifers should be too.

- When you say the Bible is silent, do you mean the word *abortion* is never mentioned or that we can't draw any inferences from what's taught there?
- Tell me why you think the Bible's authors don't expressly mention abortion. What are your reasons for thinking that?
- Help me understand your view. Are you saying that whatever the Bible doesn't expressly forbid it allows? If so, have you considered that the Bible does not directly condemn many things including female infanticide and drive-by shootings?

3. Embryonic stem cell research is more promising than adult stem cell research.

- Oh? How so?
- What's your evidence for thinking that?
- Have you considered that adult stem cells are currently treating over seventy-five known diseases while embryonic cells are presently treating none? Given a choice between a treatment that is lethal for tiny human subjects and one that is not lethal, why not go with the nonlethal option, especially since it's more effective at treating disease?

4. Calling all cloning reproductive confuses two very different things— therapeutic cloning to treat disease and reproductive cloning to make babies.

- Tell me what you mean by cloning. (That is, tell me how it's done.)
- How is the specific act of cloning different in therapeutic cases versus reproductive ones?
- So if the act of cloning is identical in both cases and results in a living human embryo, why am I wrong to say that all cloning is reproductive?
- Have you considered that the only difference between the two types of cloning is how we treat the resulting embryo? (Therapeutic cloning destroys him for research. Reproductive cloning lets him be born alive.)

5. The unborn are human, but they are not persons.

- What's the difference? Do you mean there's a group of humans whom we can set aside to be killed while others can't be?
- Why should anyone accept the claim there can be such a thing as a human that's not a person?
- Have you considered what your view does to the concept of human equality?

6. Embryos and fetuses have no desire to go on living and thus have no right to life.

- When you speak of "desire," do you mean one of which a being is consciously aware?
- Why must one have a conscious desire for something before one can justly lay claim to it?
- Have you considered that a slave (due to cultural conditioning) may not desire his freedom, yet he's still entitled to it in virtue of his humanity?

7. The pro-life view that embryos have value and a right to life is inherently religious. It's forcing the government to take a position on whether or not fetuses have souls. Religious claims of this sort have no place in government policy.

- What is a "religious claim"?
- Why is the claim that an embryo has value and a right to life any more religious than saying a teenager does?

• Have you considered that a government that bans abortion does not thereby take a position on whether the fetus has a soul any more than it takes a position on whether thirty-five-year-olds do by banning their killing?[3]

8. All truth is socially constructed in language communities.

• Do you mean we can't get outside language to know what's truly real?
• Why do you think that?
• Have you considered that if you are right, your own view is simply a construct of *your* language community? If that's true, why should I accept it?

9. Right-to-lifers are hypocritical to oppose abortion unless they also adopt unwanted babies.

• How do you know we aren't adopting them?
• But suppose we are not. How does my alleged unwillingness to adopt a child justify an abortionist killing one?
• Have you considered how bizarre it would sound if I were to say, "Unless you agree to marry my wife, you have no right to oppose my mistreating her?" Or, "Unless you agree to adopt my toddler by noon tomorrow, I shall execute him?"

10. Those abortion pictures you showed during your talk were fake and offensive!

• Really? Which ones, and how so?
• Given you think my pictures are fake, can you tell me what real abortion photos look like? How would the children in true abortion pictures differ in appearance from the ones I showed here?
• Help me understand. You aren't sure what real abortion pictures look like, but you are sure my pictures are fake?
• Have you considered that if abortion is morally no big deal, there's little reason to be offended by pictures of it?

Again, the goal is to engage your critics, not silence them. Stop worrying about winning a debate. Just keep asking good questions. "Christians should get out of the habit of trying to refute every fantasy a nonbeliever

---

[3]See Ramesh Ponnuru, *The Party of Death: The Democrats, the Media, the Courts, and the Disregard for Human Life* (Washington, DC: Regnery, 2006), 101.

imagines or every claim he manufactures out of thin air," writes Koukl. "Don't take up the defense when the other person is the one making the claim. Why let him off so easily?"[4]

So the next time you hear that embryos are just hunks of cells, don't run for cover. Step up and ask, "Why would you believe a thing like that?"

Next thing you know, you'll be back in the driver's seat.

REVIEW QUESTIONS

1. Describe Gregory Koukl's Columbo tactic.

2. List the three basic Columbo questions. What is the purpose of each?

3. When your critic is hammering you with an endless barrage of assertions, what should you do to get back in the driver's seat?

HELPFUL RESOURCES

Gregory Koukl. *Tactics in Defending the Faith.* DVD and workbook; order from Stand to Reason, www.str.org/1-800-2-REASON.

Stephen Wagner. *Common Ground Without Compromise: 25 Questions to Create Dialogue on Abortion.* Signal Hill, CA: Stand to Reason Press, 2008.

David Lee and Stephen Wagner. *Abortion: From Debate to Dialogue: A Justice for All Exhibit Guide.* Wichita: Justice for All, 2005. Contact JFA at JFAWeb.org to request a copy.

---

[4]Gregory Koukl, "Take a Tip from Lt. Columbo," http://www.str.org/site/News2?page=NewsArticle&id=5621.

10

THE COAT HANGER OBJECTION: "WOMEN WILL DIE FROM ILLEGAL ABORTIONS"

Every death from abortion is a tragedy we mourn. But why should the law be faulted for making it more risky for one human to take the life of another completely innocent one?

AS SOON AS JUSTICE Sandra Day O'Connor announced her retirement from the Supreme Court in 2005, a notice appeared on the home page for the National Organization for Women (NOW). The notice, complete with pictures, read as follows:

> These are the faces of women who died because they could not obtain safe and legal abortions. If Roe v. Wade is overturned, these pictures could include your daughter, sister, mother, best friend, granddaughter. Don't let George W. Bush and the U.S. Senate put another anti-abortion justice on the Supreme Court.[1]

Kris Hamel, founding member and organizer of DANFORR (Detroit Action Network For Reproductive Rights) claims that before *Roe v. Wade* legalized abortion in 1973, "an estimated 5,000 to 10,000 women died each year in the United States as a result of a million unsafe, illegal abortions."[2]

NOW and Hamel are making an implied threat: Keep abortion legal or women will again be forced to procure dangerous illegal abortions in the

---

[1] The notice has since been removed, but a WorldNet Daily article discusses it at http://www.worldnetdaily.com/news/article.asp?ARTICLE_ID=45100.
[2] Quoted in Diana Drillable Murray, "Anti-abortion Chain Marks Roe v. Wade Anniversary," *The Oakland Press*, January 22, 2007.

back alleys of America. Besides, the law can't stop all abortions, so why not keep things just the way they are?

The appeal for safe and legal abortion has strong emotional pull. Who in their right mind wants any woman to die needlessly? Nevertheless, it's not a good argument for keeping abortion legal.

First, it begs the question. That is, unless you begin with the assumption that the unborn are not fully human, you are making the highly questionable claim that because some people will die attempting to kill others, the state should make it safe and legal for them to do so.[3] Why should the law be faulted for making it more risky for one human being to take the life of another, completely innocent one? Should we legalize bank robbery so it is safer for felons? As abortion-choice advocate Mary Anne Warren points out, "The fact that restricting access to abortion has tragic side effects does not, in itself, show that the restrictions are unjustified, since murder is wrong regardless of the consequences of prohibiting it."[4]

Second, the objection that the law cannot stop all abortions is silly. Of course it can't, any more than laws against rape stop all rape. But it can stop most. For example, researchers Barbara Syska, Thomas Hilgers, and Dennis O'Hare estimate that the number of illegal abortions prior to 1967 ranged from thirty-nine thousand in 1950 to two hundred and ten thousand in 1961, with a mean of ninety-eight thousand.[5] Within seven years of legalization, abortion totals jumped to over 1.2 million annually![6] True, there will always be lawbreakers, but the issue here is first and foremost the status of the unborn: Are they human beings? If so, we should legally protect them the way we would any other group that is unjustly harmed. Stephen Schwarz writes:

> Perhaps what the objection has in mind is that there would be widespread resistance to outlawing abortion. That should not be a factor in deciding law. "We will protect you as long as it is not too difficult to do so, as long as it meets with popular approval." Imagine saying this to a minority suffer-

[3]Francis J. Beckwith, *Defending Life: A Moral and Legal Case Against Abortion Choice* (New York: Cambridge University Press, 2007), 95.
[4]Mary Anne Warren, "On the Moral and Legal Status of Abortion," in *The Problem of Abortion*, 2nd ed., ed. Joel Feinberg and Susan Dwyer (Belmont, CA: Wadsworth, 1984), 103. Cited in ibid.
[5]Barbara Syska, Thomas Hilgers, and Dennis O'Hare, "An Objective Model for Estimating Criminal Abortions and Its Implications for Public Policy," in *New Perspectives on Human Abortion*, ed. Thomas Hilgers, MD., Dennis J. Horan, and David Mall (Frederick, MD: University Publications of America, 1981), 178. Cited in Beckwith, *Defending Life*, 120.
[6]Stanley K. Henshaw, et al, "Abortion Services in the United States, 1991 and 1992," *Family Planning Perspectives*, Vol. 26, No. 3 (May-June 1994), 101.

ing discrimination. Persons must be given equality before the law because it is demanded by justice, not because (or only if) it is easy.[7]

Third, women aren't *forced* to have illegal abortions; they *choose* to have them. As a pro-lifer, I mourn the loss of any woman who dies from abortion. But I reject the premise that women *must* seek illegal abortions. Suppose the laws are changed to protect the unborn. Why should anyone believe that just because a woman wants an abortion, she can't stop herself from having one?[8] Such a view demeans women in general. "A woman is no more forced into the back alley when abortion is outlawed than a young man is forced to rob banks because the state won't put him on welfare," says Gregory Koukl. "Both have other options."[9]

Finally, while some women died from illegal abortions prior to *Roe v. Wade*, the claim that thousands died each year is just false. Dr. Mary Calderone, former medical director for Planned Parenthood, wrote in 1960 that illegal abortions were performed safely by physicians in good standing in their communities. True, this doesn't prove no woman will ever die from an illegal abortion, but it does call into question the claim of high mortality rates prior to legalization. Here's Calderone's quote in context:

> Fact No. 3—Abortion is no longer a dangerous procedure. This applies not just to therapeutic abortions as performed in hospitals but also to so-called illegal abortions as done by physicians. In 1957 there were only 260 deaths in the whole country attributed to abortions of any kind. In New York City in 1921 there were 144 abortion deaths, in 1951 there were only 15; and, while the abortion death rate was going down so strikingly in that 30 year period, we know what happened to the population and the birth rate. Two corollary factors must be mentioned here: first, chemotherapy and antibiotics have come in, benefiting all surgical procedures as well as abortion. Second, and even more important, the conference estimated that 90 per cent of all illegal abortions are presently being done by physicians. Call them what you will, abortionists or anything else, they are still physicians, trained as such; and many of them are in good standing in their communities. They must do a pretty good job if the death rate is as low as it is. Whatever trouble arises usually comes after self-induced abortions, which comprise approximately 8 percent, or with the very small percentage that go to some kind of non-medical abortionist. Another cor-

[7]Stephen Schwarz, *The Moral Question of Abortion* (Chicago: Loyola University Press, 1990), 209.
[8]Steve Wagner develops this point in *Common Ground Without Compromise: 25 Questions to Create Dialogue on Abortion* (Signal Hill, CA: Stand to Reason Press, 2008), 92.
[9]Greg Koukl, "I'm Pro-Choice," http://www.str.org/site/News2?page=NewsArticle&id=5313.

ollary fact: physicians of impeccable standing are referring their patients for these illegal abortions to the colleagues whom they know are willing to perform them, or they are sending their patients to certain sources outside of this country where abortion is performed under excellent medical conditions. The acceptance of these facts was such that one outstanding gynecologist at the conference declared: "From the ethical standpoint, I see no difference between recommending an abortion and performing it. The moral responsibility is equal." So remember fact number three; abortion, whether therapeutic or illegal, is in the main no longer dangerous, because it is being done well by physicians.[10]

Dr. Christopher Tietze, a statistician whose work was prominently featured in Planned Parenthood's own publications during the sixties and seventies, called the claim of five thousand to ten thousand deaths a year "unmitigated nonsense." Noting that forty-five thousand American women of reproductive age die each year from all causes, Tietze stated, "It is inconceivable that so large a number as 5,000-10,000 are from one source."[11] His own estimates put the number of illegal abortion deaths at five hundred annually for the years leading up to *Roe v. Wade*.

Make no mistake, every one of those deaths is a tragedy. But as Stephen Schwarz points out in *The Moral Question of Abortion*, "the true response to back-alley abortions is to be outraged at all abortions, to condemn all abortions—not to propose one kind (legal) in place of another (illegal)."[12]

REVIEW QUESTIONS

1. What does argument from the dangers of illegal abortion assume about the unborn?

2. Why is it silly to claim that the law can't stop all abortions?

3. What's wrong with saying women will be forced to get illegal abortions? How is the claim demeaning to women?

4. How well does the claim of five thousand to ten thousand deaths a year square with statistical data?

5. What does Stephen Schwarz say is the true response to illegal abortion?

---

[10]Mary S. Calderone, "Illegal Abortion as a Public Health Problem," *American Journal of Public Health*, July 1960.
[11]Statement made at Harvard Divinity School, Kennedy Foundation International Conference on Abortion, Washington, DC, September 1967. Cited in Daniel Callahan, *Abortion: Law, Choice & Morality* (New York: Macmillan, 1970), 134. See also Christopher Tietze and Sarah Lewis, "Abortion," *Scientific American*, Vol. 220 (1969), 21, 23; *New York Times*, January 28, 1968.
[12]Schwarz, *The Moral Question of Abortion*, 205.

11

THE TOLERANCE OBJECTION: "YOU SHOULDN'T FORCE YOUR VIEWS ON OTHERS"

Next time somebody says you shouldn't impose your beliefs on others, ask, "Why not?" Any answer he gives will be an example of his imposing his beliefs on you!

IN CHAPTER 1, Pam told Emily it was wrong to impose views on others—when it comes to abortion, every woman must decide for herself.

There was no mistaking the specifics of Pam's argument: Right and wrong are relative to the individual; it's up to us to make the rules. No one has a right to judge others. It's not our place to say what's right for another person. As stated in Chapter 5, claims like these are grounded in a worldview known as *moral relativism*. Relativism, in its most basic form, says there are no objective moral standards, only personal preferences.

Relativism, however, is seriously flawed for at least three major reasons.[1] First, it is often self-refuting. That is to say, it cannot live by its own rules. Second, relativism cannot reasonably say why anything is wrong, including intolerance. Third, it is impossible for anyone to consistently live as a relativist.

RELATIVISM IS OFTEN SELF-REFUTING

For all their talk of tolerance, relativists almost always lapse into making moral judgments. For example, when Pam said it was wrong for Emily to

---

[1] For a full refutation of relativism, see Gregory Koukl and Francis Beckwith, *Relativism: Feet Firmly Planted in Mid-Air* (Grand Rapids, MI: Baker, 1998). The dialogue that follows is based on the tactics taught by Koukl in that book.

impose her views on others, she imposed *that* view on Emily. She couldn't live with her own rule!

At the time Emily was too frustrated to notice. But suppose they take up the conversation again. Here's how Emily can reply when Pam plays the tolerance card:[2]

Pam: Like I said before, I personally oppose abortion. I really do. But you go way beyond that and tell people what's right and wrong for them. You're imposing your views on them.

Emily: What's wrong with that?

Pam: Huh?

Emily: Well, you think what I'm doing is wrong, don't you? If not, why are you correcting me?

Pam: No, I just want to know why you are imposing your views on others by telling them what they should and shouldn't do.

Emily: Are you saying I shouldn't do that? That it's wrong? If so, then why are you imposing *that* view on me?

Pam (regrouping): I'm confused. All I'm trying to say is that if you don't like abortion, don't have one. But you shouldn't force your views on others.

Emily: Is that your view?

Pam: Yes.

Emily: Then why are you forcing it on me when you know I disagree? By your own definition, that's not very tolerant, is it?

Pam: What do you mean? I think women should have a choice and you don't. It's *your* view that's intolerant.

Emily: Okay, so you think I'm wrong. What is it you want pro-lifers like me to do?

Pam: I think you should be more tolerant and let women decide for themselves.

Emily: What's your own view on abortion?

Pam: As I said, I dislike it, but I think every woman should decide for herself.

Emily: So you are saying that if I don't see things your way, I'm wrong, right? Tell me why you think that view is tolerant.

Pam: What?

Emily: Pam, with all due respect, unless I agree with you, you will not tolerate my view. That's why you keep correcting me. You speak of tolerance and respecting other views, but the minute someone takes a view different than your own, you cry foul. It seems you think tolerance is a virtue *if and only if people agree with you.*

---

[2] The tone you set for these types of exchanges should be polite and calm, never combative.

Relativists are often blind to their own intolerance. Once while driving my sons to a baseball game at Dodger Stadium, a young woman in a white pickup truck began tailgating me. Visibly angered by my pro-life bumper sticker that read "We Can Do Better Than Abortion," she stayed on my tail for a mile or so. Finally she pulled beside me and extended a certain part of her anatomy skyward to convey her feelings. She then cut in front of me.

When I saw her bumper sticker, I couldn't stop laughing. It said, "Celebrate Diversity." In other words, in a pluralistic society we should tolerate the diverse views of others. Ironically, she saw no contradiction between her unwillingness to tolerate (or celebrate) *my* point of view and her bumper sticker that said we should tolerate *all* points of view. That is what I mean when I say relativists can't help making moral judgments.

Sometimes those judgments are couched deeply in the language of tolerance, making them difficult to spot. Shortly after the terrorist attacks of September 11, 2001, *New York Times* journalist Thomas Friedman wrote an op-ed piece saying that the real war we're fighting is not against terrorism or Bin Laden but against exclusive religious truth claims of any kind.[3] Christians, Jews, and Muslims who make these claims are guilty of single-minded fanaticism, in his view. A more enlightened culture should realize that God speaks multiple languages and is not exhausted by just one faith. All religious claims are equally true.

Notice the inherent contradictions in Friedman's own exclusive truth claim. First, if all religions are equally true, why is he correcting Christians for holding a view different than his? It's not like they have much wiggle room. Jesus didn't say there were many ways to heaven, just one—him. Nevertheless, Friedman is demanding that Christians rewrite their faith as he dictates. This is not religious tolerance but a classic case of intolerance. His message to Christians is, "Agree with me or else!" Who is the real absolutist here?

Second, Friedman's own religious view self-destructs. If all religions are true, then Christianity is true. But Christianity says that other religions are not true. Either Christianity is right about that or it's mistaken. Either way, all religions can't be true.[4]

---

[3]Thomas Friedman, "The Real War," *New York Times*, November 27, 2001.
[4]Gregory Koukl, "Tactics in Defending the Faith," www.str.org.

RELATIVISM CAN'T SAY WHY ANYTHING IS WRONG, INCLUDING INTOLERANCE

Pam has a real problem. If morals are up to us, then who is she to say that Emily should be tolerant? Perhaps Emily wants to be intolerant. What's wrong with that?

Pam really can't say why anything is wrong. Suppose Emily asks, "Pam, is it wrong to torture toddlers for fun?" What is she going to say in reply— "Well, I wouldn't want to do that to my kid"? That's a lame response because Emily can shoot back with, "Pam, that's not what I asked you. I didn't ask if you *liked* torturing toddlers for fun—I asked if it was *wrong* to torture them for fun."

If it is up to us to decide (rather than discover) right and wrong, there is no real difference between Mother Teresa and Adolf Hitler. They just had different preferences. Mother Teresa liked to help people. Hitler liked to kill them. Who are we to judge?

But we can't help judging, and that's the point.

IT'S IMPOSSIBLE TO LIVE AS A RELATIVIST

As C. S. Lewis points out, a person who claims there is no objective morality will complain if you break a promise or cut in line.[5]

Relativists inevitably take moral positions just like the rest of us. Consider this e-mail sent to me by a blogger named Kevin:

> The problem is that anti-choicers are invariably intolerant of the pro-choice position. It's not enough for them not to favor abortion in their own cases, or even to make themselves a nuisance by bugging other people who make other choices for themselves. Inevitably, they seek to force others to live by the values of the anti-choicers, through legal restrictions, harassment, and often violence or murder. That's the difference between tolerance and intolerance, between holding a view and using force to make others comply with it. That's the difference more anti-choicers need to understand.[6]

So, is Kevin saying pro-lifers are *wrong* to live out their convictions in the public square? If so, who is he to impose *that* view on us? And what exactly does he want pro-lifers like me to do—become an abortion-choicer

---

[5]C. S. Lewis, *Mere Christianity* (New York: Touchstone, 1996), 19.
[6]E-mail correspondence with author, September 2005.

like him? Moreover, Kevin has it all wrong: Pro-lifers aren't imposing their views with intimidation (except for the very few who resort to violence); they're *proposing* them in hopes that the American electorate, at some level, will vote them into law.[7] That's called democracy. Yet Kevin's own (tolerant) position seems to be, "Agree with me or get out of the public square."

In short, I understand his position perfectly: We pro-lifers can believe anything we want as long as we don't *act* as if our view is true. As I wrote him at the time, his own view is anything but tolerant:

> Privately, you'll let me and other pro-lifers say that no human being regardless of size, level of development, or dependency should be killed without justification, but if we try to act on our convictions through the democratic process, you scream foul. In the real world of politics and law, the only view you seem willing to tolerate is your own. At the same time, do you really think abortion-choicers don't force their own views? Try running that by private medical schools who are now being told by "pro-choice" advocates "you *must* provide or refer for abortion training, regardless of your personal moral convictions." Try running it by the 29 states where the people, acting through their duly elected officials, passed laws against partial-birth abortion, only to be told by the federal courts—with the blessing of "pro-choice" groups—"you *must* allow that procedure." Kevin, with all due respect, why not abandon your perch of alleged moral neutrality and admit that you'd like to restrict the advance of the pro-life worldview as much as I'd like to restrict the advance of the abortion choice one. Everyone takes a position here and you'd like yours to win and mine to lose.[8]

Despite Kevin's protestations to the contrary, this is not a debate between anti-choice and pro-choice or tolerance versus intolerance. I'm sure he and I are both anti-choice (intolerant) on many things like spousal abuse, racial discrimination, and the dumping of toxic wastes in our rivers. He is also anti-choice (I assume) on the question of killing toddlers for fun. At the same time, we're both pro-choice on women choosing their own husbands, careers, pets, and cars that they drive, to name just a few things. Thus, the

---

[7]For more on this topic, see Mary Ann Glendon, "The Women of Roe v. Wade," *First Things*, June/July 2003, 14–18.

[8]E-mail correspondence with author, September 2005, edited for clarity. At the time of the e-mail, partial-birth abortion was still permitted even in states that had passed laws against it. That changed in 2007 with the Supreme Court case *Gonzales vs. Carhart*, which upheld a federal ban on PBA.

real issue that separates us is not choice versus anti-choice but, what is the unborn? Is he a member of the human family?

Until that question is answered, it's premature to preach tolerance.

REVIEW QUESTIONS
1. Define relativism.
2. What are some common phrases relativists use?
3. List relativism's three fatal flaws.
4. Why is Thomas Friedman's own religious truth claim self-refuting?
5. When relativists say you shouldn't impose your views, what question should you ask?

12

THE SINGLE ISSUE OBJECTION: "PRO-LIFERS SHOULD BROADEN THEIR FOCUS"

How does it follow that because pro-life advocates oppose the unjust killing of innocent human beings, they must therefore take personal responsibility for solving all of life's ills?

SPEAKING AT A PRO-LIFE convention in Alberta, a local cleric chastised pro-lifers for focusing too narrowly on abortion when they ought to consider broader "life issues" such as occupational safety, AIDS, poverty, and capital punishment. The result, the cleric said, is a "fractured Christian witness that hurts the cause."[1]

The cleric is typical of many on the political left who insist that because pro-life advocates oppose the willful destruction of an innocent human being, they must therefore assume responsibility for society's other ills. In other words, you are not truly pro-life unless you treat the deforestation of the Amazon with the same moral intensity that you do the unjust killing of a human fetus. This is careless thinking and highly unfair to those who take abortion seriously.

Imagine the gall of saying to the Canadian Cancer Society, "You have no right to focus on curing cancer unless you also work to cure AIDS, heart disease, and diabetes." Or try telling the American Heart Association, "You cannot reasonably oppose cardiac arrest unless you fund research aimed at

---

[1]The material in this section is adapted from my article "Pro-Life Groups Would Make Fatal Mistake Heeding Advice," *The Report Magazine*, June 19, 2000; http://www.campaignlifecoalition.com/womens_march/klusendorf.html.

stopping all loss of life." Ridiculous indeed, but how is this any different from what the cleric told pro-life advocates?

Consider what he is demanding. Local pro-life groups must take their already scarce resources and spread them even thinner fighting every social injustice imaginable. This would be suicide for those opposed to abortion. As Frederick the Great once allegedly said, "He who attacks everywhere attacks nowhere."

Contrary to what some think, the abortion debate is not principally about poverty, capital punishment, the redistribution of wealth, or protection of the environment. It's about one issue: What is the unborn? The answer to that question trumps all other considerations.

In the final analysis, the cleric's remarks are not an outrage but a distraction. You might as well blame politicians like Winston Churchill and FDR for focusing too narrowly on defeating the Nazis, to the neglect of other issues.[2] Given a choice, I'd rather pro-lifers focus on at least one great moral issue than waste their precious resources trying to fix all of them.

FOCUS ON THE UNDERLYING CAUSES?

The Alan Guttmacher Institute (AGI) supports elective abortion. The organization claims that pro-lifers are "misguided" when they focus their attention on restrictive legislation. Instead, they should broaden their efforts to address the underlying causes that influence women to abort in the first place. An AGI press release states:

> In addition to outright bans, state legislators are introducing and enacting abortion restrictions at an alarming rate. In 2005 states enacted into law twice as many abortion restrictions as the year before, including laws that would require parental consent or notification for teens' abortions and mandatory counseling and waiting periods. This misguided approach makes it more difficult for some women to obtain abortions, but does not address the underlying cause of abortion—unintended pregnancy. The United States has one of the highest unintended pregnancy rates in the developed world. Instead of pursuing an antiabortion agenda designed to chip away at the foundation of *Roe v. Wade*, states wishing to reduce the need for abortion should focus their efforts and resources on improving

---

[2]For the moment we will assume there are not two million American families who want to adopt unwanted infants, as is the case. See "Adoption Group Sets Record Straight About Abortion Film," National Committee for Adoption press release, December 5, 1990.

access to contraceptive services and helping women use contraceptives more consistently and effectively over time.[3]

As my colleague Steve Weimar points out, this is like saying that the "underlying cause" of spousal abuse is psychological; so instead of making it illegal for husbands to beat their wives, the solution is to provide counseling for men. There are "underlying causes" for rape, murder, theft, and so on, but that in no way makes it "misguided" to have laws banning such actions.

But why is the AGI even concerned about reducing the number of abortions? If removing the fetus is morally no different than cutting one's fingernails, then who cares how many abortions there are? The reason to reduce abortions is that a life is being taken, but if that's the case, then outlawing abortion to protect life makes perfect sense.[4]

SETTLED LAW?

A more sophisticated pitch for pro-lifers to broaden their focus comes from abortion-choice activists and politicians inside the Washington, DC beltway. The right to an abortion, so the argument goes, is here to stay. It's fully integrated into the social fabric of American culture, and reversing it would cause untold chaos. Therefore, pro-life advocates should accept current political realities and focus their energies on broader efforts to help poor women, thus reducing the need for abortion.

During the Senate confirmation hearings for John Roberts (2005) and Samuel Alito (2006), liberal Democrats were all over the press insisting that the right to an abortion articulated in *Roe v. Wade* was "settled law" that should not be challenged by future members of the Supreme Court. During a call-in radio show, for example, Senator Patrick Leahy said of prospective Supreme Court nominees, "I don't see how somebody who said that they didn't consider *Roe v. Wade* settled law [could] get confirmed."[5]

This is an odd claim for many reasons, but I'll mention just two. First, if we shouldn't challenge settled law, *Roe* itself is undermined. In the decade preceding that 1973 ruling, nineteen states liberalized their abortion laws, and thirty-one others did not, despite being heavily lobbied to do so. Of

[3]"South Dakota Bans Abortion; More States Introduce Bans, Other Restrictions," AGI press release, March 15, 2006; http://www.guttmacher.org/media/inthenews/2006/03/15/index.html.

[4]Steve Weimar works with me at Life Training Institute. He conveyed these thoughts in an e-mail.

[5]"Democrats Seek View on Roe from Roberts," *Washington Times*, July 29, 2005; http://washtimes.com/news/2005/jul27/20050727-115929-7321r/.

those states that relaxed their laws, most allowed abortion for rape, incest, fetal deformity, and health of the mother, but none permitted abortion-on-demand through all nine months of pregnancy the way that *Roe* and its companion case, *Doe v. Bolton*, do.[6] Indeed, leading up to *Roe*, the majority of states either left their long-standing abortion restrictions alone (some of which dated back to the 1870s when physicians and early feminists called on state legislators to stop the unwarrantable destruction of human life) or they took specific steps to reaffirm them.[7] None of this history mattered to the *Roe* Court as it swept away the abortion laws—both liberal and conservative—of all fifty states. So much for respecting settled law.

Second, we should remember that laws permitting slavery and racial segregation were settled for generations. Was it wrong to repeal them? The Supreme Court affirmed slavery in *Dred Scott v. Sanford* and racial segregation in *Plessy v. Ferguson*. Both were defended with appeals to settled law. For example, John W. Davis argued before the Supreme Court in his 1953 defense of school segregation that fifty years had passed since the Court settled the segregation question in *Plessy*. He insisted the issue was now beyond dispute:

> . . . somewhere, sometime to every principle comes a moment of repose when it has been so often announced, so confidently relied upon, so long continued, that it passes the limits of judicial discretion and disturbance. That is the opinion which we held when we filed our former brief in this case. We relied on the fact that this Court had, not once but seven times, I think it is, pronounced in favor of the "separate but equal" doctrine. We relied on the fact that the courts of last appeal of some sixteen or eighteen states have passed upon the validity of the "separate but equal" doctrine vis-à-vis the Fourteenth Amendment. We relied on the fact that Congress has continuously since 1862 segregated its schools in the District of Columbia.
>
> We relied on the fact that 23 of the ratifying states—I think my figures are right; I am not sure—had by legislative action evinced their conviction that the Fourteenth Amendment was not offended by segregation; and we

---

[6]The Court in *Roe v. Wade* said that the states could restrict third-trimester abortion if and only if those restrictions did not interfere with a woman's "health." The court in *Doe v. Bolton* (decided the same day as *Roe*) defined health so broadly you could drive a Mack truck through it. The Court said that "health" must be defined "in light of all factors—physical, emotional, psychological, familial, and the woman's age—relevant to the well being of the patient. All these factors relate to health." Thus, for all practical purposes, abortion is legal through all nine months for any reason or no reason. For more, see Francis J. Beckwith, *Defending Life: A Moral and Legal Case Against Abortion Choice* (New York: Cambridge University Press, 2007), 18–21.

[7]For history on U.S. abortion law, see John T. Noonan, *A Private Choice: Abortion in America in the Seventies* (New York: Free Press, 1979).

said, in effect, that that argument—and I am bold enough to repeat it here now—that, in the language of Judge Parker in his opinion below, after that had been the consistent history for over three-quarters of a century, it was late indeed in the day to disturb it on any theoretical or sociological basis. We stand on that proposition.[8]

The Court rejected Davis's case for settled law in *Brown v. Board of Education of Topeka*, and Senator Leahy has said he's glad that it did.[9] However, if *Dred Scott* and *Plessy* weren't settled beyond challenge, then neither are *Roe* and *Doe*.

If pro-life advocates want to win debates over abortion, they must stay focused like a laser beam on the question, what is the unborn? The people calling for pro-lifers to broaden their efforts are not our friends. They are a distraction from the real issue. If our detractors truly understand the evil of abortion, there's no way they will tell us to stop talking about it.

They will insist that we make it unthinkable.

REVIEW QUESTIONS

1. The Alberta cleric told pro-lifers to broaden their focus. What's wrong with his request?

2. Why is the Allan Guttmacher Institute's claim that pro-lifers should focus on underlying causes rather than legislation a silly request?

3. Why is the appeal to settled law not persuasive?

---

[8]Davis made these remarks during the reargument of *Brown v. Board of Education*, December 1953. Cited in *Landmark Briefs and Arguments of the Supreme Court of the United States: Constitutional Law*, Vol. 49A, ed. Phillip B. Kurland and Garland Casper (Arlington, VA: University Publications of America, 1975), 490.
[9]For Leahy's statement, see note 5.

13

THE HARD CASES OBJECTION: "RAPE JUSTIFIES ABORTION"

How should we treat innocent human beings who remind us of a painful event? That single question clarifies everything.

WHENEVER POSSIBLE, I take questions from the audience after my talks. I don't need to guess what the first one will be because it's nearly always the same.

"Okay, suppose a woman is raped. If she gives birth, the child will remind her of the rape. Do you think abortion is wrong in that case?"

Two types of people ask this question, the learner and the crusader. The learner is genuinely trying to work through the issue and resolve it rationally. The crusader just wants to make you look bad.

In either case, I begin with the following:

That's an important question, and you are absolutely right: She may indeed suffer painful memories when she looks at the child, and it's foolish to think she never will. I don't understand people who say that if she'll just give birth, everything will be okay. That's easy for them to say. They should try looking at it from her perspective before saying that. Even if her attacker is punished to the fullest extent of the law—which he should be—her road to recovery will be tough.

Then, very delicately, I ease into my reply by asking a question:

Me: Given we both agree that the child may provoke unpleasant memories, how do you think a civil society should treat innocent human beings who remind us of a painful event? (I pause and let the question sink in.) Is it okay to kill them so we can feel better?

Listener: Well, no, I guess not.

Me: And why is that?

Listener: Because they are human?

Me: That's right. So if the unborn are human beings, how do you think we should treat them when they remind us of something painful?

Listener: Hmmm. I don't know.

Me: Think of it this way. Suppose I have a two-year-old up here with me. His father is a rapist, and his mother is on anti-depressant drugs. At least once a day, the sight of the child sends her back into depression. Would it be okay to kill the toddler if doing so makes the mother feel better?

Listener: No.

Me: And is that's because he's a human being?

Listener: Yes.

That first question—"how should we treat innocent human beings who remind us of a painful event?"—gets to the crux of the issue that must be resolved: What is the unborn? Only after clarifying the primary issue do I make my case.

Me: Here's the point I'm getting at. If the unborn are human, killing them so others can feel better is wrong. Hardship doesn't justify homicide. Admittedly, I don't like the way my answer feels because I know the mother may suffer consequences for doing the right thing. But sometimes the right thing to do isn't the easy thing to do.

Listener: These are hard things to think about.

Me: I agree. Here's one more example that may help. Suppose I'm an American commander in Iraq, and my unit is captured by terrorists. My captors inform me that in ten minutes, they'll begin torturing me and my men to get intelligence information out of us. However, they are willing to make me an offer. If I will help them torture and interrogate my own men, they won't torture and interrogate me. I'll get by with no pain. Can I take that deal? No way! I'll suffer evil rather than inflict it. Again, I don't like how the answer feels, but it's the right one. Thankfully, the woman who is raped does not need to suffer alone. Pro-life crisis pregnancy centers are standing by to help get her through this. We should help, too.

What I've said so far usually satisfies the learner. She may still feel uncomfortable thinking about the rape victim suffering for doing good, but she's begun to grasp the moral logic that's in play.

The crusader, on the other hand, will hear none of it. He's out to score debate points. He appeals to the hard case of rape, but his appeal is flawed because it is not entirely truthful.

Here's why. The abortion-choice position he defends is not that abortion should be legal only when a woman is raped but that abortion is a fundamental right she can exercise for any reason she wants during all nine months of pregnancy. Instead of defending this position with facts and arguments, he disguises it with an emotional appeal to rape. But this will not make his case. The argument from rape, if successful at all, would only justify abortion in cases of sexual assault, not for any reason the woman deems fit. In fact, arguing for abortion-on-demand from the hard case of rape is like trying to argue for the elimination of all traffic laws because a person might have to break one rushing a loved one to the hospital.[1] Proving an exception does not prove a rule.

To expose his smoke screen, I ask a question: "Okay, I'm going to grant for the sake of discussion that we keep abortion legal in cases of rape. Will you join me in supporting legal restrictions on abortions done for socioeconomic reasons that, as studies on your side of the issue show, make up the overwhelming percentage of abortions?"[2]

The answer is almost always no, to which I reply, "Then why did you bring up rape except to mislead us into thinking that you support abortion only in the hard cases?"

Again, if an abortion choice crusader thinks that abortion should be a legal choice for all nine months of pregnancy for any reason whatsoever, including sex selection and convenience, he should defend that view directly with facts and arguments. Exploiting the tragedy of rape victims is intellectually dishonest.

Sometimes the abortion-choice crusader totally disregards the horror of rape when it's convenient to his argument. Steve Wagner recounts one such example from the University of New Mexico in 2006.[3] A pro-life advocate was making her case in front of a jeering crowd. At one point, the crusaders present demanded to know if she had ever been raped. She

---

[1]Beckwith uses this example in *Politically Correct Death: Answering Arguments for Abortion Rights* (Grand Rapids, MI: Baker Books, 1993), 69.

[2]Warren Hern, *Abortion Practice* (Boulder, CO: Alpenglo Graphics, 1990), 10, 39. Dr. Hern is America's leading abortionist, and he writes, "The impression of clinical staff is that all but a few women seek abortions for reasons that can broadly be defined as socioeconomic, and many cite strictly economic reasons," 10.

[3]Steve was at the event and relayed the details to me in an e-mail.

replied, "Yes." They responded with more jeering. They didn't stop for even a moment. They kept calling her a pawn of the Republican Party.

My point is that I've seen the abortion-choice crusader totally disregard the horror of rape when the victim doesn't agree with his own views on abortion.

REVIEW QUESTIONS

1. Why do you think it's important to show sympathy for the woman before making your case?
2. What is the most important question to ask when the topic of rape comes up?
3. Describe the difference between the learner and the crusader.
4. What question can you use to diffuse the crusader and expose his smoke screen?

14

THE "I DON'T LIKE YOU" OBJECTION: "MEN CAN'T GET PREGNANT" AND OTHER PERSONAL ATTACKS

Even if pro-lifers are the worst people in the world, others must still refute their arguments. Anything less is intellectually dishonest.

SUPPOSE I OWE A NEIGHBOR twenty-four thousand dollars that I refuse to repay. After patiently asking for the money, he takes me to court, where he systematically lays out the evidence against me. He presents the judge with the written loan agreement I had signed promising to repay the money within two years at a thousand dollars a month. He then shows bank statements indicating that no checks from me have been deposited into his account. Finally, he presents copies of "past due" notices sent to me via certified mail. When the judge asks me to explain my side of the dispute, I reply, "My neighbor is the worst person in the world. His dog barks all night, his kids are ugly, and he once made a pass at my wife. On top of that, he goes to that fanatical church down the street where they handle snakes and carry on like a bunch of crazies. And did you see that car he pulled up in? It's as ugly as his kids are. How can you trust someone like that to tell you the truth?"

Suppose my neighbor is all of those things and worse. Is the judge going to buy my argument? Of course not.

HOLLYWOOD ROLE MODELS

Sometimes the abortion debate gets personal in ways that have nothing to do with the issue at hand. At a 1995 Rock for Choice concert in Pensacola Florida, vocalist Eddie Vedder of Pearl Jam shrieked from the stage:

> I'm usually good about my temper, but all these men trying to control women's bodies really [profanity deleted] me off. They're talking from a bubble. They're not talking from the street, and they're not in touch with what's real. Well, I'm [profanity deleted] mean, and I'm ugly, and my name is reality.[1]

He later said that unlike pro-life advocates, he would never force his beliefs on anyone.

During an HBO special, comedian Roseanne Barr told the audience:

> You know who else I can't stand is them people that are antiabortion. . . . I hate them. They're ugly, old, geeky, hideous men. They just don't want nobody to have an abortion, cause they want you to keep spitting out kids so they can molest them.[2]

Okay, Roseanne, let's assume for the sake of argument that you're right: Pro-lifers, including the women among us, are just a bunch of hideous old men who molest kids. How does this in any way refute the pro-life claim that abortion takes the life of a defenseless child? Clearly, it does not. The attack, therefore, is completely irrelevant to the *argument* that the pro-life advocate is making.

In short, Roseanne Barr and Eddie Vedder are attacking the character of pro-lifers instead of defending their own positions. We call this the *ad hominem* fallacy. It is fallacious reasoning because even if the personal attack is true, it does nothing to refute the pro-lifer's argument that the unborn are members of the human community.

Consider the following exchange:

Abortion-choicer: You pro-lifers are just a bunch of bigots who want to force your views on others!
Pro-lifer: What's a bigot?
AC: Someone who is critical of other people's views.

---

[1]Cited in Kim Neely, "Where Angels Fear to Tread," *Rolling Stone*, May 5, 1994.
[2]Cited in Paul Duncan, "The Perils of Abortion," *Evangel*, January 1995.

PL: Are you saying people who do that are wrong?

AC: You bet they are! They're bigots, like you.

PL: Maybe you can help me clear this up. If I'm critical of the abortion-choice view, that makes me a bigot. But if you're critical of my view, that's okay?

AC: You should tolerate other views.

PL: Okay, suppose I'm a bigot. How does that refute my claim that abortion unjustly kills an innocent human being? Could the unborn still be human even if I'm a bigot?

WORDS THAT KILL?

On July 11, 2000, a knife-wielding man attacked Vancouver abortionist Garson Romalis in a downtown clinic. As journalist Andrew Coyne wrote at the time, abortion advocacy groups seized on his brush with death to score cheap political points against their opponents, notably Canadian Alliance Party leader Stockwell Day, who opposes abortion.[3]

Coyne writes that Day was quick to condemn the attack against Romalis as "outrageous and untenable," but that did not satisfy local abortion advocates. Marilyn Wilson, president of the Canadian Abortion Rights Action League, said Day had "indirectly sanctioned" the violence against Romalis with his extremist rhetoric.

Why was Mr. Day responsible for the attack? It's really quite simple: He disagrees with Ms. Wilson on abortion and has said publicly that elective abortion is the unjust killing of an innocent human being. "Day is going to try and deny that he would support any violence," she said in a press release, "but his rhetoric does incite other people who share his beliefs against abortion to violence." She then called Day a "fanatic" for "the amount of anti-choice, extremist rhetoric that's out there."

Of course, "fanatic" and "extremist" mean anyone who deviates in the slightest from Ms. Wilson's own position, which is that abortion should be legal for any reason whatsoever during all nine months of pregnancy. If you say that elective abortion takes the life of a defenseless child, as Day believes it does, your irresponsible rhetoric will cost an abortionist his life.

Ms. Wilson is using scaremongering tactics to poison the public debate over abortion. Her statements are intellectually dishonest for at least four reasons. First, let's assume that pro-life rhetoric does in fact lead to acts of violence against abortionists (though there is no good reason to suppose that

---

[3]The facts from this story, as well as some of the analysis, come from Andrew Coyne, "Opinions Are Not Crimes," *The National Post*, July 14, 2000.

this is so). Would this in any way refute the pro-life argument that elective abortion unjustly takes the life of a defenseless human being? Keep in mind that pro-life advocates do not merely state their case—they buttress it with scientific and philosophical reasoning. If Ms. Wilson thinks pro-lifers are mistaken, she should patiently explain why fetuses should be disqualified from membership in the human community. But instead of refuting the pro-life view, she attempts to silence it with personal attacks.

Second, it is blatantly unfair of Ms. Wilson to demonize pro-life advocates for espousing their sincerely held beliefs. Coyne provides a great example of why this is so. Suppose I'm an animal rights activist opposed to the sale of fur. If a deranged environmentalist firebombs a local clothing store, am I responsible? More to the point, is Ms. Wilson responsible if, upon reading her press release, a pro-abortion activist shoots Stockwell Day for the purpose of saving the community from such an awful extremist? (In a press release one day prior to the stabbing, Wilson accused Mr. Day of favoring "state-sanctioned violence against women by forcing them to bear children they may not want."[4]) If she is serious that pro-life speech incites people to violence, she should lead a campaign to ban all pro-life speech. (Actually, she would like that, but she lacks the courage to say so publicly.)

Third, it does not follow that because a lone extremist stabs an abortionist, the pro-life cause *itself* is unjust. Dr. Martin Luther King, for example, used strong language to condemn the evil of racism during the 1960s. In response to his peaceful but confrontational tactics, racists unjustly blamed him for the violent unrest that sometimes followed his public demonstrations. Mayor Richard Daley of Chicago argued that if Dr. King would stop exposing racial injustice, black people would be less likely to riot. The mayor's remarks, like those of Ms. Wilson, were an outrage. Are we to believe that a handful of rioters made Dr. King's crusade for civil rights entirely unjust? In his "Letter from the Birmingham Jail," King rebuts this dishonest attempt to change the subject:

> In your statement you asserted that our actions, though peaceful, must be
> condemned because they precipitate violence. . . . [I]t is immoral to urge
> an individual to withdraw his efforts to gain . . . basic constitutional rights
> because the quest precipitates violence. . . . Non-violent direct action seeks
> to create such a crisis and establish such a creative tension that a commu-

---

[4]Canadian Abortion Rights Action League press release, July 10, 2000.

nity . . . is forced to confront the issue. It seeks to dramatize the issue so it can be no longer ignored.[5]

Fourth, if it's extreme to call elective abortion killing, then abortion-choice advocates bear partial responsibility for the stabbing of Dr. Romalis. The fact is that pro-lifers aren't the only ones who call abortion killing. Consider these candid statements by abortion supporters and providers:

- Warren Hern, late-term abortionist: "We have reached a point in this particular technology [D&E abortion] where there is no possibility of denial of an act of destruction by the operator. It is before one's eyes. The sensations of dismemberment flow through the forceps like an electric current."[6]
- Anthony Kennedy, U.S. Supreme Court Justice, describing common dismemberment abortion techniques: "The fetus, in many cases, dies just as a human adult or child would: it bleeds to death as it is torn from limb to limb. . . . The fetus can be alive at the beginning of the dismemberment process and can survive for a time while its limbs are being torn off. . . . Dr. [Leroy] Carhart [the abortionist who challenged Nebraska's partial–birth ban] has observed fetal heartbeat . . . with 'extensive parts of the fetus removed,' . . . and testified that mere dismemberment of a limb does not always cause death because he knows of a physician who removed the arm of a fetus only to have the fetus go on to be born 'as a living child with one arm.' . . . At the conclusion of a D&E abortion . . . the abortionist is left with 'a tray full of pieces.'"[7]
- Planned Parenthood, 1961 brochure: "Abortion kills the life of a baby after it has begun. It is dangerous to your life and health."[8]
- New Mexico abortionist, 1993: "Paradoxically, I have angry feelings at myself for feeling good about doing a technically good procedure which destroys a fetus, kills a baby."[9]

ALLEGED INCONSISTENCY

Journalist Michael Kinsley thinks the pro-life case against embryonic stem cell research (ESCR) is bogus because pro-lifers are inconsistent. That is,

---

[5]See http://www.ucs.louisiana.edu/~ras2777/judpol/kingletter.html.
[6]Warren Hern and Billie Corrigan, "What About Us? Staff Reactions to D&E," paper presented at the annual meeting of Planned Parenthood Physicians, San Diego, 1978.
[7]*Stenberg v. Carhart*, 2000. Cited in David Smiling et al, "The Supreme Court 2000: A Symposium," *First Things*, October 2000. Justice Kennedy voted to uphold *Roe v. Wade* in *Planned Parenthood v. Casey* (1992) and in various other Court decisions.
[8]*Plan Your Children for Health and Happiness*, Planned Parenthood brochure, 1961.
[9]New Mexico abortionist cited in Diane Gianelli, "Abortion Providers Share Inner Conflicts," *American Medical News*, July 12, 1993.

because pro-lifers do not oppose IVF (in vitro fertilization) technology the way they do embryonic stem cell research, it follows that their case against ESCR collapses.

But as Steve Weimar points out, this clearly won't work:

> Kinsley makes the dubious claim that not speaking against in-vitro fertilization makes embryonic stem cell research justified. The logical conclusion though from his line of reasoning is that both in vitro and ESCR are wrong, not that both are OK. Secular people argue this way all the time. They try to find an inconsistency and then claim that everything is permissible.
>
> An example of this faulty reasoning is justifying bad behavior (such as sexual promiscuity) for women because men get a pass on the same bad behavior. But just because men do something immoral, doesn't justify women doing the same immoral activity. Seems to me that the solution is to hold men to the same standard, rather than lowering standards for women.[10]

For Kinsley to disqualify the pro-life case, he must show that the embryos in question are not human. Attacking pro-lifers for being inconsistent, even if the attack is a fair one, does nothing to advance that proposition; it only clouds the real issue.

But Kinsley's attack is not a fair one. What follows from the case against ESCR is *not* that pro-lifers must oppose the *creation* of embryos with IVF, but that pro-lifers will oppose the *destruction* of IVF embryos that are no longer wanted. And that's exactly what nearly all informed pro-lifers do oppose. True, pro-life advocates aren't currently introducing laws to ban the destruction of IVF embryos, but that's because such laws are unachievable in the current political environment. If the political situation changes, pro-lifers should and will introduce them. For the present, there's nothing inconsistent about pro-lifers fighting an evil they may be able to stop (an increase in federally funded ESCR) instead of one they can't (the destruction of IVF embryos).

A CRASS FORM OF REVERSE SEXISM

Finally, some pro-life advocates are attacked for their gender. Men are told, "You can't get pregnant, so leave the abortion issue to women." Besides its obvious sexism, the statement is seriously flawed for several reasons.

---

[10]Steve Weimar's quote was published on the Life Training Institute (LTI) blog November 29, 2007; http://lti-blog.blogspot.com/2007/11/kinsley-still-wrong-on-escr-sk.html.

First, arguments do not have genders, people do.[11] Since many pro-life women use the same arguments offered by pro-life men, it behooves the abortion advocate to answer these arguments without fallaciously attacking a person's gender.

Second, if men can't speak on abortion, *Roe v. Wade*, the Supreme Court case legalizing abortion, was bad law. After all, nine men decided it. Abortion-choice advocates should also call for the dismissal of all male lawyers working for Planned Parenthood and the ACLU on abortion-related issues. Since abortion advocates are unwilling to do this, we can restate their argument as follows: "No man can speak on abortion unless he agrees with us." Once again this is a classic case of intolerance.

Third, lesbians and post-menopausal women cannot naturally get pregnant. Must they be silent on the issue? Think of the bizarre rules we could derive from this argument: "Since only generals understand battle, only they should discuss the morality of war." Or, "Because female sportscasters have never experienced a groin injury, they have no right to broadcast football games on national television."

Again, abortion advocates must offer facts and arguments to support their position. Attacking people personally, even if those attacks are true, will not prove their case or refute ours.

REVIEW QUESTIONS

1. How does a personal (*ad hominem*) attack differ from an argument?
2. Suppose pro-lifers are terrible people. What follows?
3. Abortion-choice activists sometimes blame pro-lifers for using inflammatory rhetoric. Why is this claim unfair?
4. How do the quotes from abortionists neutralize that claim?
5. "Men can't speak on abortion!" List three reasons why this claim is problematic.

---

[11]Francis J. Beckwith, *Politically Correct Death: Answering Arguments for Abortion Rights* (Grand Rapids, MI: Baker Books, 1993), 90.

15

THE BODILY AUTONOMY OBJECTION: "IT'S MY BODY, I'LL DECIDE"

Does a mother have no more duty to her own child than she does to a total stranger who is unnaturally hooked up to her?

DURING OUR DEBATE AT U.C. Davis in June 2006, Dr. Meredith Williams, who performs some abortions, repeatedly called abortion tragic and said that she, too, wanted to reduce the practice provided no laws were passed restricting it.

But why abortion is tragic and why she wanted to reduce it she couldn't say. If the unborn is just a "parasite," as she claimed more than once during our debate, isn't removing that parasite a good event rather than a tragic one? The more abortions the better! She can't have it both ways.

Throughout our exchange, Dr. Williams couldn't decide whether women have an absolute right to bodily autonomy or not. For the first part of our exchange, she more or less argued that they do. However, during the cross-examination she backed off that claim when I pressed her with this thought experiment provided by Dr. Rich Poupard:

> Let's say a woman has intractable nausea and vomiting and insists on taking thalidomide to help her symptoms. After having explained the horrific risks of birth defects that have arisen due to this medication, she still insists on taking it based on the fact that the fetus has no right to her body anyway. After being refused thalidomide from her physician, she acquires some and takes it, resulting in her child developing no arms. Do we believe that she did anything wrong? Would we excuse her actions based on her

right to bodily autonomy? The fetus after all is an uninvited guest, and has no right even to life let alone an environment free from pathogens.[1]

When Dr. Williams said the woman was wrong to do that, I replied, "So if the mother *harms* her unborn child with thalidomide that's wrong, but if she *kills* it with elective abortion that's fine? But who are you to say that? If the mother's right to bodily autonomy is absolute, it's none of our business what she does with the fetus, right?"

THE BODILY AUTONOMY ARGUMENT

As we saw in Chapter 1, many popular arguments for abortion are question-begging. That is, they simply assume that the unborn are not human beings.

The bodily rights argument is an exception. Its central claim is that pregnant mothers have an absolute right to do whatever they want with their bodies regardless of what it does to the children they carry. To quote a popular slogan, "Not the church, not the state, every woman master of her fate."

A scholarly version of the argument was first put forward by MIT Professor Judith Jarvis Thomson in a 1971 essay entitled "A Defense of Abortion." In her essay, Thomson bites the bullet: She concedes for the sake of argument the humanity of the unborn. However, she contends that no woman should be forced to use her body to sustain the life of another human being. Just as you have no right to demand use of your neighbor's kidney should yours fail, the unborn, though human, does not have the right to use the woman's body if she wishes to withhold such support.

Thomson begins her case this way:

> I propose, then, that we grant that the fetus is a person from the moment of conception. How does the argument go from here? Something like this, I take it. Every person has a right to life. So the fetus has a right to life. No doubt the mother has a right to decide what shall happen in and to her body; everyone would grant that. But surely a person's right to life is stronger and more stringent than the mother's right to decide what happens in and to her body, and so outweighs it. So the fetus may not be killed; an abortion may not be performed.

---

[1]Rich Poupard, "Do No Harm (Except for That Killing Thing)," http://lti-blog.blogspot.com/2007/01/do-no-harm-except-for-that-killing.html.

Thomson says the pro-life case seems plausible, but then she asks us to imagine the following:

> You wake up in the morning and find yourself back to back in bed with an unconscious violinist, a famous unconscious violinist. He has been found to have a fatal kidney ailment, and the Society of Music Lovers has canvassed all available medical records and found that you alone have the right blood type to help. They have therefore kidnapped you, and last night the violinist's circulatory system was plugged into yours, so that your kidneys can be used to extract poisons from his blood as well as your own. The director of the hospital now tells you, "Look, we're sorry the Society of Music Lovers did this to you—we would never have permitted it if we had known. But still, they did it, and the violinist now is plugged into you. To unplug you would be to kill him. But never mind, it's only for nine months. By then, he will have recovered from his ailment, and can safely be unplugged from you." Is it morally incumbent on you to accede to this situation? No doubt it would be nice of you if you did, a great kindness. But do you have to accede to it? What if it were not nine months, but nine years? Or still longer? What if the director of the hospital says, "Tough luck, I agree, but you've now got to stay in bed, with the violinist plugged into you, for the rest of your life. Because, remember this. All persons have a right to life, and violinists are persons. Granted you have a right to decide what happens in and to your body, but a person's right to life outweighs your right to decide what happens in and to your body. So you cannot ever be unplugged from him." I imagine that you would regard this as outrageous.[2]

There's no mistaking Thomson's claim: Just as one may withhold support and detach himself from the violinist (we are asked to assume), so too the mother may withhold support and detach herself from the child. Abortion is such a detachment.

DO THE PARALLELS WORK?

Thomson wants us to believe that pregnancy is similar to the mother being hooked up to the violinist. But are these situations truly similar in morally relevant ways? If so, Thomson's case seems virtually unassailable. If not, the analogy fails and her argument crumbles.

---

[2]Judith Jarvis Thomson, "A Defense of Abortion," *Philosophy and Public Affairs* 1 (1971), 47–66. Cited in Francis J. Beckwith, *Politically Correct Death: Answering Arguments for Abortion Rights* (Grand Rapids, MI: Baker, 1993), 128.

There are good reasons to reject Thomson's alleged parallels.

First, we may not have the obligation to sustain strangers who are unnaturally plugged into us, but we do have a duty to sustain our own offspring. "The very thing that makes it possible to say that the person in bed with the violinist has no duty to sustain him, namely, that he is a stranger unnaturally hooked up to him, is precisely what is absent in the case of the mother and her child," writes Stephen Schwarz.[3]

Gregory Koukl asks, "What if the mother woke to find herself surgically connected *to her own child?* What kind of mother would willingly cut the life-support system to her two-year-old in a situation like that? And what would we think of her if she did?"[4] In short, Thomson assumes that a mother has no more duty to her own offspring than she does to a total stranger.

Second, the child is not an intruder. He is precisely where he naturally belongs at that point in his development. If the child doesn't belong in the mother's womb, where does he belong? "That a woman looks upon her child as a burglar or an intruder is already an evil, even if she refrains from killing her," writes Schwarz.[5]

Third, Thomson tries to justify abortion as merely the withholding of support. But it is also something else, the killing of a child through dismemberment, poison, or crushing. Thomson may (we assume) withhold support from the violinist; she may not actively kill him. "Assume that the woman has no duty to sustain the child," writes Schwarz. "This means only that she has the right to withhold her support from him. It does not give her the right to kill the child—which is what abortion is. . . . Thomson seizes on the withholding of support aspect of abortion, suppressing the deliberate killing aspect."[6]

Consider the following example provided by Schwarz. I return home to find a stranger in my house who will die unless I take care of him. Assume that I have no duty to give my support. May I then throw him out even if it means tossing him off a high cliff or into a deep lake where he will drown? Of course not. That I throw him out in the name of withholding support does not mean that I don't do something else—kill him. That the woman throws the child out in the name of withholding support does not mean that she does not also do something else—kill the child.[7]

[3]Stephen Schwarz, *The Moral Question of Abortion* (Chicago: Loyola University Press, 1990), 118.
[4]Gregory Koukl, "Unstringing the Violinist," http://www.str.org/site/News2?page=NewsArticle&id=5689.
[5]Schwarz, *The Moral Question of Abortion*, 122.
[6]Ibid., 116.
[7]Ibid., 117.

As Beckwith points out, "Euphemistically calling abortion the 'withholding of support' makes about as much sense as calling suffocating someone with a pillow the withdrawing of oxygen."[8] If the only way I can exercise my right to withhold support is to kill another human being, I may not do it.

Fourth, barring cases of rape, a woman cannot claim that she bears no responsibility for the pregnancy in the same way she bears no responsibility for the violinist. Merely going to bed at night does not naturally cause anyone to wake up attached to a total stranger. However, when a couple engages in sexual intercourse, they engage in the only possible activity that naturally leads to the formation of a child.[9] Hence, she is not like the woman who finds herself plugged into the violinist against her own will.

But suppose the woman is forced into pregnancy through rape. In this case, she's not voluntarily performed an action she knew could result in a child. Wouldn't abortion be justified to relieve her burden?

Given Thomson concedes the humanity of the unborn, the fundamental question is whether we can kill innocent human beings to relieve our own suffering. True, the child came into being through a violent act, but that has no bearing on how he should be treated. The fact that the woman has been violated does not justify killing the child. "Suppose someone illegally dumped garbage into my yard," writes Patrick Lee. "May I then rake the garbage into my innocent neighbor's yard? Or may I pass counterfeit money to an innocent party because I innocently received it myself?"[10]

Moreover, although carrying the child to term is burdensome and may involve serious social and psychological costs, that burden is nowhere near the harm the child would suffer being killed. Most harms of pregnancy are reversible while the harm done to the child through abortion is irreversible and total.

Fifth, pregnancy, unlike the violinist analogy, is not a prison bed. As Dr. Bernard Nathanson points out, "Few pregnant women are bedridden and many, both emotionally and physically, have never felt better. For these, it is a stimulating experience, even for mothers who originally did not want to be pregnant."[11]

---

[8]Francis J. Beckwith, *Politically Correct Death: Answering Arguments for Abortion Rights* (Grand Rapids, MI: Baker, 1993), 133.
[9]David Lee and Stephen Wagner, *Abortion: From Debate to Dialogue: A Justice for All Exhibit Guide* (Wichita: Just for All, 2005), 47.
[10]Patrick Lee, *Abortion and Unborn Human Life* (Washington, DC: The Catholic University of America Press, 1996), 121–122.
[11]Bernard N. Nathanson and Richard Ostling, *Aborting America* (New York: Doubleday, 1979), 123.

Sixth, unlike the violinist analogy, the mother-child relationship is not parasitical. A parasite is an alien being who should not be present. The mother's child was conceived with her own flesh and blood and is where he naturally belongs at that stage in his development. True, a child who is breast-feeding draws nourishment from another person, but this relationship can hardly be called parasitical. This is because the child's relation to the mother is indeed a proper one.[12]

IS THE CHILD A RAPIST? IS ABORTION SELF-DEFENSE?

Eileen McDonagh takes Thomson's bodily rights argument to a whole new level. In her book *Breaking the Abortion Deadlock: From Choice to Consent*, she writes that pregnancy is not caused by sexual intercourse but by the unborn entity implanting itself in its mother's uterus.[13] Although the unborn may in fact be fully human, the important issue is not what the fetus *is*, but what it *does* to the woman's body. What it does is massively intrude upon her body and expropriate her liberty, placing her health at risk. If the fetus implants in her uterus without consent, using her organs for its own survival, it commits an act of aggression similar to rape, slavery, and kidnapping. If a woman has a right to defend herself against a rapist, she also should be able to use deadly force to expel a fetus.

For McDonagh, consent is everything. Her major premise is that just because a woman consents to sex does not mean she consents to pregnancy. If the woman does not consent to fetal tyranny over her body, the law must recognize the pregnancy as a serious and wrongful injury. Just as a woman may refuse to donate blood to her own child, so she may refuse to donate her body to a fetus. Meanwhile, women who do not consent to pregnancy are entitled to state-funded protection from the aggressor fetus. When a fetus seriously injures a woman by imposing wrongful pregnancy (due to a lack of consent), she has a right to use deadly force to stop it; but she also has a right to state assistance. Just as the government pays police to prevent rapists from invading the bodies of women without consent, so it should pay abortionists to stop fetuses from kidnapping women's bodies.

McDonagh's parallels, however, fare no better than Thomson's.

First, why should anyone accept the fact that a rapist or a mugger has

---

[12]Ibid., 122.
[13]Eileen McDonagh, *Breaking the Abortion Deadlock: From Choice to Consent* (New York: Oxford University Press, 1996).

the same relationship to a mother's body as does her own child? As discussed above, the fetus is not an intruder. Rather, it is in its rightful place, where it naturally belongs. Thus, the very thing that makes it possible for McDonagh to repel the rapist, namely, that he is an aggressor who unnaturally invades her body, is precisely what is absent in the case of the mother and her child. We do not have a moral obligation to sustain muggers, but we do have an obligation to sustain our own children.

Moreover, McDonagh's comparison of pregnancy to violent assault unfairly biases the argument. Pregnancy dramatically changes a mother's body, but in ways it was designed and equipped to handle. Though at times difficult, it hardly compares to the damage done by rape and other physical assaults. For that matter, puberty and aging also change the body, but no one thinks of these as violent attacks. Modern pregnant women can continue to work, play, travel, work out, and take care of other children. In the 1960s, it was feminists themselves who worked to eradicate the older assumption that pregnant women were somehow ill and should be "taken care of." Rightfully so, since the overwhelming majority of pregnancies are not life-threatening.

Second, McDonagh is mistaken about the relationship between consent and consequences. Many of our choices have consequences that we don't consent to, but which we must nonetheless accept. Take, for example, a basic surgical consent form. Patients consent to a surgical procedure. They do not consent to any particular consequences of the surgery, as for example, being cured. They merely consent to the surgery. The whole point of informed consent is that our choices often have undesirable consequences. If you are aware of these consequences, then by consenting to the surgery, you are stating your willingness to accept them.

When my two oldest sons were small, our house was the wrestling capital of the neighborhood. In one particular case, the younger son (age seven) was wrestling with his older brother (age eight). During the course of their romp, the older fell on the younger sibling's head, pressing it into the carpet. The younger protested, "Daddy, Jeffrey hurt me!" When reminded that wrestling puts one at risk for pain, he replied he just wanted to wrestle, not get hurt!

Why should it be any different with sex? We consent to things we have control over—in this case, having sexual intercourse. We do not consent to the consequences, good or bad. Imagine someone arguing, "I consented to having sex, but I didn't consent to contracting a sexually transmitted disease."

To cite another example, suppose I break my neighbor's sliding glass door while playing baseball with my sons. Upon inspecting the damage, I reply to my neighbor, Mr. Lopez, "I'm sorry that I broke your slider, I really am. But I'm not going to pay for it. You see, I consented to play baseball with my sons, but I didn't consent to break your window."

If I said that, he would think I was completely nuts. We can only consent to our initial actions, not to the consequences that follow.

To say that a person consents to pregnancy is like saying a person consents to winning a lottery ticket. This is a misuse of words. You may consent to buying a ticket, but you don't consent to winning. Winning and losing are entirely outside the realm of your control. You only consent to what is within your realm of control.

Third, the fetus is the effect, not the cause, of pregnancy. McDonagh rejects the notion that having sex makes the woman responsible for the child. The mother and father don't cause pregnancy, she says; the fetus does by aggressively planting itself in the mother's womb.

In a rather bizarre analogy, she likens the situation to a woman who is mugged while jogging through a park at night. Although she places herself in a situation where mugging is possible, the jogger is not responsible for the actions of her assailant.

But the analogy is not at all parallel to a pregnant woman and her child. The fetus, even if unwanted, cannot be responsible for its own existence. Scientifically, conception, not implantation (as McDonagh asserts), begins and defines life, and the fetus wasn't around to engineer that event. As Frederica Mathewes-Green points out, there can be no "mugger" until two "joggers" combine genetic material to create him.[14] On what grounds, then, can any parent who willingly engages in a sexual act that leads naturally to the creation of a dependent child deny responsibility for him?

Finally, McDonagh's claim that a woman can refuse to donate her body to a fetus in the same way she may refuse to donate blood or a kidney to another person ignores the all-important distinction between withholding consent and actively killing another person, which is what abortion does. It is one thing for a parent to refuse to donate blood to her own child. It is

---

[14]I owe this observation to Fredericka Mathewes-Green, from her review of Eileen McDonagh's book, *National Right to Life News*, August 12, 1997.

quite another to slit her child's throat in the name of withholding "consent." If the only way I can withhold consent is to actively kill another person, I may not do it. My duty not to destroy an innocent person (in this case, my *own* child) takes precedence over my right to withhold consent.

IS THE RIGHT TO BODILY AUTONOMY ABSOLUTE?

The bodily rights argument is compelling if and only if a pregnant woman's right to control her own body is absolute, meaning she can do whatever she wants with her body regardless of the impact on her unborn offspring.

But this is clearly false. Consider the example provided by Dr. Rich Poupard earlier. If a pregnant woman demands that a physician give her medication known to cause birth defects, is he required to provide it? Or suppose that same woman wants to continue her Accutane therapy for acne. Accutane is highly toxic to developing human fetuses, and the U.S. government actually insists that a woman of childbearing age use two forms of contraception if she is sexually active prior to using the medication. Indeed, before she fills the prescription, she must verify the type of contraception she is using. Yet no one questions this as an assault on her bodily autonomy.

"In each of the above examples," writes Poupard, "the mother is seeking a medication that does not harm her, has a beneficial effect that she desires, and yet she has no recognized right to be given them" based on her alleged right to bodily autonomy. "The only reason these medications are denied to the pregnant mother who may be seeking them is the effect on her fetus."[15] Thus, while the mother's claim to bodily autonomy is important, it is not absolute and does not supersede her obligation to the child.

Of course, there is one absurd exception to all this. The same physician who refuses to give a pregnant woman a drug that *harms* her offspring may very well prescribe one that *kills* her offspring. "When I treat a mother that is pregnant," Poupard says, "I often state to them [sic] that I have two patients to worry about now, not just one. If I knowingly recommended using a medication that would potentially cause harm to the 'second patient,' I would be guilty of malpractice and would have performed a very unethical act. However, if I recommend that she kill the second patient, I am a great defender of women's rights. What a strange world we live in."[16]

---

15 Poupard, "Do No Harm (Except for that Killing Thing)."
16 Ibid.

A DEVASTATING EXAMPLE—FROM THE OTHER SIDE

An abortion-choice blogger named Paul W. presents an interesting thought experiment that demonstrates the weakness of bodily rights argument. Speaking to those who support the mother's claim for absolute bodily autonomy, he writes:

> My position is this: if a fetus is a person, the right of a woman to voluntarily get pregnant and her right to not give birth can't both be absolute—or at least, she can't have a very general, entirely absolute right to control of her own body that includes those things and other similar things.
>
> Here's the thought experiment: suppose that a woman could get pregnant, and stay pregnant indefinitely, while the fetus inside her did develop into an actual person. Perhaps a physically dwarfed person, the size of a baby, but developing the basic kinds of cognition and emotions that children and adults have. Suppose this physically dwarfed, stunted person lives in its mother's belly for decades, fully aware of who it is and where it is—it is trapped in its mother's belly. Suppose it wants to get out and live something like a normal life, but she won't let it. She says "it's my vagina, and I don't have to let you through it."
>
> Suppose, even, that the woman chooses to do all of this on purpose, because she likes the idea of having a helpless small person stuck inside her body for its entire life. She lives to a ripe old age of 90, at which time the person inside her has lived a full 70 years of fully aware helpless misery—and then she dies and her 70-year-old "child" dies with her—because right up to the end, it's her body and that's how she wants it.
>
> In that scenario, the child is the mother's slave—its bodily autonomy is overridden by her rights, and it lives a miserable existence its entire life at her whim. Supposing a woman had the ability to do that, would she really have the right to?
>
> I really don't think so. You do not have a right to voluntarily create a person and then refuse to grant that person human rights, to the point of creating a helpless slave and keeping it in that situation indefinitely.[17]

Paul W.'s thought experiment is no stretch at all when we consider the actual case of Melissa Ann Rowland of Salt Lake City. In 2004, Rowland was prosecuted for refusing an emergency cesarean section to save the lives of her unborn twins. According to the hospital staff, Rowland refused

---

[17]This thought experiment was posted at http://punkassblog.com/2006/04/26/git-yer-damn-hands-off-my-body-philosophically-speaking/#comment-156.

the C-section because of the scar it would leave on her body. She stated she preferred to "lose one of the babies than be cut like that." Emergency room doctors and nurses repeatedly tried to persuade Rowland to have the C-section, but she insisted on going outside for a smoke instead. She finally yielded to their demands, but by then it was too late. One baby died, and the other required intense medical intervention to survive. The surviving twin, like his mother, tested positive for cocaine. The medical examiner's report stated that had Rowland consented to the surgery when doctors originally urged her to, "the baby would have survived." Rowland was subsequently charged with murder.[18]

Kim Gandy of the National Organization for Women said she was "aghast" that Rowland was criminally charged. She has a point. If unborn humans have no legitimate claims on their mothers' bodies, why not let a drug addict mom avoid the scar?

DO PARENTS HAVE SPECIAL DUTIES TO THEIR CHILDREN?

Suppose I walked up to a baby-making machine and pressed the START button. Would I be responsible for the ensuing child?

According to McDonagh and Thomson, moral obligations to one's own offspring are consensual or voluntary. This is a strange response. Moral obligations, by their very nature, are non-consensual. That's precisely what makes them moral *obligations*. So the question becomes, what moral obligation does a mother have to her own child? Put another way, is there a proper moral expectation that a mother provide life-sustaining care for her offspring?

Given that both authors more or less concede the personhood of the unborn, a mother has the same moral obligations to her fetus as she does toward her born child. What obligation does she have to her born child? To give whatever sacrificial care is needed to ensure the survival of the child. The exact nature of that demand varies depending on the specific needs of the child, determined by age, development, and level of dependency.

Fathers must pay child support to children they never "consented" to raise. Parents of handicapped children have a duty to provide life-sustaining care to their child even into adulthood, if necessary. At the same time, par-

---

[18]The details in this story come from Jonathan Turley, "When Choice Becomes Tyranny: Abortion Rights Lobby Steps over the Line in Utah," *Jewish World Review*, March 23, 2004.

ents are prosecuted for abandoning their children, even if they no longer "consent" to raise them.

In short, the law places upon parents, especially mothers, burdensome responsibilities toward their offspring that make serious demands on personal freedom. That's because the moral obligation to care for one's own child exists apart from our consenting to do so.

Assume that Thomson's and McDonagh's view is correct. What kind of morality are we left with? Is there really no obligation to others who are dependent on us? To borrow an example provided by Dr. Nathanson, suppose only the breast-feeding of infants was available, as is true in many cultures. Or take an exact case from pediatrics where the infant can tolerate only the mother's milk for nourishment. Is the mother justified in either case in "unplugging" the baby from her breast (and hence committing infanticide) on the grounds that she is not obligated to use her body to sustain the life of another?[19]

As Beckwith points out, society clearly does hold people responsible for moral obligations whether they want to assume responsibility for them or not. To cite an obvious example, drunk drivers are held responsible for killing people while driving under the influence whether they intended to kill or not. This is because although they may not have *wanted* to harm anyone, they *willed* it by driving intoxicated. Likewise, the mother's responsibility for her offspring stems from the fact that she engaged in an act, sexual intercourse, that she fully realized could result in the creation of another human being, even if she took precautions to avoid such a result. She may not have wanted to become pregnant, but she willed it by giving consent to the sexual act. Hence, she has a moral obligation to sustain her offspring whether she voluntarily accepts this obligation or not.[20]

David Boonin replies that pro-life advocates are wrong to assume that parents have special duties to the child simply because they engaged in a voluntary action, sexual intercourse, that caused the child to exist in an imperiled condition. Boonin's primary argument is that we must distinguish between being responsible for someone's neediness and being responsible for the fact that they exist, with the *result* that they are in need.[21] In the first case, Boonin says, we have a special responsibility to provide assistance, but

---

[19]Nathanson and Ostling, *Aborting America*, 123.
[20]Beckwth, *Politically Correct Death: Answering Arguments for Abortion Rights*, 129.
[21]David Boonin, *A Defense of Abortion* (Cambridge: Cambridge University Press, 2003), 133ff. I owe this succinct summary of Boonin's argument to Patrick Lee, "A Christian Philosopher's View of Recent Directions in the Abortion Debate," *Christian Bioethics* (April 2004), Vol. 10, Issue #1, 7–31.

not in the second. He then argues that abortion is an instance of the second type of neediness, not the first.

For example, suppose a doctor saves a patient's life with a particular drug, but the side effects of the medication trigger a fatal kidney dysfunction. The patient's only hope is to use someone else's kidney to filter his own blood. Suppose further the doctor has the correct blood type to assist the patient. Boonin argues that although the physician is responsible for the patient's continued existence, he is not responsible for the patient's dependency condition. Thus, the physician is not required to donate the use of his kidney to save his patient. Boonin sees a parallel here to the fetus. Sure, we cause them to exist, but we do not precisely cause their dependency condition.

However, Boonin's doctor analogy fails. Patrick Lee writes that the reason the physician has no special duties to the patient has nothing to do with factors analogous to pregnancy. "The physician did not bring this patient into being, but in a generous act extended his life. The fact that the doctor thus extended the life of this patient, but with the *result* that the patient *later* develops this urgent need, is quite distinct from conceiving a child—where, at the same time, the parents both cause the child to be *and* place him in an imperiled (dependent) condition." He then suggests this counter-example to Boonin:

> Suppose I am in a motorboat in a lake and speeding past the pier I knock three or four children into the lake. I suppose Boonin would agree that certainly here I am responsible for their being in a dependency condition, and that I owe it to them to go back and try to help them out of the water, lest they drown. However, following Boonin's principles, I might also claim that I was only responsible for their being in the water, not for their being in an imperiled condition. It is not my fault, I might argue, that they do not know how to swim, and so their dependency condition is a consequence of what I do, but it is not something I am responsible for. But clearly, it is specious to distinguish between my causing them to be in the water (for which I am responsible) and their being in a dependency condition due to their inability to swim (for which, the claim would be, I am not responsible). But, likewise, it is specious to distinguish between a child's existing (for which I am responsible) and his existing in an imperiled condition (for which the claim is, I am not responsible).[22]

---

[22]Lee, ibid.

Moreover, Lee writes that parents do have special duties to their off-spring prior to voluntarily assuming those duties. Suppose that a mother takes her baby home after giving birth only because she could not afford an abortion. Or perhaps she could not find a doctor willing to perform one. In both cases, notes Lee, she has not voluntarily assumed responsibility for the child, nor has she consented to a personal relationship with it. Still, it would surely be wrong for her to abandon the child in the woods (perhaps the only way to make sure it is not returned to her), even though the child's death would only be a side effect.[23]

NO DUTY TO SUSTAIN?

Again, the bodily autonomy proponent assumes that parental responsibilities toward one's offspring are voluntary. Given the mother is the only one who can sustain the child, so the claim goes, it is morally permissible for her to deny the use of her body, even if her child dies as a result.

Rich Poupard offers a final thought experiment to challenge this argument:

> Suppose that a woman who faces an unplanned pregnancy decides to gift her child for adoption to another couple. In other words, she agrees to allow the child use of her body during the period of gestation but explicitly states that she is unwilling to care for the child after the birth event.
>
> This mother takes a vacation in a cabin in the mountains when a freak snowstorm strikes and closes down all the roads in and out of the area for at least two weeks. The cabin has adequate food and water stores for the mother, but there is no baby formula, baby bottles, or supplements available for a newborn baby. As the storm strikes, the mother goes into labor and delivers a healthy baby girl. The only way the newborn can survive is to feed on the milk naturally provided by her mother's breasts. There is no formula to feed her, and no means to give the child hydration except for breastfeeding. Does the mother have any moral obligation to use her body (against her stated desire) to feed this child? Per Boonin, although the mother is responsible for the existence of the child, she is not responsible for the child's neediness. The mother is not responsible for the circum-stance that has placed that child in need, despite the fact that the mother can easily fulfill that need in a natural, healthy way. According to Boonin, this mother appears to have no obligation to share her body with her own child, even if the baby girl dies from dehydration.

---

[23]Ibid.

If that weren't chilling enough, Poupard amends the thought experiment to show what else can be justified under Boonin's reasoning:

> What if the mother also brought a young kitten with her to the cabin? The kitten would be in the same position as the baby girl. Instead of allowing her own child to drink her milk, she elects instead to give it to her young kitten. After all, she wants and desires the kitten, and she has already stated that she did not wish to care for the child after the birth. She reminds herself of the slogan "My Body, My Choice" as she watches her child die.
>
> If the authorities find her child dead from dehydration two weeks later, how would we judge her actions? What if we found her child dead but her wanted kitten doing well? Would we consider her actions a powerful assertion of her right to autonomy, or see it as a morally unconscionable act of selfishness? It would be very difficult for the mother to justify allowing her own child to die based on her desire to keep her body to herself in this circumstance. Furthermore, assuming that the mother does have an obligation to feed her child in the scenario above, it would indicate a weakness of her bodily autonomy rights in other situations. The right for bodily autonomy is not enough to override the moral obligation we have to our children.[24]

ABORTION, BODILY RIGHTS, AND ART

In April 2008, Yale student Aliza Shvart sparked controversy with her senior art project. She claimed that over a nine month period she intentionally impregnated herself with donor sperm, then took abortifacient drugs to end any possible pregnancies. She hoped to display the remains (collections of blood that may or may not have contained fetal remains) as part of her project.

She caused no small stir. The university claimed the project was faked. Shvart denied faking anything. Local and national media denounced the project. One Yale student who supports abortion wrote, "Her project, surely, will become the poster child for irresponsible and disrespectful abuse of the right to abortion and a counter-example to the notion that a woman knows what is best for her own body."[25]

But how can defenders of the bodily rights argument for abortion say any of this? The abortion-choice position they defend says that when it

---

[24]Poupard posted this at the LTI blogspot in 2006, but the blogspot in total was accidentally deleted later that year. A new LTI blogspot began in 2007 (http://lti-blog.blogspot.com).
[25]O'Hagan Blades, "Casualty of Controversy: The Pro-choice Movement," *Yale Daily News*, April 24, 2008.

comes to reproduction, women know what's best for their bodies and thus can choose to do what they want with them, regardless of the impact on their unborn offspring. If they are right, they can't gripe if Shvart wants to intentionally impregnate herself so she can display the aborted remains. True, they can say it's bad *taste*, but how can they say its *wrong*?

Abortion-choicers are stuck. They can't pick and choose which reproductive choices they'll allow when the foundation for their view is that women have a fundamental right to make any reproductive decision they want.

IN REVIEW

1. Abortion is not merely the withholding of support but the direct killing of a child. If the only way I can withhold support is to kill another person, I may not do it.

2. We may not have the obligation to sustain strangers who are unnaturally hooked up to us, but we clearly do have a duty to sustain our own offspring.

3. Even if the child is an intruder, that only justifies removing her from the woman's body, not killing her. If the only way I can remove an intruder from my home is to kill him by throwing him off a cliff, I may not do it.

4. It is unfair for Thomson to portray pregnancy as a nine-month prison bed. Many women enjoy the experience.

5. We clearly do have certain moral obligations to others even if we do not voluntarily assume them. Since Thomson assumes that the unborn child is human, why should the parent's duty to care for the child differ before birth?

REVIEW QUESTIONS

1. What is the central claim of the bodily rights argument?

2. How does the bodily rights argument differ from other arguments for abortion? That is, what major pro-life premise does it grant?

3. What is Judith Jarvis Thomson's claim in her famous violinist argument? (Summarize in a sentence.)

4. Thomson wants us to believe that pregnancy is similar to the mother's being hooked up to the violinist. In what ways are her alleged parallels not parallel?

5. Eileen McDonagh says that just because a woman consents to sex does not mean she consents to pregnancy. Why is this claim not persuasive?

6. Consider the case of Melissa Ann Rowland, the mother who refused a C-section because she did not want a scar on her body. What problem does her case present to bodily rights advocates?

HELPFUL RESOURCES

Francis J. Beckwith. *Defending Life: A Moral and Legal Case Against Abortion Choice.* New York: Cambridge University Press, 2007.

Patrick Lee. "A Christian Philosopher's View of Recent Directions in the Abortion Debate." *Christian Bioethics* (April 2004), Vol. 10, Issue #1, 7–31.

Stephen Schwarz. *The Moral Question of Abortion.* Chicago: Loyola University Press, 1990.

PART FOUR

Pro-Life Christians
Teach and Equip

16

EQUIP TO ENGAGE:
THE PRO-LIFE PASTOR IN THE
TWENTY-FIRST CENTURY

Human nature is up for grabs, and pastors committed to biblical truth must step up and fulfill four vitally important tasks.

PRO-LIFE CHRISTIANS CONTEND THAT although humans differ in their respective degrees of development, they are nonetheless equal because they share a common human nature that bears the image of their Creator. Humans have value simply because they are human.

This biblically informed pro-life view explains human equality, human rights, and moral obligations better than its secular rivals. Nevertheless, it's under assault in ways barely imagined a decade ago. The very definition of humanness is up for grabs.

UNDERSTANDING THE TIMES

The April 1 headline was no joke: "British Team Makes Mixed Human Animal Embryos." In the first experiment of its kind, scientists added human DNA to empty cow eggs. "We have created human-animal embryos already," excited researchers told *The London Times*.[1]

The embryos were 99 percent human and didn't survive beyond a few cell divisions, but the implied message to the world was clear: Science is fooling around with the biological nature of human beings.

---

[1] Mark Henderson, "British Team Makes Mixed Human Animal Embryos," *The Times Online*, April 1, 2008; Mark Henderson, "We Have Created Human-Animal Embryo Already," *The Times Online*, April 2, 2008, http://www.timesonline.co.uk/tol/life_and_style/health/article3663033.ece. For more background on hybrid embryos, see Rick Weiss, "Britain to Allow Creation of Hybrid Embryos," *Washington Post*, September 6, 2007.

Not everyone objects to that. Three groups eagerly await the next batch of hybrid embryos: (1) scientists who will use them for grisly medical research; (2) trans-humanists who wish to alter the biological nature of human beings in hopes of radically advancing our evolutionary development; and (3) radical animal rights advocates who consider any claim of human exceptionalism to be dangerous and intolerant and who look to the creation of these hybrids to knock humans off their privileged perch.[2]

At the same time, scathing attacks on human dignity, once restricted largely to academia, are now creeping into popular media. Peter Singer, who thinks killing disabled newborns is only wrong if it adversely affects other interested parties,[3] writes in *The Dallas Morning News*, "During the next 35 years, the traditional view of the sanctity of human life will collapse under pressure from scientific, technological and demographic developments. By 2040, it may be that only a rump of hard-core, know-nothing religious fundamentalists will defend the view that every human life, from conception to death, is sacrosanct."[4] A *New York Times* editorial writer unabashedly states, "We are all of us, dogs and barnacles, pigeons and crabgrass, the same in the eyes of nature, equally remarkable and equally dispensable."[5] Darwinism, it seems, proves humans are no more and no less valuable than barnacles. Who can escape with his dignity intact?

Disabled newborns apparently can't. In 2008, the *Hastings Center Report*, arguably the most prestigious bioethics journal in the world, published yet another article in support of the Groningen Protocol, a proposal from Dutch physicians whereby an independent committee selects severely disabled babies and children (up to age twelve) for lethal injections.[6] When the protocol was initially made public in 2005, *The New York Times* and the *New England Journal of Medicine* both published articles sympathetic to the proposal.[7] Once a fringe belief, infanticide is now trendy among the intelligentsia and mainstream journalists.

---

[2]See, for example, "Human-Animal Hybrid Embryos Approved for Research in Britain," *Science Daily*, September 7, 2007; Wesley J. Smith, "The Transhumanists: The Next Great Threat to Human Dignity," *National Review Online*, September 20, 2002; Wesley J. Smith, "Destroying Human Exceptionalism by Creating Human/Chimp Hybrids," blog post at Second Hand Smoke, July 25, 2006, http://www.wesleyjsmith.com/blog/2006/07/destroying-human-exceptionalism-by.html.
[3]Interview with Singer found at http://www.princeton.edu/~psinger/faq.html.
[4]Singer is quoted in "10 Ideas on the Way Out," *The Dallas Morning News*, November 27, 2005.
[5]John Darnton, "Darwin Paid for the Fury He Unleashed," *The San Francisco Chronicle*, September 25, 2005.
[6]Hilde Lindemann and Marian Verkerk, "Ending the Life of a Newborn: The Groningen Protocol," *Hastings Center Report*, 38, 1, 42–51.
[7]See Gregory Crouch, "A Crusade Born of a Suffering Infant's Cry," *The New York Times*, March 19, 2005; Eduard Verhagen and Pieter J. J. Sauer, "The Groningen Protocol—Euthanasia in Severely Ill Newborns," *New England Journal of Medicine*, March 10, 2005. Dr. Verhagen and Dr. Sauer are both leaders in the Dutch

While pro-lifers struggle to hold the line against infanticide, an aggressive scientism is trumping morality in debates over cloning and embryonic stem cell research (ESCR). As currently practiced, ESCR destroys living human embryos. Nevertheless, the public, either out of ignorance or self-interest, supports doing it anyway.[8] The idea is that if we *can* do it, we *should* do it. As mentioned in Chapter 4, even some so-called "pro-life" politicians are falling for this dangerous idea. For example, Utah Senator Orrin Hatch, defending ESCR, states, "It would be terrible to say because of an ethical concept that we can't do anything for you."[9] Hatch left two things unexplained. First, if science trumps ethics in the quest for cures, aren't grisly medical experiments on two-year-olds justified if we can cure disease? Second, what about the embryos themselves—were they human subjects? Hatch assumed, without a shred of argument, that "we" and "you" do not include *them*. It's a safe bet politically. Even in conservative bastions like Utah, when Americans are asked to choose between microscopic embryos and their own sick kids, the kids win every time—at least the born ones do.

Theologically, the "new atheism" treats all religious truth claims as harmful and intolerable, even in the home. It's atheism with attitude, and its principal goal is to drive anything that smells like the metaphysics of religion, including belief in human exceptionalism, from the public square. Authors like Richard Dawkins, Sam Harris, and Christopher Hitchens (to name a few) insist there is no truth outside the realm of nature. The human animal is merely the product of blind physical processes that did not have him in mind. Naturalistic claims about humankind aren't new, but the angry, condescending tone in which new atheists deliver them certainly is.

Radical environmentalists have also joined the attack on human exceptionalism. For many, humanity is a dreadful curse on the planet. "This myth [of human exceptionalism] is at the root of our environmental destruction—and our possible self-destruction," writes University of Washington psychology professor David P. Barash.[10] If that weren't bad enough, *Time* quotes abortionist and anthropologist Warren Hern of the University of Colorado when he calls our species an "ecotumor" or "planetary malignancy" that is

---

euthanasia movement. Cited in Wesley J. Smith, "Pushing Infanticide," *The Center for Bioethics and Culture Network Newsletter*, February 20, 2008; http://www.cbc-network.org/enewsletter/index_2_20_08.htm.

[8]See polling related to 2008 election at http://www.harrisinteractive.com/harris_poll/index.asp?PID=807.

[9]Cited in Ramesh Ponnuru, "Hatching Clones," *National Review Online*, April 29, 2003.

[10]David P. Barash, "When Man Mated Monkey," *Los Angeles Times*, July 16, 2006.

recklessly devouring its host, the poor Earth.[11] Hern's outrage is puzzling. If humans are tumors, why is he surprised when they act in destructive ways?

Most damaging, personhood rights are replacing human rights. Many prominent bioethicists do not believe that membership in the human species gives any of us value. Rather, what matters is whether any organism, animal or human, is a "person," a status achieved by having sufficient cognitive abilities. Thus, a sentient puppy has more value than a day-old infant. Peter Singer writes, "The fact that a being is human does not mean we should give the interests of that being preference over the similar interests of other beings. That would be speciesism, and wrong for the same reasons that racism and sexism are wrong. Pain is equally bad, if it is felt by a human or a mouse."[12] The acceptance of personhood theory meant that a majority of Americans strongly favored the intentional killing of Terri Schiavo simply because her cognitive abilities were less than our own.[13] That whole ordeal put in place a premise that it's okay to kill people who don't improve.

Finally, for many Americans, personal experience and an indefensible quest for compromise have muddled objective thinking on abortion. Between 1973 and 2005 (the last year for which we have reported data), American women procured an estimated 48,589,993 abortions.[14] Aborting women aren't the only ones personally impacted. Depending on the circumstances, a boyfriend, husband, or parent may also play a role in the abortion decision.

Others want the debate to just go away. A 2006 Pew Research poll reveals that most Americans, including most Christians, don't understand the fundamental questions at the heart of the abortion debate. Sixty-six percent of Americans and six out of ten Christians prefer compromise and a "middle ground."[15]

But when it comes to taking human life without justification, there is no middle ground. How many human beings should we allow to be killed? Should we compromise on how many children we allow to be sexually molested? Should we find middle ground on how many abused children we allow?

---

[11]Barbara Ehrenreich, "On the Bright Side of Over-Population," *Time*, September 26, 1994.
[12]Singer interview, http://www.princeton.edu/~psinger/faq.html.
[13]For a survey of polling data, see http://www.religioustolerance.org/schiavo7.htm.
[14]National Right to Life has compiled survey data from both the Centers for Disease Control and the Alan Guttmacher Institute to arrive at this estimate; http:www.nrlc.org/abortion/facts/abortionstats.html.
[15]"Pragmatic Americans Liberal and Conservative on Social Issues: Most Want Middle Ground on Abortion," Pew Research Center, August 3, 2006; http://people-press.org/report/283/pragmatic-americans-liberal-and-conservative-on-social-issues.

Christians who argue for a settled compromise on abortion assume that the unborn are not fully human, at least not the way other children are. After all, if the unborn is a human being, doesn't the right to life belong to him as much as it does to us? On the other hand, if the unborn is not a human being, then why have any restrictions on abortion? Compromise makes no sense on either side of the issue.[16]

WHAT CAN PASTORS DO? FOUR ESSENTIAL TASKS

Rather than giving up the fight for human value, the pro-life pastor commits himself to four essential tasks. First, he preaches a biblical view of human value and applies that view to abortion, embryonic stem cell research, and cloning. Second, he equips his people to engage the culture with a persuasive defense of the pro-life view. Third, he restores lost passion for ministry with cross-centered preaching. Fourth, he confronts his own fears about preaching inconvenient truth.

TASK #1: THE PRO-LIFE PASTOR PREACHES A BIBLICAL VIEW OF HUMAN VALUE

As stated in Chapter 8, the biblical worldview explains human dignity and equality: all humans have value because they bear God's image (Gen. 1:26; 9:6; Jas. 3:9.) At the same time, the science of embryology establishes that from fertilization forward, the unborn are unquestionably human. Hence, biblical commands against the unjust taking of human life (Exod. 23:7; Prov. 6:16–19) apply to the unborn as they do to other human beings. Like everyone else, they bear the image of their Creator.

Pastors should not assume that church members understand or agree with this biblical view of human value. I speak at some of the finest Christian schools around the country. Yet without exception, I encounter pockets of students who think human beings can be killed because they're the wrong size or the wrong level of development. When I ask them to say why anything has a right to life, they give a totally secular answer: "It depends on if you have a brain and are self-aware."

Make no mistake: the debate over the question, what makes humans

---

[16]That's not to say that pro-lifer lawmakers (and voters) who make short-term, tactical moves to save some lives now until they can save more later are compromising with evil. They are not. Rather, they are choosing the greatest good possible given current political realities. If I don't have the votes to save all children, I should at least work incrementally to save some, thus limiting the evil done. But for those who understand the moral logic of the pro-life view, a settled compromise with evil is out of the question.

valuable? not only impacts disputes over cloning, abortion, and embryo research but our presentation of the gospel as well. For example, if my unchurched neighbor thinks human beings are the product of undirected physical forces and thus are nothing more than a pile of physical parts, what's that going to do to his concepts of sin, judgment, and the afterlife? If when my body dies I die, my fundamental problem isn't sin, it's survival. On the other hand, if I possess a moral and rational nature that reflects my Maker, the choices I make in this life have eternal significance.

TASK #2: THE PRO-LIFE PASTOR EQUIPS HIS PEOPLE TO ENGAGE THE CULTURE

Theology gives church members a biblical foundation for their pro-life beliefs. Apologetics gives them the tools to take those biblically informed beliefs into the marketplace of ideas.

Churchgoing adults and youth must be taught to make a basic scientific and philosophic defense for the lives of the unborn as outlined in Chapters 1–3, including strategies for handling the tough questions discussed in Chapters 9–15.

They must also be taught courage.

When Summer White was fifteen, she wrote a paper for a class at a Phoenix area public high school. This was no ordinary paper. In it she carefully defended her pro-life views by arguing that embryonic stem cell research (ESCR) unjustly takes the life of a defenseless human being. She was the only one in her class to take that position.

Summer defended her case two ways. First, she argued that the embryos in question were human beings and should not be killed to benefit other people. Second, she argued that we don't have to kill embryonic human beings to find cures for disease. Adult stem cell research, which does not require killing the donor, is already treating human illness, and there is nothing controversial about it.

Her teacher sent the paper back with no credit.

What was Summer's crime? She claimed to be right. Never mind that she presented evidence to back up her case. Never mind that her teacher did not even try to refute what Summer had written. She was told it all came down to this: ESCR was a matter of personal opinion. Thus her paper was rejected. When Summer appealed to the school administration, they presented her with a proposal: to get a grade, all she had to do was rewrite her paper and simply say it was her personal opinion that ESCR is wrong.

Do you think for even a moment Summer White took that deal? No chance. "It did not take any extra thought to leave that proposal on the table," she writes. "With my 4.0 in jeopardy, I bounced one thought around in my head: how many ways could I say no?" She concludes, "As for me, I will not budge; perhaps I will take a beating for it. Well then, it is my honor. . . . It is my prayer I do not only speak for myself when I say I prefer my grade to be in jeopardy over my faith."[17]

We need more Christian young people like this who know what they believe and why they believe it. But we won't get them by accident. They must be trained within our local churches. If pastors don't equip their Christians to think clearly on abortion and embryonic stem cell research, churchgoers will get the message that these things are okay. Unlike Summer White, they'll remain tongue-tied when they need to speak up. Worse still, they may get abortions or encourage others to do so. Either way, our collective Christian witness is badly damaged.

TASK #3: THE PRO-LIFE PASTOR RESTORES PASSION FOR MINISTRY THROUGH CROSS-CENTERED PREACHING

Millions of Christians have given up on a passionate pursuit of God-glorifying ministry because they feel disqualified by past sexual sins that may include abortion, fornication, pornography, etc. Ignoring these sins does not spare people guilt; it spares them healing. The starting point for human healing is the gospel of Jesus Christ.

The gospel teaches how a holy God designed a good world in which the humans he made to worship him and enjoy communion with him willfully rebelled against their Creator. Although these rebel humans deserved God's almighty wrath, he held back his righteous judgment and sent Jesus to take the punishment they deserved. By God's design, Jesus—the sinless one—was killed on a cross to atone for mankind's sin. Yet the story doesn't end there. Three days later, God affirmed Christ's sin-bearing sacrifice by raising him from the dead.[18]

[17]Summer White discusses her paper at the following links: http://vintage.aomin.org/Summer2.html and http://vintage.aomin.org/Summer1.html.
[18]I owe this concise summary in part to James Hamilton, "The Greatest Danger Facing the Church," http://jimhamilton.wordpress.com/2006/06/26/the-greatest-danger-facing-the-church.

As a result of Christ's sin-bearing work on their behalf, God's people are declared justified or righteous by God the Father, who then adopts them as his own sons and daughters. Who, then, can bring a charge against God's elect? Paul's answer is clear: No one can, for it is God who justifies the ungodly (Rom. 4:5; 8:33). It is his gift, completely undeserved, so that no one can boast (Eph. 2:8–9).

Like all sinners, post-abortion men and women need this gospel. With it, they live each day assured that God accepts them on the basis of Christ's righteousness, not their own. They experience unspeakable joy, knowing that their past, present, and future sins are not counted against them.

Tragically, the pastor who ignores abortion for fear of laying a guilt trip on people distorts the redemptive gospel he's sworn to preach. His silence on the issue does not spare post-abortion men and women guilt—it spares them healing. Unconfessed sin is keeping these wounded souls from full fellowship with their Savior. As Gregg Cunningham points out, the kindest thing a spiritual leader can do is help bring people out of denial and into confession so they can experience healing. Refusing to preach, teach, and counsel that abortion is a sin—however laudable the pastor's reasons for remaining silent—only complicates the recovery process. Indeed, the Scriptures are clear that confessing our sins brings healing, while covering them up only deepens our deception and guilt (1 John 1:8–9; Prov. 28:13).

Wise pastors avoid the twin extremes of heavy-handed (and graceless) preaching on one hand and ignoring sin on the other. Instead, they opt for a biblical third alternative. They preach, teach, and show that abortion is sinful, then point to the remedy—the cross of Christ.

TASK # 4: PRO-LIFE PASTORS CONFRONT THEIR FEARS

1) Fear of distraction. Pastors sometimes ask, "Won't addressing abortion distract the church from the gospel?" This is a legitimate concern. Our preaching must always direct sinful human beings to the righteousness that God alone provides. The good news is that we can use the topic of abortion to point people to the very gospel they so desperately need.

At the same time, we should remember that God's gospel is addressed to a particular audience, human beings. But our attempts to communicate that gospel suffer when the very definition of what it means to be human is up for grabs. Indeed, it's hard to preach that man is a sinner, that man needs to repent, and that man can be saved only through Christ when nobody knows what a man is anymore.

Teaching Christians to engage the ideas that determine culture is not a distraction from the gospel. Rather, it removes roadblocks to it. In hundreds of hours of conversation, I've found that abortion is an excellent bridge to discussing worldviews and the gospel. It brings up nearly every issue that matters to Christians such as: What is a human? What's wrong with us? Have we sinned? Where did we come from? Does God care? These questions are critically important because, as J. Gresham Machen points out, false ideas are at the root of unbelief:

> It is true that the decisive thing is the regenerative power of God. That can overcome all lack of preparation, and the absence of that makes even the best preparation useless. But as a matter of fact God usually exerts that power in connection with certain prior conditions of the human mind, and it should be ours to create, so far as we can, with the help of God, those favorable conditions for the reception of the gospel.
>
> False ideas are the greatest obstacles to the reception of the gospel. We may preach with all the fervor of a reformer and yet succeed only in winning a straggler here and there, if we permit the whole collective thought of the nation or of the world to be controlled by ideas which, by the resistless force of logic, prevent Christianity from being regarded as anything more than a harmless delusion.
>
> Under such circumstances, what God desires us to do is to destroy the obstacle at its root. . . . What is today a matter of academic speculation begins tomorrow to move armies and pull down empires. In that second stage, it has gone too far to be combated; the time to stop it was when it was still a matter of impassionate debate.
>
> So as Christians we should try to mould the thought of the world in such a way as to make the acceptance of Christianity something more than a logical absurdity. . . . What more pressing duty than for those who have received the mighty experience of regeneration, who, therefore, do not, like the world, neglect that whole series of vitally relevant facts which is embraced in Christian experience—what more pressing duty than for these men to make themselves masters of the thought of the world in order to make it an instrument of truth instead of error?[19]

In short, it's not either/or: We can preach the gospel *and* confront false ideas, including the one that says humans have no intrinsic value.

---

[19]J. Gresham Machen, "Christianity and Culture," *The Princeton Theological Review*, Vol. 11, 1913.

2) Fear of driving people away who might otherwise hear the gospel. Despite the mistaken notion that we are somehow responsible for saving souls with clever programs designed to sell non-Christians on church attendance (the Bible paints a different picture—it's God's gospel, and he draws those who are his), it's just plain false that addressing abortion responsibly drives people away. My own speaking experience confirms this.

In 2005, Campus Crusade students and staff at West Virginia University aggressively promoted my talk "The Case for Life." Instead of driving people away, the talk drew four hundred students, including many non-Christians. (By the way, Crusade's promotional efforts were brilliant—the staff made sure that students got university credit for attending the talk!) After presenting my case for the pro-life view, I concluded by saying something like this:

> Tonight you've heard a rational defense of the pro-life view. True, I did not hit you with Bible verses, but make no mistake: I believe that the pro-life position squares nicely with a Christian worldview. And I think that worldview is true and reasonable to believe. I'm not going to give an altar call tonight. Quite frankly, I've not given you enough information to fully consider the claims of Christ, though CC staff members are standing by to help you with any questions you might have. My goal tonight is really quite modest. I want you to examine just one question: If the Christian worldview on abortion is true and reasonable to believe, shouldn't we at least explore what that worldview has to say on other important matters like the death and resurrection of Jesus Christ and his claim to be the only way to salvation? Biblical faith is not belief in spite of evidence; it's belief based on evidence, as the writer of Hebrews explains. Hopefully I've shown tonight that Christian belief is relevant to at least one key issue we face today. If you'll take a closer look, I think you'll see that it's relevant to a whole lot more.

There was no jeering, no hissing, and no angry confrontations, just good questions after the meeting officially ended.

None of this surprises me. In fact, Christian leaders have it all wrong. Pro-life presentations, properly presented, don't drive people from considering the gospel. Rather, they suggest to nonbelievers that maybe, just maybe, the Christian worldview has something relevant to say to the major questions of our day. And any worldview that can make sense of those questions is worth a second look.

Here's one more example. When I gave a pro-life presentation at the University of North Carolina Law School, a young female professor responded (in front of her students), "I did not come to this event with the same pro-life views you hold. In fact, I came here today expecting an emotionally charged religious presentation. Instead, you gave one of the most compelling arguments I have ever heard. Thank you."

True, she didn't fall on her knees and confess Christ on the spot. But now she's begun wrestling with biblical truth. To use a baseball example, you don't have to hit a home run with every conversation. Sometimes just getting on base is enough. And you'll certainly do just that whenever you clarify the moral logic of the pro-life view.

3) *Fear of offending people with abortion-related content.* The challenge for the local pastor almost always comes down to this: Do I trust God to protect his ministry through me when I preach inconvenient truth?

It's amazing how people will tolerate a strong pro-life presentation if you make your case graciously and incisively. Kindness goes a long way and often pays off with changed lives. Consider this e-mail from fifteen-year-old Brittany, received after I spoke to an assembly of a thousand high school students in Baltimore:

> Dear Scott,
>
> Yesterday you came and talked to my high school, Archbishop Spaulding, about pro-life. It made a big difference on how I thought about abortion. I was totally for abortion and I thought that pro-life was just plain stupid.
>
> I have totally changed my mind after I listened to the pro-life point of view. Upon watching the short video clip of aborted fetuses, I felt my stomach turn and I thought, "How could anybody do this? How could anyone be so cruel and self absorbed as to kill an unborn baby who doesn't have a say in that decision?"
>
> Then I thought, "Oh my gosh, I think that!" I was totally ashamed at how selfish I had been. Before the assembly, I didn't want to listen to what you had to say. I was going to nap during your speech . . . until I saw that video. Now, I am totally changed forever. Keep doing what you do!

In conclusion, as a pro-life pastor in the twenty-first century, determine to preach truth and equip your church family to engage the culture with a robust but graciously communicated, biblical worldview. Always stress grace. Give hope to those wounded by abortion. Ask God to fill your heart for lost and hurting souls. Then speak and show the truth in love. They can take it.

REVIEW QUESTIONS

1. List at least four cultural challenges to the biblical view of human value.
2. What are the four tasks of the pro-life pastor?
3. How does Michael Kinsley's view on human life differ from the biblical one?
4. In reply to Mr. Kinsley, what points should pastors make from the pulpit?
5. Why is ignoring the sin of abortion harmful to those people who have participated in it?
6. Some pastors fear that preaching on abortion will distract the church from its true mission. Why is this not so?
7. What's wrong with the claim that talking about abortion will drive people away from hearing the gospel?
8. How do well-crafted pro-life presentations help establish the biblical world-view as true?

HELPFUL RESOURCES

Randy Alcorn. *Why Pro-Life?* Sisters, OR: Multnomah, 2004.

Jerry Bridges. *The Gospel for Real Life*. Colorado Springs: NavPress, 2002.

C. J. Mahaney. *Living the Cross-Centered Life: Keeping the Gospel the Main Thing.* Sisters, OR: Multnomah, 2006.

John Piper. *Brothers, We Are Not Professionals: A Plea to Pastors for Radical Ministry.* Nashville: Broadman & Holman, 2002.

17

HEALED AND EQUIPPED: HOPE FOR POST-ABORTION MEN AND WOMEN

If you've had an abortion, you don't need an excuse. You need an exchange—his righteousness for your sinfulness.

HER TEARS FLOWED LIKE A RIVER. "Scott, you have no idea what I've done. No matter how many times I tell God I'm sorry, I still feel guilty. What hope is there for me?"

I'm going to share with you what I share with all post-abortion women and men. It's not original with me, but if you've experienced abortion and seek resolution, it's the best news in the whole world.

In a sentence, Jesus wants to exchange something with you. In return, you'll receive something infinitely precious.

If that interests you, read on.

As mentioned in the last chapter, the starting point for human healing is the gospel. What is the gospel? John Piper summarizes it this way: "The Gospel is the news that Jesus Christ, the Righteous One, died for our sins and rose again, eternally triumphant over all his enemies, so that there is no condemnation for those who believe, but only everlasting joy."[1] It's stated succinctly in 1 Thessalonians 5:9–10—"For God has not destined us for wrath, but to obtain salvation through our Lord Jesus Christ, who died for us so that whether we are awake or asleep we might live with him."

That's the gospel. It's the best news ever. And you'll never outgrow your need for it.

---

[1]John Piper, "The Gospel in Six Minutes," video clip available from www.desiringgod.org; transcript at http://www.desiringgod.org/ResourceLibrary/Articles/ByDate/2007/2389_The_Gospel_in_6_Minutes.

But it can't be had on the cheap. As James R. White points out, "God's love shines with its full and proper glory only when it is seen in its biblical context—against the backdrop of God's holiness and hatred of sin."[2]

THE BAD NEWS . . . WE'RE ALL SINNERS

Man's problem is that God's holy and righteous character cannot wink at sin. He must punish it. Our sin, no matter how small, is an assault on his infinite majesty. Though we don't like to talk about it, human beings are in big trouble with God. The Bible is clear: "None is righteous, no, not one. . . . All have sinned and fall short of the glory of God" (Rom. 3:10, 23).

But the bad news is even worse than we first imagined. The problem is not only that we *do* bad things, but that we *are* bad by nature. Left to ourselves, we are rebellious, disobedient, and hardened against God. Worse still, we are powerless to fix things. Paul tells us that, like the rest of humankind, we're dead in our sins and are objects of God's wrath (Eph. 2:3). We don't seek him, and we don't want to seek him. God's judgment is coming. We're getting exactly what we deserve.

BUT WAIT—THERE'S GOOD NEWS

After leaving no doubt about man's true condition, Paul sets forth the remedy. The only hope for sinful man is "the righteousness of God through faith in Jesus Christ" (Rom. 3:22). Though we were dead in our transgressions and sins and deserved his wrath, God did what we could not do for ourselves—he made us alive in Christ. In Romans 5 Paul writes, "while we were still weak, at the right time Christ died for the ungodly." As a result, we're saved from the wrath we justly deserve (vv. 6, 9). God, the rightful judge of all, now accepts us on the basis of Christ's righteousness, not our own.

That's great news for those who repent, but it's not the message most people want to hear. The secular culture considers it a sin to tell people, "You are wrong. What you believe is wrong. Turn to the only one who can save you." And yet there's no fix for our guilt until, through a miracle of grace, we renounce all hope of justifying ourselves.

"There is salvation in no one else" but only in Jesus (Acts 4:12). All other options, including our attempts to please God through good works, leave us dead in our sins.

---

[2]James R. White, *The God Who Justifies* (Minneapolis: Bethany, 2001), 46.

NOT BY OUR OWN DEEDS

A gifted friend and colleague responsible for saving many unborn lives once explained his motivation for pro-life activism this way (paraphrase): "Jesus gave a very clear answer when asked by the rich young ruler, 'What must I do to inherit eternal life?' Jesus told him to obey the Commandments—don't murder, love the Lord your God and love your neighbor, care for the defenseless, and so on. Jesus then says in the Sermon on the Mount that 'everyone who hears these words and does them' will be saved in the day of destruction. I'm doing my very best to make the grade."

By that standard my friend doesn't stand a chance. Yes, Jesus did point the rich young ruler to the Ten Commandments, but he did so to expose the young man's utter inability to keep them. The same is true of the Sermon on the Mount (Matthew 5–7). No one can live up to the demands that Christ presents there. Am I pure in heart? Do I hunger and thirst after righteousness? Show mercy when I ought? Love my enemies? There's no wiggle room here. To please God in these matters, my righteousness must exceed that of the scribes and Pharisees. It must be perfect.

The problem is, if you're anything like me, you're nowhere close. Look how tough Christ is on us (paraphrase): "Think you're free of adultery? Guess again. Every time you lust after a woman, you commit adultery in your heart. Think you don't murder? Each time you are angry with your brother, you kill in your heart." Couple that with Paul's teaching in Romans 3:10 that "none is righteous, no, not one," and you start to get the picture of how desperate our situation truly is. On our own, there really is nothing we can do to escape the righteous wrath of almighty God. Someone else has to take the rap for us and provide the righteousness we don't have.

Thankfully, someone did. The righteousness that God demands is the righteousness that he alone provides through Jesus Christ. Paul is clear: It is God who justifies the ungodly (Romans 4:5; 8:30, 33), and he both initiates and completes the salvation of his people. The work is totally his. No wonder Paul writes that "no man may boast," for it's by grace we've been saved through faith (Ephesians 2:8–9).

Here's where my friend has it backwards: I don't engage in good deeds to *earn* God's favor. I do good deeds because I *have* God's favor. But I have it because Jesus bore the punishment for my sin so I wouldn't have to. There's no way my good deeds will ever make up for my bad ones. The only thing that removes my judicial guilt before God is the righteousness of Christ applied to my account. With that in mind, I approach Christian service not from a sense of guilt but of gratitude. I'm doing a whole lot better than I deserve thanks to the sin-bearing work of Christ on my behalf.

JUSTIFICATION: HOW CAN I GET RIGHT WITH GOD?

Biblically speaking, justification is a legal declaration by God the Father whereby my sins are pardoned and Christ's righteousness is applied to my account. Justified sinners are not made righteous with an infusion of holiness; they're declared righteous solely because of the sin-bearing work of Christ. Justification is about my status before God: I am no longer con-demned because Jesus both paid the penalty for sin in my place and lived the life of perfect obedience that God requires. Put differently, justification is a matter of imputation: My guilt is imputed to Christ; His righteousness is imputed to me.

Who, then, can bring a charge against God's elect? The apostle Paul's answer is clear: No one. For it is God who justifies. It is His gift, completely undeserved, so that no one can boast.

"BUT YOU HAVE NO IDEA WHAT I'VE DONE"

We can't add to our justification. It's already a finished work. Confusion about this leads to spiritual depression and, in some cases, years of emotional pain.

Martin Luther's legendary dunghill example as explained by James R. White answers the question decisively not only for post-abortion women and men but for all Christians. (I say legendary because we are not sure where or whether Luther used it.) In fifteenth-century Europe, farmers, needing a way to fertilize their fields, would pile up refuse from their farm animals. These dunghills dotted the landscape, leaving a stench that was anything but pleas-ant. Luther allegedly used this commonplace example to demonstrate the difference between justification and sanctification. According to the illustra-tion, our sinful state is like a dunghill—ugly and offensive, having nothing in itself that would commend it to anyone, let alone God. Justification is like the first snowfall of winter that covers everything, including the dunghill, in a blanket of pure white. The smell is gone. The repulsive sight is gone. The dunghill is still intrinsically a dunghill, but now it's covered.[3]

---

[3]Ibid., 119–123.

Likewise, in justification we receive the pure and spotless righteousness of Christ, a blanket that covers our sin in the sight of the Father. We're declared righteous solely because Jesus bore the penalty for sin in our place. However, we remain sinners inwardly.

Meanwhile, sanctification (also God's work) is an ongoing process that changes us internally, conforming us more and more to the image of Christ. Our behavior and thought patterns improve. Vices are replaced with virtues. Habitual sins are confronted and challenged. But moral improvement is not what makes us right before God. What removes our judicial guilt is the legal declaration of God the Father that our sins are no longer counted against us.

What incredibly great news! No longer are we God's enemies—we are now his own adopted and dearly loved children.

My message to that hurting post-abortion woman was simple: You don't need an *excuse*; you need an *exchange*—your sinfulness for Christ's righteousness. The Bible speaks of this exchange in 2 Corinthians 5:21: "For our sake he made him to be sin who knew no sin, so that in him we might become the righteousness of God."

"Take heart," I told her, "if you're in Christ, the penalty for your past, present, and future sin has already been paid. God accepts you because you are clothed in the perfect righteousness of his Son."

If that does not make us want to shout for joy, no matter how bad our past and present difficulties, I'm afraid nothing will!

Permit me one final example from Gregory Koukl:

The story is told of a king who, having discovered a theft in the royal treasury, decrees that the criminal be publicly flogged for this affront to the crown. When soldiers haul the thief before the king as he sits in his judgment seat, there in chains stands the frail form of the king's own mother. Without flinching, he orders the old woman to be bound to the whipping post in front of him. When she is secured, he stands up, lays down his imperial scepter, sets aside his jeweled crown, removes his royal robes, and enfolds the tiny old woman with his own body. Baring his back to the whip, he orders that the punishment commence. Every blow meant for the criminal lands with full force upon the bare back of the king until the last lash falls.

In like manner, in those dark hours the Father wrapped us in His Son who shields us, taking the justice we deserve. This is not an accident. It was planned. The prophet Isaiah described it 700 years earlier: 'Surely our griefs He Himself bore. . . . He was pierced through for our transgressions. He was crushed for our iniquities. The chastening for our well-being fell upon Him, and by His scourging we are healed. All of us like sheep have gone astray. Each of us has turned to his own way. But the Lord has caused the iniquity of us all to fall on Him.'"[4]

Greg is right. Only Jesus can pay, and he does pay. He has completed the transaction. He has canceled the debt. It is finished. It only remains for us to trust in his promise.

That's the great exchange: your sin for his righteousness.

WHAT NOW?

If you've sinned by participating in an abortion-related decision, the solution to your guilt is not denial—it's forgiveness. Like all sinful human beings who desire reconciliation with God, your place is at the foot of the cross.

Here's how to get started.

First, stop making excuses. If you are a woman who conceded to have an elective abortion, stop blaming your boyfriend, ex-boyfriend, or husband. If you are that boyfriend, ex-boyfriend, or husband, stop blaming the woman you impregnated. Step up and admit that you took a human life and that you did so without justification. You feel guilty because you are guilty.

Second, resist the temptation to solve your guilt problem with "good" behavior. The truth is, your good deeds will never make up for your bad ones. You can't fix what's wrong, and you must give up all hope of ever fixing it on your own. There's only one solution: You need a substitute who can pay your sin debt and fulfill the demands of God's holy law. Thankfully, Jesus did both so that you could be completely forgiven and restored. True, once you experience forgiveness, you'll want to serve God with good works, even though you will fail to live out your convictions in many ways. However, your motivation for doing good deeds will be a heart of thanksgiving for what God has already accomplished, not a feeble attempt to impress him with your own good stuff (which, in light of your own sinfulness, isn't very good at all).

Third, place your trust completely in the only substitute who can save you—Jesus, the sinless one, who paid your debt in full. Biblical faith is not a blind leap in the dark. It's trust based on evidence. Ask God to forgive

---

[4]Gregory Koukl, "No Other Man Did This," http://www.str.org/site/News2?page=NewsArticle&id=6804& printer_friendly=1.

your rebellion and give you a new heart to love and cherish Christ above all. Seek out other Christians who've also been forgiven, and draw strength from them. Yes, that means joining a church.

Finally, establish a firm foundation for your Christian life. Learn the basics of Christian doctrine and thought. Consider reading C. J. Mahaney's *Living the Cross Centered Life* and Jerry Bridges's important book *The Gospel for Real Life*. Both will help you learn the foundation upon which your new faith is built.

John Newton, author of the hymn "Amazing Grace," was a slave trader before Christ found him. He later said, "Two things I know. I am a great sinner, and Christ is a great Savior."

I suggest you follow Newton's example. Each day look yourself in the mirror and admit that you're the worst sinner you know. Then, in your very next breath, triumphantly declare, "But Christ came to save sinners."

In other words, your sin's been exchanged.

REVIEW QUESTIONS

1. Summarize the gospel in a single sentence.
2. Before the good news of the gospel can be fully appreciated, what must we understand about God's holiness and our sinfulness?
3. Why is the bad news of our sinful condition even worse than we first imagine?
4. What is the only hope Paul sets forth for sinful humans?
5. How does God's law as explained by Jesus in the Sermon on the Mount destroy all hope of justifying ourselves?
6. Why is there no room for us to boast (Eph. 2:8–9)?
7. What is justification? How does it relate to our legal status before God?
8. How does sanctification differ from justification? How are they similar?
9. What is the great exchange Paul speaks of in 2 Corinthians 5:21?
10. On what basis does God accept us, sinful though we are?

HELPFUL RESOURCES

C. J. Mahaney. *Living the Cross-Centered Life: Keeping the Gospel the Main Thing.* Sisters, OR: Multnomah, 2006.

Jerry Bridges. *The Gospel for Real Life.* Colorado Springs: NavPress, 2003.

———— and Bob Bevington. *The Great Exchange: My Sins for His Righteousness.* Wheaton, IL: Crossway Books, 2007.

D. Martyn Lloyd-Jones. *Spiritual Depression: Its Causes and Its Cures.* Grand Rapids, MI: Eerdmans, 1965.

William Backus and Marie Chapian. *Telling Yourself the Truth.* Minneapolis: Bethany House, 2000.

18

HERE WE STAND: CO-BELLIGERENCE WITHOUT THEOLOGICAL COMPROMISE

Evangelicals are not forsaking their theological distinctives when they work with Catholics, Jews, Muslims, and atheists to stop abortion.

EVANGELICAL CHRISTIANS committed to sound doctrine must distinguish themselves theologically from people who reject fundamental truths of the Protestant Reformation.[1] Those truths must never be discarded so as to achieve a greater unity with non-evangelicals.

That raises an important question: Do evangelicals forsake their core beliefs when they unite with Catholics, Jews, and other religious groups to address cultural issues?

Let me begin with an observation. Cultural reform efforts are not primarily about religious doctrine but social justice. To work, they must be broad and inclusive. For example, cultural reform efforts that were designed to abolish slavery and establish civil rights for all Americans were led by large ecumenical coalitions. These coalitions, despite their theological differences, committed themselves to a common goal: establishing a more just society. The same is true of the current struggle to abolish abortion. Although we must reject religious pluralism (the belief that all religions are equally valid), we should work alongside those who oppose the destruction of innocent human life, regardless of their religious persuasions.

Not all evangelicals agree with this view, however. Steve Camp, a gifted

---

[1] I first published portions of this chapter in the "Viewpoint" column of the *Christian Research Journal*, Vol. 29, No. 3 (2006). For further information or to subscribe to the *Christian Research Journal* go to www.equip.org.

Christian musician who gets high marks for the substantial theological content of his songs, thinks evangelicals who work with non-evangelicals to reform culture are guilty of co-belligerence and that this behavior compromises the Great Commission. "There can be no real 'cultural impact' apart from the transforming power of the gospel of Jesus Christ the Lord," argues Camp on his website.[2] Christians, therefore, should focus on preaching the gospel, not on cultural reform:

> Evangelical Co-Belligerence is culturally impotent in dealing with the depraved hearts, minds and souls of a pagan world. Satan is pleased when any discourse designed for Christ and His gospel is turned into a political rally to pacify unsaved people in their sin while at the same time creating a superficial morality that is not based upon the salvific work of Christ alone! The tragic result is unredeemed people are left to feel comfortable and safe in a "Christian morality"—yet, they are still lost, still dead in their sins.[3]

This view, though common, does not stand up to scrutiny. First, it does not follow that because cultural reformers cannot make a culture blameless before God, we shouldn't try to make it better for the weak and oppressed. I do not know of a single pro-life leader who argues that cultural reform can save souls eternally; only the gospel does that. However, the fact that cultural reform cannot get a man to heaven does not mean that it cannot (in many cases through political means) save him from injustice here on earth. In short, pro-life advocates like me do not work for change in culture to save the world from spiritual death but to save the most vulnerable members of the human family, the unborn, from physical death.

Second, the goal of cultural reform is not necessarily to change the hearts of individuals but to restrain their evil acts. Martin Luther King Jr. put it well: "It may be true that the law cannot make a man love me but it can keep him from lynching me, and I think that's pretty important." King's overall point is worth seeing in context:

> Now the other myth that gets around is the idea that legislation cannot really solve the problem and that it has no great role to play in this period of social change because you've got to change the heart and you can't

---

[2]Steve Camp, "Are We Playing Politics with God?"; http://www.a1m.org/page.php?page=template1.php&pageid=f7b69a48e099e9e5825c44bda6624425.
[3]Ibid.

change the heart through legislation. You can't legislate morals. The job must be done through education and religion. Well, there's half-truth involved here. Certainly, if the problem is to be solved then in the final sense, hearts must be changed. Religion and education must play a great role in changing the heart. But we must go on to say that while it may be true that morality cannot be legislated, behavior can be regulated. It may be true that the law cannot change the heart but it can restrain the heartless. It may be true that the law cannot make a man love me but it can keep him from lynching me and I think that is pretty important, also. So there is a need for executive orders. There is a need for judicial decrees. There is a need for civil rights legislation on the local scale within states and on the national scale from the federal government.[4]

According to Scripture, the purpose of government is not to save people eternally but to restrain evil acts (Romans 13:1–4). The primary purpose of the church, meanwhile, is to preach the gospel of Christ. However, if Christians do not also challenge government to fulfill its duty to protect the weak and defenseless, who will?

Third, the notion that "there can be no real cultural impact apart from the transforming power of the gospel of Jesus Christ" sounds good, but it's simply incorrect. The moral evil of American slavery did not end because of mass conversions to Christ. It ended when believers and nonbelievers joined forces to stand against it and paid for it with the lives of 360,000 Union soldiers. Was the abolition of slavery not "real" cultural improvement? True, it did not make those who participated right with God, but it did take the whips off the backs of oppressed people. That is moral and cultural improvement by any reasonable standard.

Fourth, why should anyone suppose that it's wrong for evangelicals to mobilize other than for preaching the gospel? If a group of Christian doctors fails to rid a Third-World country of AIDS or malnutrition, does that mean they wasted their time and should have devoted themselves to preaching or evangelizing? Christian pro-life activists are no more selling out their faith than are Christian doctors who devote their lives to treating the sick. It's also permissible for Christians to mobilize with non-Christians to promote social justice. Prior to the Civil War, Protestant clergy worked with non-Christians organizing the Underground Railroad to free black slaves. Later Dr. King's followers marched directly from the church to the streets where

---

[4]Taken from Martin Luther King Jr.'s address at Western Michigan University, December 18, 1963; http://www.wmich.edu/library/archives/mlk/transcription.html.

they joined nonbelievers eager to promote racial equality. Were both these examples ill-advised attempts to usher in a false sense of Christian morality? Anyone who thinks that God's people are wasting their time pursuing social justice may want to take a look at how important it is to God (Ps. 94:1–23; Prov. 24:1–12; Isa. 1:16–17, 21–23; 58:6–7; 61:8; Jer. 5:26–28; 9:24; Matt. 25:41–46).

Fifth, why should anyone suppose that pro-life advocacy detracts from the biblical command to go and make disciples? Simply put, the answer to a lack of evangelical fervor for the gospel is not to withdraw our political advocacy for the weak and vulnerable but to encourage Christians to do a better job of presenting the gospel. We don't have to stop rescuing the innocent to do that.

Pro-life advocacy, in fact, often serves an important evangelistic function because it reawakens people's moral intuitions. A skilled Christian apologist knows how to use this for the sake of the gospel. For example, once a man next to me on a plane concedes that right and wrong on these issues are real things and not just matters of personal taste, he's now ready for me to ask, "So where do these moral rules come from?" They can't just exist in a vacuum. If objective morals exist, so does an objective moral lawgiver. At this point I'm ready to ask, "Have you ever committed moral crimes? And do you think that people who commit moral crimes deserve to be punished?"[5] Now we're at the threshold of the gospel. I may not persuade my conversation partner to convert on the spot, but I likely will get him to think about his moral culpability within the context of a Christian worldview. Pro-life advocacy also awakens Christians to care more about evangelism generally. The students at Focus on the Family Institute are proof. Each semester they're taught apologetics, after which they participate in a pro-life outreach on a secular college campus. When surveyed after the event, the Focus on the Family students overwhelmingly say their pro-life training inspired them to evangelize more, not less.

But even when in select cases pro-life Christians focus primarily on saving lives and work with nonbelievers to do it, they do nothing wrong. The fire department, for example, is not "distracted" when it spends time putting out fires rather than preaching the gospel. The purpose of the fire department is not theology but rescue. Its job is to save lives. The same is

---

[5] I got these questions from Gregory Koukl, "Am I Going to Hell?"; http://www.str.org/site/News2? page=NewsArticle&id=5098.

true of the pro-life movement. Its primary goal is not to save souls, though Christian pro-lifers rejoice whenever that happens. Its mission is to protect lives from immediate physical danger. When houses are burning, we put out the fire. We form bucket brigades of concerned Christians, Jews, Muslims, and atheists. We don't need a theological litmus test to do that. We take all the help we can get.

Sixth, the claim that cultural reform efforts hinder the gospel because they leave unredeemed people feeling "safe" (falsely) in "superficial Christian morality" is misguided. Are we to conclude that God's ability to save his elect goes up when cultural morality goes down? That is counterintuitive and hardly consistent with a proper view of God's sovereignty. The fact that a person thinks he is moral (as Saul of Tarsus once did) in no way limits God's ability to save him. Most sinners think they are good prior to God granting them the gift of repentance. Following the critics' logic, if an increase in cultural morality means fewer souls make it to heaven, shouldn't Christians pray for evil to abound that more may be saved (cf. Rom. 3:8; 6:1–2)?

I'm often told that getting people to realize that certain acts are wrong only treats the symptom; it may well coerce them into living a more moral life, but without Christ, it will only serve to deaden their sense that they are sinners requiring forgiveness. Using this same logic, one could argue that doctors who cure people of cancer are only treating a symptom and, in reality, are giving unsaved patients a false sense of security about their eternal states. One also could argue that evangelical leaders in the Sudan are wrong to partner with Catholics and Jews in reforming a militant Islamic culture (one bent on butchering its wives and children) because their co-belligerence only creates a superficial morality, one that leaves unregenerate men dead in their sins.

Gregory Koukl writes, "When someone tells me that laws can never change a fallen person's heart, I ask them if they apply that philosophy to their children. Does the moral training of our children consist merely of preaching the Gospel to them? Wouldn't we consider it unconscionable to neglect a child's moral instruction with the excuse that laws can never change a child's rebellious heart?"[6]

Seventh, why shouldn't evangelicals work with Catholics or non-evangelicals against abortion? Gregg Cunningham of the Center for Bio-Ethical Reform affirms that many Christians are inconsistent on this point. For

---

[6]Gregory Koukl, "No Hint of Politics," http://www.str.org/site/News2?page=NewsArticle&id=6876.

example, if a critic of evangelical co-belligerence had a two-year-old daughter who stumbled into a swimming pool and needed immediate medical attention, he would gladly work with Catholic paramedics to save her life. If she were injured and needed surgery, it wouldn't matter for a moment if the best surgeon were a Catholic operating out of a Catholic hospital. If the critic of co-belligerence will work with Catholics to save his own child, what's wrong with working with them to save somebody else's (unborn) child?

Gregg Cunningham writes, "The Good Samaritan did not preach salvation to the beating victim, he risked his own life to save a fellow traveler. Jesus used this example to illustrate our duty to love our neighbor. It is cold comfort to a dead baby that we allowed him to die to avoid working with Catholics."[7]

Finally, critics of co-belligerence need to substantiate their claim that evangelicals are spending too much time on cultural reform. What is their evidence for this? Can they list even ten churches in the United States with a thousand members or more who systematically train their members to persuasively defend a biblical worldview on pro-life issues? If not, perhaps we need to spend more time on cultural reform, not less.

REVIEW QUESTIONS

1. How do cultural reform movements differ from theological ones?

2. In order for cultural or social reform movements to work, what must be true of them?

3. How does the purpose of government differ from that of the church?

4. Some Christians say that changing the culture won't save souls. What's wrong with this claim? How does it distort the true purpose of pro-life efforts to reform culture?

5. Why is the claim "there can be no real cultural impact apart from the transforming power of the gospel of Jesus Christ" mistaken? What historical examples refute it?

6. In what way does pro-life advocacy serve an important evangelistic function?

7. What's wrong with the claim that cultural reform efforts hinder the gospel because they leave unredeemed people feeling "safe" (falsely) in "superficial Christian morality"?

8. In what ways are evangelicals who refuse to work with Catholics on pro-life issues inconsistent?

---

[7]Gregg Cunningham, personal correspondence with author, May 2001.

HELPFUL RESOURCES

Joe Carter. "A Herd of Unicorns: The Myth of Evangelical Political Engagement." *Evangelical Outpost,* May 1, 2008; http://www.evangelicaloutpost.com/archives/ 2008/05/a-herd-of-unico.html.

John Frame. "In Defense of Christian Activism"; http://www.frame-poythress.org/ frame_articles/2006InDefense.html.

Martin Luther King Jr. "Letter from the Birmingham Jail"; http://www.Stanford. edu/group/King/frequentdocs/birmingham.pdf.

Gregory Koukl. "No Hint of Politics." *Solid Ground,* November-December 2004; http://www.str.org/free/solid-ground/SG0411.htm.

Albert Mohler. "Standing Together, Standing Apart: Cultural Co-belligerence without Theological Compromise." *Touchstone,* July-August 2003; http://www.touchstonemag.com/archives/article.php?id=16-06-070-f.

19

CAN WE WIN? HOW PRO-LIFE CHRISTIANS ARE MAKING AN EXTRAORDINARY IMPACT

Yes, if pro-life Christians equip themselves to engage.

DURING A MINISTRY SYMPOSIUM IN 1984, I heard a Christian historian say he thought the Berlin Wall would come down in ten years.

I nearly laughed out loud. As it turns out, he was wrong. It came down in five years.

Despite the bleak picture I've sketched in some parts of this book, I'm convinced that our cause is not nearly so bleak when our message is clearly communicated. Though I don't think we're in for a quick fix, it's apparent that pro-lifers are making an impact right now.

During the last decade, leading philosophers like Leon Kass, Francis J. Beckwith, Robert P. George, Christopher Tollefsen, Patrick Lee, Hadley Arkes, Scott Rae, and J. P. Moreland (to name only a few) have published comprehensive defenses of the pro-life view.[1] Topics include detailed philosophical discussions of natural rights, the substance view of human persons, the proper role of science, and the relationship between law and morals. At the popular level, Stand to Reason has published training material designed to equip pro-lifers for effective service, while Ramesh Ponnuru and Wesley J. Smith have educated readers about the disregard for human life in the

---

[1]Titles include Leon Kass, *Life, Liberty and the Defense of Dignity: The Challenge for Bioethics* (San Francisco: Encounter Books, 2002); Francis J. Beckwith, *Defending Life: A Moral and Legal Case Against Abortion Choice* (New York: Cambridge University Press, 2007); Robert P. George and Christopher Tollefsen, *Embryo: A Defense of Human Life* (New York: Doubleday, 2008); Patrick Lee, *Abortion and Unborn Human Life* (Washington, DC: Catholic University Press in America, 1996); Hadley Arkes, *Natural Rights and the Right to Choose* (New York: Cambridge University Press, 2002); J. P. Moreland and Scott Rae, *Body and Soul: Human Nature and the Crisis in Ethics* (Downers Grove, IL: InterVarsity Press, 2000).

courts, big bio-tech, and the media.[2] Local pro-life advocates are using what's been written to engage friends and critics in thoughtful discourse.

Jon A. Shields, assistant professor of government at Claremont McKenna College, argues that conservative pro-life advocates increasingly deploy "sophisticated philosophical arguments" in their efforts to convince Americans that embryonic stem cell research and abortion are wrong.

Shields's main theme is the intellectual maturation of the pro-life movement and the mental stagnation of the abortion-choice one. "The burden for pro-choice advocates . . . is to demonstrate that the change a human undergoes as she develops from a fetus to a newborn [is] so different from all future developments that it alters her ontological status entirely. They must also show that the value of a human being depends on the characteristics that he or she acquires rather than on the kind of thing that it is."[3]

This is a serious problem for abortion-choice advocates. Rosamund Rhodes, director of bioethics at Mt. Sinai School of Medicine and a supporter of legal abortion, says her side must explain "how or why the fetus is transformed into a franchised 'person' by moving from inside the womb to outside or by reaching a certain level of development."[4]

Meanwhile, pro-life organizations are making an impact with those most at risk for abortion—students ages thirteen to twenty-four. Life Training Institute presents compelling pro-life content at Catholic and Protestant high schools nationwide while engaging in debates with leading abortion-choice advocates at secular universities. Students for Life of America has seen attendance at its annual conference swell to 875 in 2008, up from barely a hundred five years earlier. The group now has four hundred plus chapters. On the Web, Abort73.com gets one hundred thousand visitors a month viewing abortion pictures and written defenses of the pro-life position. At universities across the United States and Canada, pro-life students are getting big-time help from Justice for All and The Center for Bio-Ethical Reform, each of which uses large, professionally designed exhib-

---

[2]See Stand to Reason's *Making Abortion Unthinkable: The Art of Pro-Life Persuasion* by Greg Koukl and Scott Klusendorf. Order at www.str.org. Also see Ramesh Ponnuru, *The Party of Death: The Democrats, the Media, the Courts, and the Disregard for Human Life* (Washington, DC: Regnery, 2006) and Wesley J. Smith, *The Consumer's Guide to a Brave New World* (San Francisco: Encounter Books, 2004).
[3]Jon A. Shields, "Bioethical Politics," *Society*, March/April 2006. Cited in Albert Mohler, "Who's Afraid of an Argument? The Insecurities of the Abortion Rights Movement," http://www.albertmohler.com/commentary_read.php?cdate=2006-02-20.
[4]Cited in Shields, ibid.

its to graphically depict abortion. Whenever these exhibits go up, abortion becomes the talk of the school.

Shields observed one such exhibit at the University of Colorado at Denver and noted how Justice for All staffers graciously communicated their pro-life views with reasoned arguments, eventually engaging many students in conversation about abortion and the meaning of human life. Although rank-and-file students observing the exhibit often reciprocated the kindness of the pro-life staffers, the abortion-choice counter-demonstrators responded with profane chants and insults. One counter-demonstrator screamed at the pro-lifers, then walked away without giving them a chance to respond. Shields sees a pattern here, as many abortion-choice activists, especially on campus, seem "unwilling or unprepared" to confront the growing philosophical sophistication of pro-life advocates:

> On college campuses across the country . . . pro-choice student groups refuse to debate their opponents despite the persistent efforts of pro-life students. As one student from the University of Albany put it when I asked him about the reluctance of pro-choice students to discuss abortion, "we have to beg them." Such frustration is fueled by NARAL and Planned Parenthood where élites discourage their campus affiliates from debating or even talking to pro-life students.[5]

According to Shields, the secular left prefers to undermine discussions on vital bioethical questions "such as when a human organism deserves state protection—by depicting them as fundamentally religious and therefore beyond legitimate public debate."[6]

To be clear, not all defenders of elective abortion play hit and run with pro-lifers. Thoughtful critics of the pro-life view exist, and though I disagree with their conclusions, they make interesting contributions to the national debate.[7] But they aren't always easy to find.

Shields's analysis is a devastating critique of abortion-choice activists. He makes the case that they're not just stagnated but closed-minded. When they increasingly refuse to debate, it's prime evidence they're in a defensive posture. Pro-life advocates are making progress because we have a case to make; many of our critics have given theirs up.

---

[5]Ibid.
[6]Ibid.
[7]See, for example, David Boonin, *A Defense of Abortion* (New York: Cambridge University Press, 2003).

THREE IMPORTANT GOALS

I do not pretend to have a sufficient strategy for winning the abortion battle. Strategies come and go, and most are discarded before the ink is dry. But I do believe there are some necessary steps we must take if we are going to win. Here are three that we can begin implementing right now.

RECRUIT MORE FULL-TIME PRO-LIFE APOLOGISTS

Gregg Cunningham once said, "There are more people working full-time to kill babies than there are working full-time to save them. That's because killing babies is very profitable while saving them is very costly. So costly, that large numbers of Americans who say they oppose abortion are not lifting a finger to stop it. And those that do lift a finger to stop it do just enough to salve the conscience but not enough to stop the killing."[8]

That's a stunning indictment of our movement, and it's easy to think, "That's not me." But like it or not, I can't dispute Gregg's point. We simply don't have enough full-time pro-life workers, and unless we get serious about finding them, our movement will remain a part-time volunteer movement incapable of taking on the heavily funded professionals from Planned Parenthood, the ACLU, large parts of the Democratic Party (and some Republicans too), and other groups who are paid handsomely to defend killing babies. Churches have no problem recruiting missionaries for overseas adventures, and that's a good thing. Why not also recruit young people from our churches to study law and seek political office while others are encouraged to seek careers in pro-life apologetics. (Biola University and Trinity International University provide graduate-level training in Christian apologetics and bioethics.)

Anyone who thinks we'll never find qualified young people is mistaken. Ten years ago, an energetic Canadian college student approached me at the end of a pro-life training symposium I led in Toronto. "When I grow up, I want your job. I want to be your clone." I was glad for her enthusiasm but had no idea just how serious she was. When she returned to the University of British Columbia (UBC), this eighteen-year-old freshman helped reorganize the campus pro-life group, and in November 1999 she and other pro-life students set up a display at UBC depicting the truth about abortion. These young pro-lifers were hardly extremists, and nothing they did was illegal.

---

[8]Cunningham has stated this often since 1990 in public presentations.

They were sensitive to set up warning signs about the graphic abortion photos on the main walkways. They offered a toll-free telephone number to students facing a crisis pregnancy. They never shouted at anyone. They patiently stood by the signs and gave solid answers to tough pro-abortion questions. In short, they were gracious witnesses against the evil of abortion.

Nonetheless, their on-campus display was viciously attacked and torn down by three pro-abortion students (so much for pro-choice "tolerance"). The entire attack was caught on video. Shockingly, the Canadian government refused to bring criminal charges against the attackers, one of which was a Student Council representative. Undaunted, the pro-life students, led by Stephanie Gray, the student I met in Toronto, sued for damages. They also raised money to replace the destroyed signs. (The signs are large and expensive.) A short time later, the display went back up. As a result of their careful planning and courteous demeanor, large numbers of students witnessed the display, and the event made the headlines in several Canadian publications. Upon graduation, Stephanie launched (along with Jo Jo Ruba) The Canadian Center for Bioethical Reform and has since spoken at many post-secondary institutions such as the University of Toronto, York University, the University of Calgary, Johns Hopkins University, and George Washington University. Stephanie has debated leading abortion-choice advocates such as Ron Fitzsimmons, executive director of the National Coalition of Abortion Providers, and Dr. Jan Narveson, philosophy professor and recipient of the Order of Canada. Oh, and did I mention she raised all her own funding to do it? That's exactly what we need—courageous pro-life students with tough minds and tender hearts who are groomed to be leaders.

Here's one more example. Eight years ago, Steve Wagner was a twenty-five-year-old music teacher at a private school in Los Angeles, but he loved pro-life apologetics. In 2001 he took a huge leap into the unknown and began raising financial support so he could do full-time pro-life speaking. It wasn't easy getting the money, but nevertheless, for the last seven years he's provided some of the finest pro-life training available. One pastor remarked that Steve's presentation "is the best youth workshop I have ever attended." Now, he's literally written the book on effective pro-life conversations, which I cited from several times in this work.[9]

---

[9]See Steve Wagner, *Common Ground Without Compromise: 25 Questions to Create Dialogue on Abortion* (Signal Hill, CA: Stand to Reason Press, 2008).

Here's what's discouraging: Neither Steve nor Stephanie gets much in the way of organized church support. Nearly all of it comes from individual donors.

If we're serious about getting more full-time pro-life apologists like Stephanie and Steve into the field, we're going to have to do more than donate pocket change to their efforts.

SYSTEMATICALLY TRAIN YOUTH

Two summers ago, I paid my two oldest sons—ages sixteen and fifteen at the time—to study apologetics with me instead of getting summer jobs. I had them read books on Christian doctrine (lay-level), apologetics, and pro-life advocacy. Some people thought I was nuts, but it made perfect sense to me. Parents have no problem shelling out up to twenty-five thousand dollars per year to send their kids to universities where Christianity is openly attacked, so why trouble myself over a fraction of that so my kids can have their beliefs affirmed?

I speak in Protestant and Catholic high schools all over the United States. Over and over again, students tell me they've never heard a pro-life talk like mine. At each place, students see pictures depicting abortion and hear a compelling case for the pro-life view. Gatekeepers such as teachers and administrators worry that the kids can't handle abortion-related content, but the gatekeepers are wrong. I'm often told by students, "I finally know how to defend what I believe. Thank you!"

That reminds me of one of my saddest moments that was briefly one of my happiest. In the summer of 2002, I had the privilege of speaking to roughly nine thousand high school students at Hume Lake Christian Camps. Each week I'd drive up to camp and provide pro-life training to a new group of eight hundred and fifty youth attending from across California. It was electrifying. One day as I was driving home, I was so excited I could hardly contain my joy. Then it dawned on me. I was ecstatic because big training events like this happen so rarely and probably wouldn't happen again for years.

Most people simply have no idea how much work it takes to get a pro-life presentation into any school or youth event, even with my established credentials and appearances on Focus on the Family and other Christian media outlets. The problem isn't me—many people simply don't want to raise the abortion issue and spark potential controversy (which, by the way, is minimal when the presentation is done correctly). Thankfully, I get in front of many students each year, but that's because Steve Weimar, who sets up my speaking agenda, spends hours negotiating with schools to have me speak. And once we get in, we then must fight for the opportunity to use visuals depicting abortion. Too many people in Christian leadership fear man more than they fear God. I once asked a school principal who wanted me to speak without pictures, "Are any of the reasons you are giving me for not showing this film worth the price of children's lives that could have been saved if we'd graciously shown it?" He acknowledged that the question was a good one but gave the standard reply: "Our students just aren't ready for this."

So what are we to conclude, that a student seeing an abortion is worse than a student actually having one?

Admittedly, some pro-life advocates misuse graphic visual aids and thus demonstrate a general lack of sensitivity. For example, they may spring them on unsuspecting audiences with no warning or context, or perhaps they fail to communicate God's grace before showing them to post-abortion men and women. Either way, the solution isn't to categorically reject the pictures; the solution is to use them wisely and compassionately.

If we want to equip our kids to withstand challenges from a secular abortion-loving culture, we'll have to start taking some reasonable risks, one of which is letting them see the truth.

GO VISUAL

Any student who is old enough by law to get an abortion without parental consent is certainly old enough to view the consequences of that choice.[10] Educators universally acknowledge the value of graphic visuals when used properly. High school students, for example, are routinely shown grisly pictures of the Nazi Holocaust against the Jews. Images of mutilated bodies stacked like cordwood communicate the horror of the death camps in a way no lecture can. In fact, the producers of *Schindler's List* donated a copy of the film to every high school in America, in spite of its graphic content. At the same time, movie theaters provided free screenings (during school hours) to over two million students in forty states. Faculty members acknowledged the disturbing images but argued that students would not understand the

---

[10]True, some states have parental consent or parental notification laws, but there's a catch. If the underage girl does not want to tell her parents about a pending abortion, she can appear before a judge who will often grant permission for the procedure. We call this judicial bypass, and it operates in states with consent laws.

Holocaust unless they saw it.[11] They were so convinced of this that when a conservative congressman protested exposing *young* children to the film, forty of his colleagues in the House of Representatives signed a letter expressing outrage at his comments. "While it's true that 'Schindler's List' depicts nudity and graphic violence," the letter states, "we believe that these scenes are critical to the film's accurate portrayal of the dehumanizing horrors of the Holocaust. As noted television critic Howard Rosenberg wrote in the *Los Angeles Times*, 'Although almost too horrid to watch, these segments are absolutely essential.'"[12] The same can be said about teaching the controversial histories of the Vietnam War and the Civil Rights Movement. Teaching the abortion holocaust with any less academic rigor is intellectually dishonest. If students are mature enough for *Schindler's List*, they can certainly view a two-minute film like *This Is Abortion*, produced by the Center for Bio-Ethical Reform.[13]

I realize that some may object to these pictures on the grounds that they substitute emotion for reason and therefore should not be used in public presentations. But this objection misses the point entirely. The question is not, are the pictures emotional? They are. The real question is, are the pictures true? If so, they ought to be admitted as evidence. We ought to avoid empty appeals to emotion, those offered *in place of good reasons*. If, however, the pictures substantiate the reasons I am offering and do not obscure them, they serve a vital purpose. Truth is the issue.[14]

This is precisely the point feminist (and abortion-choice advocate) Naomi Wolf makes in a *New Republic* article:

> The pro-choice movement often treats with contempt the pro-lifers' practice of holding up to our faces their disturbing graphics. . . . [But] how can we charge that it is vile and repulsive for pro-lifers to brandish vile and repulsive images if the images are real? To insist that truth is in poor taste is the very height of hypocrisy. Besides, if these images are often the facts of the matter, and if we then claim that it is offensive for pro-choice women to be confronted with them, then we are making the judgment that women are too inherently weak to face a truth about which they have to make a grave decision. This view is unworthy of feminism.[15]

---

[11]John Davies, "Moving Pictures," *Times Educational Supplement*, September 16, 1994. See also *Social Education* (October 1995), 365–366.

[12]The letter (dated March 3, 1997) was sent to NBC officials after the film aired on television.

[13]Order at www.abortionno.org.

[14]Gregory Koukl and Scott Klusendorf, "The Vanishing Pro-Life Apologist," *Clear Thinking* (Spring 1998).

[15]Naomi Wolf, "Our Bodies, Our Souls," *New Republic*, October 16, 1995, 32.

Some pro-lifers worry that showing graphic abortion pictures lays a guilt trip on post-abortion women. True, we should always be gentle, but people wounded by abortion desperately need to be brought out of denial and into confession so they can repent and find healing and forgiveness. The fact that repentance is painful does not relieve us of our duty to teach it. At the same time, Naomi Wolf is correct: We patronize women when we assume they are too inherently weak to look at abortion objectively.

Nevertheless, the images must be used properly, meaning we should not spring them on unsuspecting audiences. When I use the two-minute film *This Is Abortion*, I tell people exactly what is in the clip and invite them to avert their gaze if they so desire. Nearly everyone watches, and no one complains. I have found this to be true in diverse settings such as debates, banquets, schools, churches, etc. With Christian audiences, I introduce my remarks by stating that Christ is eager to forgive the sin of abortion (see Chapter 17) and that my purpose is not to condemn but to clarify and equip.

People who are not heartbroken over abortion will almost never make the lifestyle concessions necessary to support crisis pregnancy centers or other pro-life efforts at a sacrificial level. Pictures change the way people feel about abortion, while facts change they way they think. Both are vital in changing behavior.

Critics of the pro-life view rightly fear provocative images. During the debate over partial-birth abortion in 1996, abortion-choice columnist Anne Roiphe wrote, "The anti-abortion forces will again display horrible pictures of the technique, which they call partial-birth abortion. Although few in the abortion rights movement take this approach seriously, it has emotional resonance and erodes public support for all abortion."[16]

She wasn't the only one to express concern. "When someone holds up a model of a six-month-old fetus and a pair of surgical scissors, we say 'choice' and we lose," writes feminist Naomi Wolf.[17]

Later, in a 1998 article in *George Magazine*, Wolf states, "The brutal imagery, along with the admission by pro-choice leaders that they had not been candid about how routinely the procedure was performed, instigated pro-choice audiences' reevaluation of where they stood." As a result, "the ground has shifted in the abortion wars."[18]

---

[16] Anne Roiphe, "Moment of Perception," *New York Times*, September 19, 1996.
[17] Naomi Wolf, "Pro-Choice and Pro-Life," *The New York Times*, April 3, 1997.
[18] Naomi Wolf, "The Dead Baby Boom," *George Magazine*, January 27, 1998.

Cynthia Gorney, author of *Articles of Faith*, a book about the abortion wars, says that serious damage has been done to the pro-abortion side. "One of the dirty secrets of abortion is it's really gruesome, but nobody would look at the pictures. With partial-birth, the right-to-life movement succeeded for the first time in forcing the country to really look at one awful abortion procedure."[19]

The quotes from Wolf, Roiphe, and Gorney are critically important. The abortion-choice people are conceding their weakest point, and we should listen.

True, many people dislike abortion pictures and find them offensive. That's to be expected, given the discomfort of admitting one's own moral culpability in the face of injustice. The more pressing question is whether the number of people put off by the graphic images exceeds those compelled into modifying their beliefs. If the debate over partial-birth abortion is any indication, we should bet on the pictures.

CONCLUDING CHALLENGE: OPEN THE CASKET ON ABORTION

Gregg Cunningham often says in public presentations that abortion represents an evil so inexplicable, there are no words to describe it. Although the pictures are difficult to look at, they convey truth in a way that words never can.

Consider this historical parallel example. In 1955, Emmett Till, a fourteen-year-old black youth, traveled from Chicago to visit his cousin in the town of Money, Mississippi.[20] Upon arrival, he bragged about his white girlfriends back in Chicago. This was surprising to his cousin and the cousin's friends because blacks in Mississippi during the fifties didn't make eye contact with whites, let alone date them! Both actions were considered disrespectful. Later that day, Emmett, his cousin, and a small group of black males entered Bryant's Grocery Store where, egged on by the other males, fourteen-year old Emmett flirted with a twenty-one-year-old white, married woman behind the counter. After purchasing candy, he either whistled at her or said something mildly flirtatious. (Reports vary.) The cousin and

[19]Cited in Larry Reibstein, "Arguing at a Fever Pitch," *Newsweek*, January 26, 1998.
[20]This story is reported in the PBS series *Eyes on the Prize*, a history of the Civil Rights Movement. For a detailed account of the Emmett Till story as a catalyst for that movement, see Clenora Hudson-Weems, "Resurrecting Emmett Till: The Catalyst of the Modern Civil Rights Movement," *Journal of Black Studies*, Vol. 29, No. 2, November 1998. Weems argues that the bloody picture of Emmett Till, even more than the actions of Rosa Parks, provoked whites to support civil rights legislation.

the others warned him he was in for trouble. A few days later, at 2:00 A.M., Emmett was taken at gunpoint from his uncle's home by the clerk's husband and another man. After savagely beating him, they killed him with a single bullet to the head.

Emmett's bloated corpse was found three days later in the Tallahatchie River. A cotton gin fan had been shoved over his head and tied with barbed-wire. His face was partially crushed and beaten almost beyond recognition. The local sheriff placed Emmett's body in a sealed coffin and shipped it to his mother back in Chicago. When Mamie Till got the body, she made a stunning announcement—there would be an open-casket funeral for her son Emmett. People protested and reminded her how much this would upset everyone. Mamie agreed but countered, "I want the whole world to see what they did to my boy." The photo of Emmett's mangled body in that open casket was published in *Jet* magazine, and that helped launch the Civil Rights Movement in America. Three months later in Montgomery, Alabama, Rosa Parks refused to go to the back of the bus when ordered to do so. She said the image of Emmett Till gave her the courage to stand her ground.[21]

It's time for pro-life Christians to open the casket on abortion.

We should do it lovingly but truthfully. We should do it in our churches during the primary worship services, comforting those who grieve with the gospel of forgiveness. We should do it in our Christian high schools and colleges, combining visuals with a persuasive defense of the pro-life view that's translatable to non-Christians.

But open the casket we must.

Until we do, Americans will continue tolerating an injustice they never have to look at.

[21]The details of the Emmett Till story are taken from the following sources: Clenora Hudson-Weems, "Resurrecting Emmett Till: The Catalyst of the Modern Civil Rights Movement," 179–188; George F. Will, "Emmett Till and a Legacy of Grace," *Washington Post*, June 19, 2005; Mark Gado, "Mississippi Madness: The Story of Emmett Till," The Crime Library, http://www.crimelibrary.com/notorious_murders/famous/emmett_till; Leonard Pitts, "Open Casket Opened Eyes," *Miami Herald*, January 10, 2003.

APPENDIX
TRAINING RESOURCES

TOP FIVE BOOKS EVERY PRO-LIFE APOLOGIST SHOULD OWN

1. Francis J. Beckwith, *Defending Life: A Moral and Legal Case Against Abortion Choice* (New York: Cambridge University Press, 2007). This outstanding book is a favorite of advanced pro-life apologists everywhere. The arguments presented are lucid and hard-hitting, but the style is suitable for both academic and advanced lay audiences. It's one of the finest (if not *the* finest) systematic defenses of the pro-life position to date.

2. Ramesh Ponnuru, *The Party of Death: The Democrats, the Media, the Courts, and the Disregard for Human Life* (Washington, DC: Regnery, 2006). Ramesh's strengths lie in outlining the political implications of the debates over abortion and embryo research and how those debates have been hijacked within the Democratic Party, the federal courts, and the media. His survey of the cultural and political landscape is breathtaking and second to none.

3. Hadley Arkes, *Natural Rights and the Right to Choose* (New York: Cambridge University Press, rev. ed. 2004). Hadley's thesis is simple: By advocating an alleged right to choose, liberals have talked themselves out of the very natural rights upon which their own freedoms are built.

4. Robert P. George and Christopher Tollefsen, *Embryo: A Defense of Human Life* (New York: Doubleday, 2008). This book defends a simple thesis: Human embryos are not different in kind from other human beings. Rather they are whole living members of the human family from the very beginning. The embryonic, fetal, child, and adolescent stages are just that—stages of development of a determinate and enduring entity—a human being.

5. Peter Kreeft, *The Unaborted Socrates: A Dramatic Debate on the Issues Surrounding Abortion* (Downers Grove, IL: InterVarsity Press, 1983). The text is a funny, yet insightful look at how the abortion issue comes down to just one question: What is the unborn? This book simplifies the abortion debate and is suitable for lay readers.

DVD TRAINING RESOURCES

1. Gregory Koukl and Scott Klusendorf, *Making Abortion Unthinkable: The Art of Pro-Life Persuasion* (Signal Hill, CA: Stand to Reason, 2001). Want to equip your Sunday school class to defend life? In just five sessions (one hour each) you'll learn to simplify the abortion debate, including the wise use of visual aids, and answer the five most common objections to the pro-life view.

2. Gregory Koukl, *Tactics in Defending the Faith* (Signal Hill, CA: Stand to Reason, 2006). Tired of finding yourself flat-footed and intimidated when discussing a Christian worldview? You can increase your confidence and stop critics in their tracks if you learn to ask the right questions. These six one-hour sessions will show you how. Though not exclusively about abortion, the tactics taught apply perfectly to the issue.

PRO-LIFE ORGANIZATIONS

1. **Life Training Institute** (www.prolifetraining.com) is Scott Klusendorf's organization, which trains pro-life advocates to defend their views. The LTI website has helpful articles on pro-life apologetics and can be used to contact Scott for speaking events.

2. **Justice for All** (www.jfaweb.org) produces a large pro-life exhibit on college campuses around the nation. If you want to make abortion the talk of your campus, JFA will train you how to do it in a gracious yet compelling way.

3. **The Center for Bio-Ethical Reform** (www.abortionno.org) pioneered the use of visual aids on college campuses, and its Genocide Awareness Project (GAP) has reached over one hundred campuses with displays depicting the humanity of the unborn and the inhumanity of abortion. The group also has offices in Canada.

4. **Priests for Life** (www.priestsforlife.org) provides resources to the entire pro-life movement, with a special emphasis on the pro-life teachings of the Catholic Church.

5. **National Right to Life** (nrlc.org) is great for legislative updates and information on life issues such as abortion and euthanasia.

6. **Abort73.com** is a comprehensive, online abortion education effort aimed specifically at students.

7. **Students for Life of America** (www.studentsforlife.org) provides college students with resources for starting a campus pro-life chapter. The organization also hosts an annual conference in Washington, D.C.

PREGNANCY CARE CENTER NETWORKS

1. **CareNet** (care-net.org) supports a network of over seven hundred pregnancy resource centers in the United States and Canada, offering free pregnancy tests, peer counseling, post-abortion support, and other practical help.

2. **Heartbeat International** (heartbeatinternational.org) serves over eight hundred affiliates in the United States and in many countries overseas, providing them with education, training, and support. The website includes a worldwide directory of pregnancy help centers.

3. **Abortion Changes You** (abortionchangesyou.com) is a site for post-abortion men and women who wish to begin the process of healing.

CHRISTIAN APOLOGETICS ORGANIZATIONS

1. **Stand to Reason** (str.org) provides articles on a wide variety of topics including abortion, homosexuality, origins, and Christian apologetics.

2. **Summit Ministries** (www.summit.org) offers a two-week summer conference for high school and college students covering topics such as apologetics, worldview analysis, ethics (including abortion), origins, and America's Christian heritage. The website contains essays on Christian apologetics and worldview.

3. **Eternal Perspectives Ministries** (www.epm.org) has Randy Alcorn's articles on apologetics, Christian living, culture, and ethics (including abortion).

4. **Reasonable Faith** (www.reasonablefaith.org) is the website of Dr. William Lane Craig. The site contains both popular and academic articles on Christian apologetics, as well as transcripts of Dr. Craig's debates with atheists.

5. **Paul Copan.com** contains essays and articles on defending the Christian worldview by one of my favorite Christian thinkers.

6. **Afterall.net** is the archived site for Dr. J. P. Moreland's essays defending theism. The site also contains reviews and summaries of Dr. Moreland's books.

7. **Garyhabermas.com** features the work of one of the premier experts on the resurrection of Jesus Christ.

8. **Breakpoint.com** is the website for Chuck Colson's voluminous writings on politics, justice, and bioethics.

The Case for Life has its own website!
Visit www.caseforlife.com for summaries of the book and
Scott's answers to your questions.

SCRIPTURE INDEX

GENERAL INDEX